SCULPTURE
Inside Outside

Published in conjunction with the
exhibition *Sculpture Inside Outside*,
organized by Walker Art Center,
Minneapolis. Following its opening at the
Walker, the exhibition will be shown at
The Museum of Fine Arts, Houston.

SCULPTURE
Inside Outside

Introduction by
Martin Friedman

Essays by
Douglas Dreishpoon
Nancy Princenthal
Carter Ratcliff
Joan Simon

Profiles of the Artists
Peter W. Boswell
Donna Harkavy

Walker Art Center, Minneapolis
Rizzoli, New York

The *Star Tribune*/Cowles Media Company provided principal corporate support for *Sculpture Inside Outside* and events associated with the opening of the Minneapolis Sculpture Garden. The Henry Luce Foundation, Inc. of New York provided major sponsorship for both the exhibition and this publication. The Lannan Foundation of Los Angeles provided important support for the commissioned pieces in *Sculpture Inside Outside*. Additional funding for the exhibition came from the National Endowment for the Arts and the Dayton Hudson Foundation for Dayton's and Target Stores.

Major support for the Walker Art Center exhibition program is provided by The Bush Foundation. Additional support is provided by the General Mills Foundation, the Honeywell Foundation, The McKnight Foundation, The Pillsbury Company Foundation, and the Minnesota State Arts Board, through an appropriation by the Minnesota State Legislature.

First published in the United States of America in 1988 by
Rizzoli International Publications, Inc.
597 Fifth Avenue
New York NY 10017

Library of Congress Cataloging in Publication Data

Sculpture inside outside.

  Bibliography: p. 278
  Includes index.
  1. Sculpture, American—Exhibitions.
2. Sculpture, Modern—20th century—United States—Exhibitions. 3. Outdoor sculpture—United States—Exhibitions.
I. Friedman, Martin L.
NB212.S36   1989
730'.973'0740176579   88-20891
ISBN 0-8478-1004-6
ISBN 0-8478-1005-4 (pbk.)

Designed by Craig Davidson
Printed and bound in Japan

All dimensions are in inches; height precedes width precedes depth

(front and back covers)
Martin Puryear
Ampersand (details)   1987–1988

(frontispiece)
Michael Singer
Cloud Hands Ritual Series 1982–83   (detail)

Contents

Seventeen Americans

Martin Friedman

One of the more intriguing aspects of the current American art scene is the proliferation of sculpture in seemingly limitless stylistic approaches, techniques, and materials. Judging from its bewildering variety of manifestations, the truest common denominator of sculpture today may be idiosyncrasy. It has a strongly individualistic, "hands-on" character that is different from the cool, seemingly depersonalized quality that emanated from the pristine cubes of Minimalism, its most immediate predecessor. There is also an element of revivalism, not just stylistically, but in the return to materials, such as wood, stone, and bronze that are associated with traditional sculpture.

However innovative in form and technique, much of the new sculpture being made has certain historical resonance. Indeed, it could be argued that along with idiosyncrasy, revisionism is its salient feature. Recycled forms and stylistic philosophies are, of course, nothing new in the evolution of Modernism, which is constantly rediscovering its own history, but it is always illuminating to observe just how much of the past persists in such contemporary phenomena. What, for example, could be more simultaneously avant-garde and *retardataire* than the use of stone, sculpture's most elemental material? Jene Highstein's irreducible ovoids, hewn in fine-grained gray granite, are assertively modern, yet evocative of remotest antiquity. The elemental forms of Peter Shelton's iron sculptures result from his relatively primitive technique of sand casting. Revivalism in sculpture is not limited to materials and techniques, but also affects style; classicism still casts a spell. Its spirit emanates from the architectural structures of Brower Hatcher, such as his stainless steel mesh dome supported by a circle of fluted columns. It persists in Judith Shea's latter-day Delphic altar, whose stone stage is occupied by a trio of enigmatic personages—an armless and headless female deity, a cast stone variation on a New Kingdom Egyptian head fragment and, as a symbol of present-day anomie, an invisible seated figure represented solely by an overcoat.

To better comprehend this aesthetically anarchic situation in which elements of the past and present can coexist within the imagery of a single artist, it might be helpful to focus on a few stylistic developments in American sculpture, from the mid-1940s, when it began to gain force

Judith Shea
Without Words   1988
bronze, cast marble, limestone
78 x 80 x 118
Commissioned for the exhibition
Sculpture Inside Outside
Collection Walker Art Center
Gift of Jeanne and Richard Levitt, 1988

Louise Nevelson
Sky Cathedral Presence   1951–1964
painted wood
122¼ x 200 x 23⅞
Collection Walker Art Center
Gift of Judy and Kenneth Dayton, 1969

and eloquence, to its situation today. Long in the shadow of painting, sculpture throughout that decade was still regarded as a second-class medium, associated more with technique than content. Despite the active presence of such internationally recognized figures as Alexander Calder, Jacques Lipchitz, and Isamu Noguchi, whose work reflected a diverse approach associated with European Modernism, American sculpture at mid-century, unlike painting, was not considered to have much expressive or formal potential. It had a hard time escaping its academic origins. Its exemplars were not generally regarded as thinking artists, as painters presumably were, but as muscular craftsmen who hauled blocks of stone around the studio.

Certain forces set into motion in the late 1940s, however, were to drastically change this perception during the next decade. Even though the New York Action Painters were attracting many like-minded adherents, a smaller group of artists, some of whom had friends among this influential group of painters, began exploring similar gestural ideas three-dimensionally. Prominent among these sculptors were David Smith, Theodore Roszak, and Ibram Lassaw, each a master of welded metal techniques which he used to create richly individualistic abstract forms. Smith's dazzling spatial calligraphy in gleaming steel freely improvised on the skeletal structures of birds and other creatures, while the rough surfaced, braised metal constructions of Roszak and Lassaw called to mind fantastic biological and botanical forms. The lure of another approach, Assemblage, was irresistible for some artists who preferred to "find" rather than fabricate the components of their sculptures, which they fashioned from fragments of wood, rusted metal, and other urban detritus. As a style, Assemblage is closer to painting than to sculpture. The dynamism of John Chamberlain's melancholy urban monuments, made of pounded, twisted, multicolored automobile carcasses, parallels Abstract

Donald Judd
Untitled—10 Stacks 1969
anodized aluminum
27 x 24 x 6 each
(height variable)
Collection Walker Art Center
Gift of Mr. and Mrs. Edmond R. Ruben, 1981

Expressionism's surging force. At another extreme are the fragile constructions of Joseph Cornell and Louise Nevelson. The symbol-filled boxes of Cornell, and Nevelson's black walls and towers, in which form and shadow seem interchangeable, represent the lyrical stream of this intuitive approach to creating form.

Of these two germinal directions, welded sculpture and Assemblage, the effects of the latter have been particularly enduring. Painters especially were quick to recognize Assemblage's liberating qualities and rapidly turned their work into three dimensions. In their efforts to erase the line between the illusionism of art and the real world, Robert Rauschenberg and Jasper Johns had few qualms about incorporating stuffed birds, goats with tires encircling their mid-sections, chairs, ladders, and prosthetic limbs in their 1950s "combines." By the beginning of the next decade, two new directions, Pop Art and Minimalism, were undermining conventional attitudes about sculpture and broadening its thematic and formal spectra. Despite its studied, ironic facade, Pop Art, in essence, was a latter-day manifestation of the venerable tradition of American Social Realism, in which subject matter reflected everyday surroundings. The Popsters' wry idealizations of familiar icons borrowed from the supermarket, the highway, and mass media were to affect the course of American sculpture as well as painting. Oldenburg's monumentalized clothespins, three-way plugs, and baseball mitts, and Segal's plaster vignettes of Americana, ranging from all-night diners to gas stations, introduced a new sense of immediacy to sculpture, vastly extending its expressive possibilities.

Though the 1960s saw a dizzying array of styles in American art, one of the most influential was Minimalism, a sharp-edged, even-surfaced mode which virtually enshrined geometry. In the hands of such sculptors as Sol LeWitt, Donald Judd, Dan Flavin, and Carl Andre, Minimalism, though never an officially declared movement, became a compelling aesthetic theology. Its concerns, such as the relationship of mass to void, of object to environment, and ultimately, of the artist to his industrially fabricated creations, were to preoccupy sculptors for years to come, and so powerful were its emanations that it was virtually impossible for any young sculptor not to be affected by them. Its forms, like those of Constructivism and Suprematism, its early twentieth-century purist antecedents, implicitly celebrated technological order. No evidence of the artist's hand contaminated Judd's elegantly proportioned metal boxes which were manufactured commercially according to his precise specifications; and LeWitt's three-dimensional grids in white metal were disquisitions on harmony and perception that represented the essence of Euclidean logic.

Reacting against so pervasive a movement was no easy matter for younger artists for whom Minimalism represented the Academy, but by the mid-1970s, a search for alternative directions was in full swing. In place of unyielding reductivism, they sought forms that were allusive to, if not downright descriptive of, the "real world." Their journeys took them along different roads as they attempted to redefine sculpture for themselves. The miniaturized forms of Joel Shapiro and Charles Simonds were as much a retreat from large-scale public art as from pure geometry. In his cast-iron pieces, Shapiro retained the elemental vocabulary of Minimalism, but used it to make quasi-abstract sculptures such as generic houses and cubicized human figures. For some artists, new sources of imagery were to be found outside the traditional realm of art history. References to archaeology, anthropology, and even to psychology permeated Simonds's miniaturized red clay villages, which were nostalgic evocations of forgotten worlds. For her sculptures as well as paintings, Nancy Graves found inspiration in cartography, zoology, and botany, disciplines whose imagery offered rich possibilities. The abstract imagery of Eva Hesse and Bruce Nauman derived directly from the physical properties of their malleable materials, such as sheets of plastic, lengths of rope, and strips of neon. As a result of such stirrings, American sculpture took on a decidedly new character—individualistic, experimental and, in its restless search for new forms, often eccentric. Though certain currents, running the gamut from descriptive to abstract, were discernible, none constituted a cohesive movement.

What we are witnessing today, in large as well as intimately scaled sculpture, is the desire of some artists to have it both ways—to simultaneously assert and dematerialize form, so that the border between mass and void becomes indeterminate. This ambivalence has several origins. In large measure it reflects the increasingly important influence of painting on sculpture. This is not a particularly new development. Since the beginning of the century, sculpture has been vulnerable to the forays

Ellsworth Kelly
Green Rocker 1968
painted aluminum
20¼ x 97¾ x 112
Collection Walker Art Center
Purchased with matching grant from
Museum Purchase Plan/National
Endowment for the Arts and
Art Center Acquisition Fund, 1969

Joel Shapiro
Untitled 1975
cast iron, wood
20 x 22 x 29½
Collection Walker Art Center
Purchased with the aid of funds from
Mr. and Mrs. Edmond R. Ruben,
Mr. and Mrs. Julius E. Davis, Suzanne
Walker and Thomas Gilmore and the
National Endowment for the Arts, 1976

of painters, with many of its most drastic transformations resulting from such invasions. Picasso and Matisse had no difficulty shifting back and forth between two and three dimensions. Closer to home, Ellsworth Kelly's thin-edged planar sculptures have always been extensions of his painting ideas. The 1960s Minimalists, many of them ex-painters, often fabricated their unitary shapes of materials whose reflective and transparent properties subvert the volumetric character of their sculptures. This is certainly true of Larry Bell's metal-edged, mineral-coated glass boxes. A painter's sensibility is equally apparent in Flavin's fluorescent light constructions that, through their radiant color, incorporate the walls on which they are placed as integral parts of the composition.

Another impetus to the dissolution of form was the seemingly nihilistic Distribution movement of the mid-1960s. Using this deconstructive approach, Barry LeVa, Robert Morris, and Richard Serra deployed fragments of metal, wood, rock, glass, and other materials in seemingly random fashion across the floor. These works have no focal point, no beginning or end.

Such concerns about the nature of sculptural form persist in the work of younger artists who, with one eye to the past, are pursuing similar ideas in their work. Although no single impulse dominates the rapidly changing spectrum of current American sculpture, it is nevertheless possible to identify a few basic stylistic approaches that contribute to its vibrant, polymorphous character. This publication and the exhibition *Sculpture Inside Outside* on which it is based attempt to highlight four such salient tendencies in the work of seventeen young Americans, the majority of whom have achieved artistic identity in the 1980s. Two of these impulses, figuration and transformed objects, are aspects of realism, while the other two, organic abstraction and architectural abstraction, refer to nondescriptive form. These are admittedly informal categorizations, and are not offered here as official art-historical nomenclature. Also, the borders between them are not sharply defined. And to complicate matters further, it is necessary to state one more caveat: within the work of many sculptors represented in this exhibition, two or more of these impulses often coexist.

For all their ambiguity, however, these stylistic categories are useful to keep in mind as one ventures forth into the occasionally disorienting landscape of present-day American sculpture. They serve as the subjects of four speculative essays in this volume. Joan Simon, Carter Ratcliff, Douglas Dreishpoon, and Nancy Princenthal, in discussing their respective topics—figuration, the transformed object, organic abstraction, and architectural art—trace the various incarnations of these impulses from the beginning of the twentieth century to the present and, in the process, refer to the work of sculptors represented in the exhibition.

Although the term figuration is often used to characterize descriptive imagery in general, from representations of the human body to still-life objects and forms in nature, Joan Simon chooses to focus solely on its associations with human anatomy. But within these strictures she manages to include quite a variety of manifestations, from Rodin's fervent turn-of-the-century realism to such absurdist manifestations as the 1950s Happenings and the autobiographical "living sculpture" performance pieces by Vito Acconci, as well as those by the enigmatic British duo, Gilbert and George.

The term figuration, as applied to the human figure, is not necessarily synonymous with realistic depiction; it refers as well to abstract form that has a strong animate quality, and such a quality has long been a property of sculpture. Anthropomorphism is as present in a stainless steel Cubi by David Smith as in a Neolithic stone stele. Whether overtly stated or subliminally implied, the impulse toward figuration is an enduring aspect of Modernism, even in periods when pure abstraction has prevailed. It remains especially potent in sculpture. Its attractions these days are irresistible to many young artists who, though rigorously schooled in abstraction, have ventured forth into this heretofore forbidden realm. Whatever their reasons, whether disaffection with what they consider to be exhausted abstract forms or the need to identify with past verities in order to deal with present-day uncertainties, they have made a choice. For them, figuration affords opportunities to pursue psychological as well as aesthetic issues.

We are especially conscious of such concerns in the work of several artists represented in this exhibition, in particular that of Judith Shea, Peter Shelton, and Robert Therrien. Shea's serene, static forms, which derive from such varied sources as dressmakers' dummies and Hellenistic sculpture, can be read on one level as mystical communication among disparate personae and, on another, as commentary on the relationship between the contemporary world and antiquity. Her mute, self-absorbed beings exist within a surrealistic dreamlike ethos in which past and present are interchangeable. In their eccentric fashion, the quasi-abstract stone and cast-iron sculptures of Peter Shelton also allude to the human body—often his own—and vary from severely elemental renditions of the whole figure to abstract variations on heads, torsos, and limbs. In his imagery, elements of the body are drastically elongated or compressed and, on occasion, are represented by visual equivalents of their movements. Less specifically anatomical are the associative elements that lurk within the serene geometry of Therrien's solemn unitary steel and bronze sculptures; one of these is the "snowman," a vintage Therrien icon consisting of three spherical forms, one over the other. Within the severe outlines of other Therrien sculptures may be found such disparate forms as church steeples, trumpets, and coffinlike objects, the last another, if unsettling, reference to the human body.

The essence of the transformed object is paradox and, as Carter Ratcliff suggests in his essay, the process of changing an object can have social as well as aesthetic implications. By removing a water glass, a chair, or a telephone from its context, altering or juxtaposing it with other objects, it takes on ambiguous status, and the notion of utility and the social values behind it are questioned. Thus the most prosaic articles are infused with subtle shades of meaning and for the viewer may assume spiritual, aggressive, or erotic properties.

For some artists "transforming" an object has ritualistic significance, perhaps reflecting a need to create personal symbols in a time when collective ones have all but lost their meaning. The creation of a transformed object may require no more than selecting, as opposed to fabricating, its components. Duchamp showed us the way: all it took to instantly aestheticize a bicycle wheel or a cage filled with marble cubes was his calm assertion that these were works of art. Although the transformed object's early twentieth-century origins are in the anti-rational imagery of Dadaism and Surrealism, a more recent American manifestation of this syndrome was seen in Pop Art, which slyly celebrated seductive consumer culture icons such as sleek cars, fast foods, beer, and laundry soap. Who better understood the transcending symbolism of such desiderata than Andy Warhol, who magically transmuted soup cans and Brillo boxes into works of art?

Working today within the seemingly ineradicable spirit of the transformed object are many young Americans whose sculptures reveal a wide range of psychological and formal approaches. But unlike the imagery of their Pop predecessors, there is surprisingly little reference in their work to immediate things and situations. No topical commentary, and certainly no streetwise irony, emanate from their creations. Donald Lipski's sculptures are witty, occasionally sinister combinations and syntheses of unlikely, mundane things—a white baby shoe impaled on a pedestal rising from the cover of a book, or a circle of shattered glass on the floor spilled like water from an overturned galvanized metal bucket. Jin Soo Kim incorporates recognizable objects in stifling tentacular constructions that crowd a room, but like Lipski's, these works transcend reality by their ritualistic character. At another extreme are the quasi-mystical tableaux of Walter Martin, who reconstitutes familiar objects in foreign materials and places them in unlikely settings. One of the most compelling is a headless dog, cast in plaster, seated before a pile of plaster bones; an old-fashioned microphone has been placed between the dog and his "audience." Even the most descriptive of these transformed objects seems remote and generalized in feeling. However detailed in execution, the surrogate forms in Martin's sculptures—pieces of fruit, bones, and bottles—exist in a vacuum, with no sense of time or place. This is also true of Robert Gober's simulacra; there is a touch of the demonic in Gober's fake porcelain sinks

David Smith
Cubi IX 1961
stainless steel
105¾ x 58⅝ x 43⅞
Collection Walker Art Center
Gift of the T.B. Walker Foundation, 1966

13

transformed into Minimalist wall sculptures, hand-made baby cribs compressed into 3-D parallelograms, and a bizarre, painstakingly fabricated, upholstered chair at two-thirds scale, each element of its floral patterned slipcover compulsively hand-painted by the artist. Another latter-day alchemist is Robert Lobe, who magically transforms nature by pounding on huge sheets of aluminum laid against rocks and tree trunks to reveal their underlying contours in gleaming, undulating relief sculptures.

The term organic abstraction describes sculptures whose shapes are metaphors for natural forms and processes. In discussing the genesis of this approach, Douglas Dreishpoon cites the early twentieth-century vision of pioneer abstractionists such as Arp and Miró, whose Surrealist-inspired biomorphism recalled all manner of natural phenomena, from mountains to microorganisms. While such ambiguous allusions to nature's external forms continue in the work of many sculptors today, there is particular emphasis on expressing the idea of metamorphosis. In their sculptures, cycles of growth and decay are symbolized in forms that swell, twist, interlock, and disintegrate. Working with the vocabulary of organic abstraction are a number of artists represented in *Sculpture Inside Outside*. Jene Highstein's giant stone eggs are powerful organic variations on the Minimalist aesthetic. The swelling volumes in wood and stone that comprise Martin Puryear's iconography are evocative of fecund forms in nature. Phoebe Adams's subtly toned sculptures that project from the wall are vibrant with complex forms cast in bronze, which include seashells, stones, and bizarre hornlike shapes. Adams's transformed objects are contained within dynamic, abstract configurations that suggest the movement of wind and swirling water. Some of Tom Butter's translucent sculptures, fabricated of lightweight shaped and molded fiberglass, are reminiscent of exotic undersea vegetation; others are delicate structures of wood and resin wrapped around empty space. If Butter's work exemplifies the most fragile, attenuated aspect of organic abstraction, then John Newman's stainless steel constructions are its most mechanistic; his sharp-contoured, aggressive forms, which sometimes look like robotic vegetation, interlock and scoop out space.

As a stylistic mode, architectural abstraction is a fairly recent phenomenon. As more sculptors involve themselves in the design of bridges, plazas, and other public areas, their visual syntax is filled with references to the forms and principles associated with construction. The shapes, materials, and processes identified with industrial fabrication, however, are also evident in more theoretical, less utilitarian creations. Broadly stated, architectural abstraction refers generally to large-scale sculptures that enclose space. More specifically, some of these utilize basic building techniques, such as stud-wall construction, while others employ sophisticated principles such as cantilevering. Siah Armajani incorporates traditional building techniques in his metaphoric sculptures whose forms,

Joan Miró
Femme debout (Standing Woman) 1969
bronze
75½ x 46¼ x 42¼
Collection Walker Art Center
Gift of the Pierre Matisse Gallery and
the T.B. Walker Acquisition Fund, 1973

in fact, are largely predicated on traditional building conventions. Equal inspiration for his metaphorical architecture comes from the visionary writings of Whitman, Melville, and Thoreau, and the elegantly ordered thoughts of Jefferson. Armajani's art, in many ways, is the truest embodiment of architectural abstraction, and for many younger artists, he has revealed its expressive possibilities. In her essay on this topic, Nancy Princenthal discusses the social and political, as well as aesthetic implications of this attitude, touching on its idealistic early twentieth-century origins in movements such as De Stijl and the Bauhaus, and citing its successive manifestations to the present.

In recent American art, the concept of architectural abstraction has come to include sculptures whose simple tensile and planar forms are associated more with structural engineering than architecture per se. The massive sheets of Cor-Ten steel that Richard Serra leans against one another and shapes into slow curves dramatically exemplify sculpture as primal engineering. Mark di Suvero's towering constructions exuberantly define, rather than displace, the space they occupy. The industrial steel beams that form them are taut vectors, each no longer or wider than it absolutely must be to perform its structural as well as visual function.

Many variations of this architectural approach are evident in *Sculpture Inside Outside*. Brower Hatcher uses structural principles intuitively in fabricating his giant steel mesh follies. Some of his sculptures take the shape of human figures, others are large, transparent geometric forms within which are suspended constellations of improbable objects made of shiny and brightly hued metal, ranging from tables, chairs, turtles, and alligators to purely geometric forms. The monumental spirals that Steven Woodward creates of plywood under pressure are as much about movement as they are about structural principles. Rising wavelike from the floor and suspended from the ceiling, these thin-edged sculptures have strong dynamic character. Michael Singer's formal vocabulary is as basic as the structural technique he uses. Its components, stones and strips of raw wood, place his work in the current of organic abstraction; its architectural qualities are apparent in his method of delicately positioning the wood strips on stones, resulting in airy, seemingly weightless structures. Like a house of cards, a Singer sculpture is a balancing act. Meg Webster's sculptures also have organic and architectural attributes. Her huge, earth-walled outdoor pieces, filled with flowering plants, reveal the influences of Minimalist reductivism and the Earth Art movement of the 1970s. Entered through slotlike doorways, her craters have a beguiling ritualistic quality, reminiscent of Rio Grande kivas and ancient fertility shrines.

The stylistic pluralism that characterizes recent American sculpture often takes unpredictable forms. Considering this pluralism within the work of an individual artist, we may encounter the uneasy coexistence of

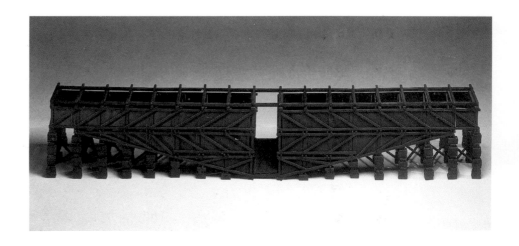

Siah Armajani
Bridge for Robert Venturi 1970
balsa wood with stain
14 x 76⅝ x 12¼
Collection Walker Art Center
Purchased with the aid of funds
from Mr. Brooks Walker, Jr., 1977

seemingly opposite directions. Although Peter Shelton's sculptures are body oriented, his interest in architectural form is equally strong. Not only does he make organic and geometricized figures in stone and cast iron, but he also locates such effigies in or next to corridors and arched enclosures formed of wood, stone, or concrete. Sometimes a change of scale or material will radically affect the way we perceive an archetypal form that an artist has made his own. Puryear's works, carved in wood, or formed of lath strips or tar-coated metal mesh, have a decidedly organic character, alluding as they do to natural forms. Yet these simple shapes assume an entirely new quality when drastically enlarged and executed in other materials. When, for example, these primal roots are elongated and translated into granite, they become architectural entities.

Difficult as it may be to generalize about recent American sculpture, which runs the gamut from associative imagery to enigmatic abstraction, a few observations can be hazarded. Because, in the aggregate, this new work is a reaction to the uncompromising purity of Minimalism, its attributes are more intuitive than analytical. This is true of its abstract as well as descriptive manifestations. For all the elemental simplicity of a Highstein stone sculpture or an earth-formed circle by Webster, the contours and surfaces reveal the effects of a shaping hand. Such preoccupation with the inherent properties of materials is unabashedly romantic, even a bit old-fashioned, especially in light of Minimalism's cool stance, but it is a significant characteristic of today's sculpture. Another characteristic is ambivalence about scale. While there is no shortage of artists willing to take on large-scale indoor as well as outdoor pieces, the psychology underlying these efforts is worth examination. Instead of equating large scale with heroic statement, as do Serra and di Suvero, a younger generation of Americans deals with the issue of size in more offhand fashion. However space-filling a structure by Singer or Hatcher may be, its character is essentially reserved, rather than confrontational. There is also, in recent sculpture, a taste for discontinuity with respect to subject matter, style, and materials. And, as we have observed, there is a casualness about quoting and improvising on forms from ancient and recent art history. Shelton's perverse juxtapositions of figures and structures, Shea's metaphysical dialogues between antiquity and the present, and the hallucinatory assemblages of Donald Lipski and Jin Soo Kim exemplify this freewheeling creative process.

Abstraction in American sculpture is certainly alive and well. As we have seen, its organic and architectural manifestations have many creative adherents. But another equally important phenomenon is worth mentioning—the reintroduction of realism, after so many decades of banishment. But this is realism with a new twist, a realism whose sources are more in psychology than academicism: though Shea borrows Greco-Roman forms and Phoebe Adams freely utilizes Bernini-like baroquery in her configurations of billowing cloth and floating objects, the results are anything but slavishly historical. Their use of descriptive form is oblique and detached; they comment on history from a distinctly modern stance, transmuting its testimonies into their unique iconographies.

A great deal of new sculpture seems to be a quest for personal symbols. This search is not limited to descriptive works, but pervades abstract manifestations as well. Much of it focuses on the processes of nature. Conceivably, this probing of elemental natural forms represents a search for stability in a time when the specter of ecological disaster looms.

Whatever their motivations, and clearly there are many, young American sculptors have few compunctions about pursuing their ideas in an open, uninhibited manner. If their imagery suggests a susceptibility to a wide spectrum of philosophical and stylistic impulses, it is also indicative of fresh insights into contemporary existence.

Figurative Imagings

Joan Simon

Peter Shelton
BLACKVAULT*falloffstone* 1988
cast concrete, steel, aluminum, stone
BLACKVAULT: 142 x 105 x 197
falloffstone: 53 x 67 x 116
Commissioned with Lannan Foundation
support for the exhibition
Sculpture Inside Outside
Courtesy the artist and L.A. Louver
Gallery, Inc., Venice, California

Imaging Thought/Imaging Figures

In a century whose art history has been essentially a streamlined movement toward abstraction and reduction, it is not surprising that figurative art, and in particular figurative sculpture, has been downplayed as an area of concern. Its history is not so neat, nor is it so evolutionary. Further, as Michael Brenson recently wrote: "For those who believe in a future where the past will finally be irrelevant or dead, figurative sculpture is nostalgic, reactionary, or a bother."[1]

Yet the figure has been persistent: it has been almost willfully ahistorical. It has cropped up in every medium and in every style, with the notable exception of Minimal Art—where it can be argued that the figure has not so much been erased but displaced, the viewer becoming the primary figure in relation to primary objects. In the past century the classical figure has been formally dissected and reconstructed (Cubism and Constructivism) and psyches as well as structures have been delved (Surrealism and Performance Art). At times the figure has been idealized or naturalistic, anatomically correct or thoroughly invented. It has been presented live, in replication, and by substitution—whole, in parts, or even as an invisible but resonant presence.

As the possible program for sculpture shifted from the nineteenth century's classical unities and singular conflation of public purpose, rhetoric, and patronage to the twentieth century's more private and changeable sets of explorations which embrace dualities and often contradictions of inner vision and external matter, the essential problem remains the same as it was for Rodin: What place can there be for the figure in sculpture, and how can the figure itself be rethought and remade? Or, as Joel Shapiro put it: "The intention isn't to do something with a head, two arms, two legs and a chest. That's just part of the vocabulary. That's just one thing you could do."[2]

Signs of Animation: The 1960s

At the beginning of the decade predominantly known for the equally cool, hands-off abstracted, and industrial aesthetics of Minimalism and Pop, Giacometti, who died in 1966, was making some of his most powerful and intimately moving portrait busts, walking men, and standing women.

George Segal
Embracing Couple 1975
plaster
33¾ x 31½ x 13
Collection Walker Art Center
Gift of Mr. and Mrs. Julius E. Davis, 1979

Marisol
Portrait of Virgil Thomson 1981
charcoal, enamel paint on wood
69 x 92 x 65½
Private collection

(opposite)
Mimi Gross
Ms. Liberty (originally included in
Ruckus Manhattan installation by
Red Grooms and Mimi Gross, at 88 Pine
Street, New York) 1975–1976
mixed media
approx. 96 high
Courtesy Marlborough Gallery, New York

By the end of the decade, de Kooning had made his very first bronze figures, and Miró and Dubuffet had taken up figurative sculpture as well.[3] While the three-dimensional art object was being pared down to vernacular materials and geometric forms and often reduced to ideas alone, it seems important to keep in mind that the figure, while not taking center stage in vanguard critical circles, was, contrary to rumors of its (and painting's) demise, alive and well in a variety of places and in a variety of traditional as well as newly invented media. Even a brief listing of body imagings would include Yves Klein's body-brush paintings, Fluxus events and Pop Happenings, Ed Kienholz's and Bruce Conner's "arsenic and old lace" assemblages of figures and picturesquely squalid real-life objects, Robert Arneson's irreverent use of clay and his own visage, Mary Frank's classical fragmented clay torsos, George Segal's haunting white plaster figures and Marisol's carved and drawn figure groupings, Alex Katz's free-standing "slice of life" portrait cutouts, and Lucas Samaras's Polaroid self-transformations.

For the purposes of this essay, though, it may be helpful to begin to look at the figure in contemporary sculpture from the rather arbitrary though certainly dramatic benchmark of the Minimalists' elimination of all figurative expression, including any evidence of the hand of the artist, from their industrially styled and architecturally scaled works of art. With hindsight, it can be said that they set the stage for the figure's return.

The Minimalists were reacting to the forceful, emotive gestures, indeed the charismatic personalities and spiritual reach of the Abstract Expressionists, and more generally to the traditions of European art, with its balancing of compositional elements, illusionism, and fictive space. The host of new three-dimensional works (also labeled Primary Structures and ABC Art before the term Minimalism became fixed)—what Donald Judd preferred to call "specific objects" to isolate them conceptually from either painting or sculpture—were to exist in real space; were to be made of real materials, often new industrial materials; and were to convey a "whole" that was both direct and complete. Judd's objections to traditional painting and sculpture were that they had become set forms, almost academic displays of complexity and virtuosity intrinsically expressive of the artistic self in action.

In his essay "Specific Objects," Judd compared traditional sculpture to the new three-dimensional work and set out a program that, while outlining a rigorously abstract and structural work ethic, also offered figurative precedents. The full-bodied, detailed anatomical figure had no place, yet the figurative object was still admissible. "There are precedents for some of the characteristics of the new work," Judd wrote. "The parts are usually subordinate and not separate in Arp's sculpture and often in Brancusi's. Duchamp's Ready-mades and other Dada objects are also seen at once and not by part."[4] The stark, real-space objects of the Minimalists

were dramatic presences. To borrow an often quoted phrase applied to the Abstract Expressionists, the Minimalists in effect set out yet another "arena in which to act." The dynamic, however, shifted in emphasis from the behavior of the producer of the art object to the behavior of the consumer. Collaboration between viewer and artwork within a specific architectural setting was essential.

The theatrical and the behavioral were to inform much of the artwork that followed and also informed comtemporaneous Minimalist dance and music. Real-time, real-space, artist-identified endeavors that were performed in the Minimalist arena included Trisha Brown's real bodies actually walking on the face of real walls—matter-of-fact methodical actions on the part of the walkers, yet stunningly objectified actions to viewers—and her more down-to-earth and intimate one-thing-added-to-another "accumulation" solos in which she assembled simple, unmodulated gestures and talk fragments. Philip Glass's unitary musical phrases, serially repeated, paralleled Minimalist methodology. (These "live" works were performed to the same audiences as Minimalist Art, and often in the same exhibition spaces.) If the full figure was not depicted in the vanguard plastic arts, it was nevertheless made evident as a separate and an equally important aspect of art productions.

Figurative images had already made their way into Pop painting, but they functioned essentially as found objects; in formal terms and in tone, photographic appropriations were flat, detached, and dehumanized. Yet Happenings, the sideshow of Pop, offered animated, celebratory human presences—and also set the terms for a variety of new kinds of figurative sculpture and sculptural painting. In particular the Happenings of Oldenburg, Rauschenberg, Dine, and Grooms, while providing an almost carnival-like atmosphere where artist and audience could join together, profoundly informed the object-making of these artists.

Dine's tools and self-images quickly adhered in his paintings, and Rauschenberg explored in just about every medium the "gap," as he put it, between "art and life." It was Grooms, however, whose buoyant, cartoonlike performances were to find themselves defined as a whole new genre—large-scale, three-dimensional picto-dramas, part stage, part caricature, part historical machine, and part movable funhouse. Built, modeled, and painted by Grooms and his Ruckus Construction Company, these larger-than-life figures on their wildly skewed stages captured the vibrancy of performance and the exuberant personality of their maker.

Oldenburg's soft sculptures, abstracted and overscaled everyday items, were also theatrical, and indeed deliberately anthropomorphic. "I am for an art," he wrote, "that is political-erotic-mystical, that does something other than sit on its ass in a museum. . . . I am for an art that takes its form from the lines of life itself, that twists and extends and accumulates and spits and drips, and is heavy and coarse and blunt and

George Segal
The Diner (detail)   1964–1966
plaster, wood, chrome, laminated plastic,
masonite, fluorescent lamp
98¾ x 144¼ x 96
(overall dimensions variable)
Collection Walker Art Center
Gift of the T.B. Walker Foundation, 1966

sweet and stupid as life itself."[5] Though monumentally expressive, Oldenburg's figurative objects were also emotionally detached. They seemed to have it both ways. Judd could admit them to the specific objects canon because "Oldenburg has taken this anthropomorphism to an extreme and made the emotive form, with him basic and biopsychological, the same as the shape of an object, and by blatancy subverted the idea of the natural presence of human qualities in all things. And further . . ." —Judd here makes a point so obvious that it is easily missed—"Oldenburg avoids trees and people."[6]

Among the contemporaries of Oldenburg who actually put people into their figurative sculpture were Marisol and George Segal—neither of whose work fit into the industrial aesthetic of the Pop enterprise, but was initially mislabeled as such. Decidedly humanistic and handmade— hers carved and drawn, his cast from live models and reworked—their assemblies of freestanding figures were theatrical, pictorial, and basic in contour yet complex in historical and emotional resonance. Marisol's use of media celebrities and her cartoonlike reductions of anatomy superficially linked her with Pop, but her intimate working of materials and frequent application of her own self-portrait more directly allied her carved sculptures with totemic figures and folk portraiture. And though Segal often staged his generalized and ghostly figures with "real" props—a Coke machine, bathtub, subway sign, or movie marquee—they suggested a studied and sober reuse of classical casts and an expressiveness of the human condition that was decidedly unlike the "no comment" figuration of Pop painting, or the giddiness of Pop performance.

Closer to Pop's emphasis on surface appearances were the life-size nude casts of John de Andrea, or Duane Hanson's cast figures, repainted and redressed in real clothing. The Super-Realist sculptors, while photographically accurate in detail and in their freeze-frame isolation of behaviors, drained all life from their verist surfaces. By comparison, and despite his claims that his art was devoid of emotion and all on the surface, Andy Warhol was perhaps Pop's most acute observer and recorder of human behavior, whether in his real-time films like *Sleep*, his photo-derived yet reworked society portraits, or in his proto-*People* magazine, *Interview*, documenting fashion, foible, and fantasy—all sorts of glamorous body images. With his own invented look and studied costume—his silver wig and vernacular American garb of sneakers, Levi's, Brooks Brothers button-down shirt, and blazer—and his wraithlike ubiquitous presence, Warhol, the first marketable and marketed performance artist, could also be said to be the first "living sculpture." (It was even suggested that he sometimes had "multiples" impersonate him at public events, and at parties.)

But it was the personae and performances of European artists, particularly Joseph Beuys and Jannis Kounellis, that began to return a truly expressive self to art-making, conjoining the spiritual, theatrical, mythical, and mundane. Breaking down the purist aesthetic of formal concerns, they reassembled an iconoclastic array of objects and gestures, live animals and archaic relics, in order to restore to the artist a sense of history as well as a social and didactic function.

The full range of essential, human emotions was not to be fully explored in contemporary sculpture—that is, of the more or less conventional sort, meaning three-dimensional independent objects—until the Post-Minimalists of the late 1960s introduced once again the hand of the artist and an "anima" to figurative sculpture—a primitive, almost naive sense of the figure as spiritual and spirited vessel, a reconnection between the maker and the made, and a visceral identification as well as a palpable atmosphere between viewer and object.

Two exhibitions in New York in 1968 were bold statements of the figure's return and both pointed to new directions that figurative sculpture could take. The shows were as different from each other as they were from the prevailing aesthetic climate. Three of Nancy Graves's Camels made their debut at Graham Gallery, and an entire inventory of Bruce Nauman's ways of remaking the self were presented for the first time at the Leo Castelli Gallery.

Nancy Graves's Camels, life-size and realistic—matted hair, dirty feet, and all—were grand imposing beasts. They were resonant of other cultures and other times, of climates and atmospheres and life itself. Like the structural anthropologists' search for underlying patterns of humanity built from analysis of particular customs, myths, and language, Graves detailed a new kind of animistic humanism built on and from the tabula rasa of Minimalism.

Graves's approach was as much about analysis—of organic form and construction techniques—as it was about full-blown, anatomically correct entities. Like Chuck Close's monumental blowups of faces, paintings reconstructed from deconstructed photographs (almost billboards announcing the figure's return to avant-garde art-making)—the veracity of Graves's Camels was built out of a methodical series of procedures, of the integration of parts to the whole, where physiognomy was almost a by-product of rigorous thought and the details of making. Graves's Camels replicated the mechanics of life forms while also capturing a living spirit. Graves would subsequently take the Camels apart, investigating in detail the skeletal, nearly abstract forms of their biological armature, and later take that investigative analysis of cumulative information to mappings not only of anatomy, but of surfaces of the moon, plant life, and other found forms, in both painting and sculpture.

In a multitude of different styles and mediums, Bruce Nauman was also exploring the anatomy of sculpture making. Wanting to put ideas back into the work, and to work directly with materials, he began to focus on his own figure and the question of identity, and in particular the role of the artist. Having done live performances, videos, and films, he began to locate his observations of body language and his bodily illustrations of spoken language in fully three-dimensional form. Among the works in his 1968 show at the Castelli Gallery were photographs such as *Feet of Clay*, in which Nauman's own feet were both models and modeled, and *From Hand to Mouth*, a body fragment literally explicating its title. *Templates of My Body Taken at Ten-Inch Intervals* also did what its title said; it was made from a sequential series of body casts, each more and more abstract as the molds were shaped into different materials, resulting in a final state in which each measurement was fabricated in neon tubing and strung together like a radiant green exoskeleton.

Nauman, like Graves, was interested in exploring and confounding insides and outsides, fronts and backs. In a series of sculptures cast from the artist's back and depicting his hands bound behind him, Nauman conflated his own identity with a more generalized proposition of the possibilities (or impossibilities) of the sculptor's activities, and in yet another reversal made the gesture once again specific by titling the piece after another sculptor. *Henry Moore Bound to Fail* was one of Nauman's more complex verbal and pictorial puns. It was fully animated yet in low relief, reminiscent both of Matisse's "Backs" and Man Ray's mysterious tied bundle, *The Enigma of Isadore Ducasse.* And its source was as indirect as

Chuck Close
Big Self-Portrait 1968
acrylic on canvas
107½ x 83½
Collection Walker Art Center
Art Center Acquisition Fund, 1969

Bruce Nauman
Henry Moore Bound to Fail   1967
wax over plaster
26 x 24 x 3½
Collection Mr. Leo Castelli

it was specific. Nauman had overheard a group of young English artists dismissing Moore and he felt that their rejection had come too soon, that there was still much to be learned from the human figure, and from Moore himself—the master who had spent a lifetime opening up internal volumes while expressing the entirety of the human form.

While many of their contemporaries had moved outdoors to expand the boundaries of sculpture, or had eliminated the object entirely from their ideas of art-making, expressing those ideas either aloud or on the page, both Graves and Nauman remained intensely in the studio, wanting to directly manipulate materials and be intimately involved in the process of making. They broke the rules of Minimalism, adding emotional, expressive states to specific objects. Both of these artists not only opened up the question of style, and the possibilities of a variety of styles and materials issuing from the hand of an individual artist, but deliberately eschewed a singular, precise, and repeatable signature. They each engaged the possibilities of working abstractly *and* figuratively in their art. Though Graves was the bold explorer into the world, and Nauman took the world's measure by his own body, both made radically important statements that reinvigorated and in a sense reinvented contemporary figurative sculpture. Drawing on the tangible, factual "wholes" and rigorous thinking of Minimal Art, the conceptual and procedural nature of Process Art, and the spirited gesture of performance, they also brought into play traditional notions of craft and unconventional presentations of what a figure might be and how and why it might be issued.

The Expressive Figure Live and Reframed: The 1970s
Behaviorism characterized the decade—initially in live performance, later in surrogate objects derived from performance, and by mid-decade in the figurative imagery of "New Image" painting. The personal was expressed in an almost episodic, isolated series of body imagings. While it was a decade in which sculpture dominated, sculpture for the most part was still operating on Minimalist steam, though it had moved to the extended field of Process and Earth Art, site-specific operations, and architecturally based constructions. For figurative sculptors it was an especially exploratory time. Jonathan Borofsky's multi-media revisions of his own self-portrait were cast in clay as lamps, were painted on walls, and made as cutouts; James Surls's surrealistic wood figures were extracted from found and carved tree trunks; and Luis Jimenez cast his Western iconography in fiberglass to create "Remington bronzes" exploded to over life-size and in blaring color.

It was a pluralist era not only because no single style dominated, but because the locales for art-making were dispersed. For a time New York lost its hegemony—there was little need for a market, especially during the first half of the decade when performance had come into its own

Magdalena Abakanowicz
Backs 1976–1982
burlap, resin
80 pieces in three sizes up to
28 x 23 x 28 each
Courtesy Marlborough Gallery, New York

as an independent medium. "Whenever a certain school, be it Cubism, Minimalism or Conceptual art, seemed to have gained a stranglehold on art production and criticism," RoseLee Goldberg wrote, "artists turned to performance as a way of breaking down categories and indicating new directions."[7]

Compared to the vaudevillian gestures of the 1960s Fluxus events and the lighthearted playfulness of Pop Happenings, the 1970s performance artists often laid the body bare and subjected it not only to intense scrutiny but to intensely brutal effect. Dennis Oppenheim "drew" on his body by leaving an open book on his chest while sunning himself—a rather mild action compared to that of Chris Burden, who had himself shot at by a sharpshooter for one piece, and crucified himself on a car for another. Oppenheim later displaced his own figure with bronze puppets that periodically would have their heads smashed by swinging into a bell, and Burden made vast perpetual motion machines to replay a violent aesthetic. Gilbert and George presented themselves as "machines;" bronzing their faces and putting themselves on a pedestal, the "living sculptures" sang music hall ditties for hours on end, mechanistically moving like overgrown figures on a music box.

Performance was the most directly communicative art form, aspiring, as Lucy Lippard wrote, "to the immediacy of political action itself. Ideally performance means getting down to the bare bones of esthetic communication—artist/self confronting audience/society."[8] The personal was the political. The body in motion was also the body politic. As the women's movement began to engage the art world, Womanhouse in Los Angeles was the site of installations and performances that detailed women's issues and anatomies. At other sites, Ana Mendieta acted out brutal rapes; Martha Wilson, Martha Rossler, and Hannah Wilke transformed their own bodies into sculptures and those sculptures into powerful photographic statements.

Judith Shea's clothing-derived fabric works evoked the bodies that might wear them, and later were cast and modeled as fully three-dimensional objects. Siah Armajani's reading rooms and other constructed public sites, though abstracted and architectural, always implied the behaviors of a potential user. And while Charles Simonds's tiny brick buildings presumed an allegorical and invisible village of "little people," in one film he himself emerged from a mound of clay and built the structures directly on his own body. Magdalena Abakanowicz made multiple figures of fiber and clay that presented the body both as an encasement and as a thing encased; Deborah Butterfield constructed freestanding horses made of sticks and mud; and Antony Gormley cast in lead organic forms like rocks and fishes, and his own body as well, to generalize with these lead skins both the containers and what might be contained.

New images abounded. Yet when these figurative images entered the painterly arena, once again they were more tentative than the declarative images of either sculpture or performance, and they were located, for the most part, on Minimalist fields. The New Image painters essentially drew in paint, almost outlining and silhouetting the idea of a figurative image. Whether that image took the form of Susan Rothenberg's horses, Jennifer Bartlett's houses, Robert Moskowitz's skyscrapers, or David True's boats, they were all in a sense behavioral traps, iconic and abstracted. The only "people" appeared in Neil Jenney's paintings, where he focused on pairing relationships (illustrating the rather simple narratives of cause and effect, he also stenciled onto the paintings' massive frames), and in Nicholas Africano's low reliefs.

Though New Image was cast as a painter's movement, it could be said that sculptures like Bryan Hunt's Empire State Buildings and his reworkings of the Great Wall of China, or Scott Burton's furniture, or Judith Shea's clothing pieces, or later Robert Lobe's re-presentations of parts of tree trunks and root systems, could have been informative in context; their works were equally abstract and figurative, outlined and summary. Joel Shapiro's sculptures of houses, bridges, and ladders were acknowledged at the time as relevant to this direction in art-making, and it was Shapiro who extended the implications of these generalized behaviorist icons to fully figurative sculpture.

Perhaps the most important and inventive figurative sculptor of his generation, Shapiro began as a Process artist in the late 1960s, exhibiting his variations on hammered lead slabs. He soon began to make small, hand-modeled balls and birds which were presented on shelves as items to hold and play with. Shapiro's gestural and behavioral procedures took the form of miniature geometric sculptures which encapsulated the domestic and the intimate, while being displayed in vast open spaces.

Shapiro's first figures, but a few inches high, relative in scale but non-relational to his "houses," were soon to grow into simple wooden constructed figures, about half life-size, whose poise and balance, in the most economical forms, were as touchingly human as the figures were straightforward assemblies of two-by-fours. In the past few years Shapiro has remade the figure, taken it apart, used blocks of wood to barely de-marcate isolated torsos or limbs, and has exhibited these partial figures lying on the floor and wildly cantilevered into space. His figures convey multiple factual truths to materials, and an equally compelling set of truths about the imagined, if barely outlined, self.

By 1980, figuration fully came to the fore and made its international debut at the 1980 Venice Biennale. Laurie Anderson performed live, Kounellis staged one of his theater pieces, the New Image painters, along with the more overtly figurative Neo-Expressionists, were featured in the *Aperto* section. Sandro Chia, Enzo Cucchi, and Francesco Clemente were represented along with Borofsky, Rothenberg, and Schnabel, whose plate paintings had incorporated the sculptural, pictorial, and behavioral—he once called the smashed plates embedded in his paintings prosthetic devices for paint strokes. And in the German pavilion, the densely structured, mythical paintings of Anselm Kiefer were introduced along with a single, carved, fully three-dimensional sculpture of a monumental male figure by the painter Georg Baselitz still partially encased in its block of wood.

The Traditional Figure Revived/The Figurative Object Recast: The 1980s
In 1981 the exhibition *New Spirit in Painting,* at London's Royal Academy, signaled the prominence of painting in general and particularly of the Neo-Expressionists' conservative, declarative style which involved aggressive ransacking of older art for imagery, wildly expressive paint strokes, and extremely large scale. A year later, the *Zeitgeist* exhibition in Berlin not only confirmed the dominance of Neo-Expressionist painting but began to showcase sculpture by many of the same artists. Chia's bronze allegorical fountain, which dominated the café, was as summary a statement of the return of an academic tradition to sculpture as Baselitz's carved figure in Venice was the first clue to its emergence.

Yet with few exceptions, the sculptures by the Neo-Expressionist painters did little to advance either the narratives of their paintings or the sculptural tradition. The carved, polychromed sculptures of Baselitz, Penck, and Jorg Immendorf seem but a footnote both to their own work and to such German Expressionist sculptors as Kirchner and Kollwitz. Mimmo Paladino, Cucchi, and Chia seemed to be illustrating their own appropriations of Italian painting, which translated into almost illustrational Beaux-Arts statuary. Of the Neo-Expressionist painters, it seems that Clemente alone has found a sculptural equivalent to the mystical, almost

Jonathan Borofsky
Hammering Man 1981
honey-combed and pressed wood,
metal, electric motor
282 x 132 x 24
Collection The Minneapolis Institute of Arts
Gift of the Aimee Mott Butler Foundation,
Regis Corporation, and Christina N. and
Swan J. Turnblad Fund

primitive remakings of his own imagined self. His papier-mâché and mud figures are as ephemerally tangible and exploratory as his watercolors, his books made on handmade paper, and his ghostly frescoes.

The American painter-sculptors are a more eccentric group, having little in common with each other, except perhaps their Conceptual Art roots. Jennifer Bartlett "extracts" the boats and houses from her paintings, has them remade in wood and concrete, and exhibits them as ensembles with her canvases as almost environmental configurations rather than isolated paintings and sculptures. Most recently, Jonathan Borofsky has made freestanding sculptures that, while comfortable within his room-size multi-media installations, can stand on their own. His monumental, mechanical, Hammering Men have appeared singly and in groups, as have his Chattering Men, both of which capture the noise and animation of the fragmented self characteristic of his installations.

If academic statuary seemed to be lifted whole as sources for the German and Italian Neo-Expressionists, two American artists perverted the academic relief, reinvesting it not only with its traditional didacticism but with an alternative political and moral force. No longer official views celebrating victory, idealism, patriotism, or good citizenship, these darker visions were as shocking stylistically as they were powerfully narrative. Robert Morris, who previously worked as a Minimal, Performance, and Environmental artist, is perhaps the signal cultural reporter-artist of the past twenty years. He began to turn to expressionist drawings with his Firestorm series of the 1970s, and escalated his apocalyptic vision into three-dimensional painting-reliefs during the 1980s. Morris's devastating juxtaposition of painted radiated land- and skyscapes, and dismembered, cast body parts evoked crematoria and the aftermath of a nuclear holocaust.

Robert Longo, who emerged as one of the "Pictures" artists (a term derived from the title of an essay by the critic Douglas Crimp) of the late 1970s, working with appropriated photographic sources and epic per-formances, began to recast his Men in the Streets drawings—isolated falling figures, ambiguously dancing or wounded—into fully three-dimensional freestanding sculptures and into large-scale cast reliefs. Illustrating the modern-day version of hand-to-hand combat in works like Corporate Wars, Longo's painting-reliefs located partial figures crushed in the urban sink. At times, he placed freestanding figures in front of photomurals of decaying urban sites.

In the early 1980s, however, a grittier, anti-heroic kind of figurative sculpture was also beginning to make itself known. If the Zeitgeist exhibition—sited in a restored Neoclassical building located on the western edge of the Berlin Wall—symbolized the reclamation of German culture and history and was to serve as the flagship of the New Academy, The Times Square Show, in a former massage parlor in New York's Times Square district, opened up the possibilities of a more populist and

Robert Longo
Corporate Wars 1982
cast aluminum, lacquer on wood relief
84 x 108 x 36 overall
Private collection

provocative direction for new art. Organized by Collab, a changeable group of young artists who had previously reclaimed sites on the Lower East Side for numerous temporary exhibitions, *The Times Square Show* included Christy Rupp's tinseled rats, John Ahearn's cast, painted reliefs of faces and torsos of his South Bronx neighbors hung high on the walls, and Tom Otterness's small, hand-size figures—both on display in the exhibition and for sale, like dime-store dolls.

By the mid-1980s, the dime-store aesthetic and the urban grit of *The Times Square Show,* and the New Academy's art historical foragings had become curiously conflated. A group of younger English sculptors was sifting through urban detritus, cleaning up their finds, putting them in sculpture, and sending those sculptures on the road. Tony Cragg assembled his plastic toy guns, food containers, and the like, sorted them by color, and deployed them on walls and floors in figurative arrangements. Bill Woodrow and Richard Deacon incorporated mechanical appliances, like washing machines, into their assemblages. The English sculptors, and such Americans as Donald Lipski, were reclaiming not only bits and pieces of domestic culture but the Assemblage aesthetic. They re-socialized and re-aestheticized their tidy messes of the found and minimally transformed, as if Duchamp's bottle-rack had been taken out of its isolationist posture, been dressed up and given some company.

In an almost escalating ambition of shopping and reframing, artists scoured the streets, the thrift shops, and finally the antique stores for figurative objects to incorporate into their art works. Both Julian Schnabel and David Salle recycled more expensive items—Schnabel replacing his antlers and broken plates with antique carpets and Kabuki back-drops (figure/ground already in place for the next "layerings" of images); Salle "collaging" Eames chairs into his paintings.

An even younger generation of artists began to isolate and re-assemble—actually reshelve—rather pristine, fresh-from-the-box "collectibles." Haim Steinbach puts his artifacts of kitsch and 1960s culture, like lava lamps, production pottery, and Halloween masks—on Minimalist-looking, Formica geometries projecting from the wall. Robert Gober remakes "porcelain" sinks, giving them an anthropomorphic mien, while attaching them to walls in the positions of bizarre plumbing fixtures. And Meyer Vaisman aestheticizes toilet seats by painting them with abstract patterns and setting them out on Minimalist cube bases. Simulationism (or Neo-Geo, or Neo-Abstraction, as this work is now called) isolates figurative objects as surrogates for invented sculpture and for art-making itself. Questioning the ideas of authenticity and any presentation of the artistic self, these sculptors quote from a variety of styles and appropriate the behaviors of shopkeepers as well as consumers. Simulationism directly confronts, incorporates, and blatantly restates the obvious fact that, particularly in recent years, art is yet another commodity to be accumulated, displayed, and consumed.

But like any newly coined term for a loose grouping of artists whose differences from each other will become more evident over time than their similarities, the doubling of identity in the Simulationist approach can be seen as either a closed system—hermetically fusing Modernist abstraction and figurative objects (as was recently the case in an exhibition called *Endgame* at the Institute of Contemporary Art, Boston)—or as a way of revitalizing both figurative and abstract sculpture. In Wallace & Donohue's construction *Jack in the Box,* whose movable slats hide or reveal a photo blowup of Jack Nicholson, surrogacy is presented as a changeable, open-ended prospect. Behind the layers of abstraction, the idea of a figurative presence still lurks.

1. Michael Brenson, "Images That Express Essential Human Emotions," *The New York Times,* 26 July 1987, p. 29.
2. Quoted in Ruth Bass, "Minimalism Made Human," *Art News,* vol. 86 (March 1987), p. 97.
3. Lynne Cook, Whitechapel Art Gallery, London, *In Tandem: The Painter-Sculptor in the Twentieth Century,* exh. cat., 1986.
4. Donald Judd, "Specific Objects" (1965); reprinted in *Donald Judd: Complete Writings 1959–1975* (Halifax: The Press of the Nova Scotia College of Art and Design, 1975), p. 183.
5. Quoted in *American Artists on Art: From 1940 to 1980,* ed. Ellen H. Johnson (New York: Harper & Row, 1982), p. 98.
6. Donald Judd, p. 189.
7. Quoted in *The Art of Performance: A Critical Anthology,* eds. Gregory Battcock and Robert Nickas (New York: E.P. Dutton, 1984), p. xvii.
8. Ibid., p. xiii.

The Transformed Object

Carter Ratcliff

Donald Lipski
Balzac #55 1988
marine buoys
241 x 288 x 468
Commissioned with Lannan Foundation
support for the exhibition
Sculpture Inside Outside
Courtesy the artist and Germans van Eck Gallery,
New York

In 1913 Marcel Duchamp mounted a bicycle wheel upside down on a wooden stool. This curious object, he later recalled, was at first "just a distraction. I didn't have any special reason to do it, or any intention of showing it."[1] In 1915 the artist applied the word "readymade" to the object he now titled, simply, *Bicycle Wheel.* Thus Duchamp found a name for a new genre of artwork. The Surrealist poet and theoretician André Breton later praised Duchamp for "acting to divert the object from its ends by coupling it to a new name and by signing it."[2] Though Breton's remarks are dense with Surrealist imagery, one can make out a list of three, possibly four, variants on the Duchampian genre.

Among them are "Max Ernst's interpreted found object" and the "Surrealist object, properly speaking," which Breton sees as a response "to the necessity of establishing . . . a veritable 'physics of poetry.'"[3] This brand of physics advanced its often inscrutable theses with unexpected juxtapositions, as in Joan Miró's *Poetic Object* (1936). Taking cues offered by the Surrealists, Joseph Cornell devised still another genre—the glass-fronted box filled with mysterious odds and ends scavenged from city shops and streets. In 1943 Pablo Picasso made *Bull's Head,* a bronze sculpture cast from a pair of handlebars, like horns, welded to the seat of a bicycle. In the decades since then, the readymade has continued to evolve with remarkable energy.

Breton prefaced his remarks on the readymade and its variants by praising Duchamp, Ernst, and others for having brought about "a total revolution of the object." Their works, he claimed, "lift the prohibition resulting from the overpowering repetition of those objects which meet our glance daily and persuade us to reject as illusion everything that might exist beyond them."[4] In other words, mass-produced objects dull our spirit by filling everyday life with "overpowering repetition;" in this numbed state, we suffer the delusion that nothing is real but the mundane world created by mechanization; however, objects transformed by Duchamp and his colleagues can show us a better reality. The transformed object liberates us because it has itself been set free, unchained from the utilitarian purpose for which it was manufactured. "Acting to divert the object from its ends," said Breton, the artist brings out its "latencies." The object's "conventional value . . . disappears behind its representational value . . . its evocative power."[5]

Marcel Duchamp
Bicycle Wheel 1951
(third version, after lost original of 1913)
metal wheel, 25½ diam., mounted
on painted wood stool, 23¾ high; 50½
high overall
The Sidney and Harriet Janis Collection
The Museum of Modern Art, New York

Marcel Duchamp
Fountain 1917
photograph from the second issue of
The Blind Man (published in May 1917
by Duchamp, Beatrice Wood,
and H.P. Rouché)
The photograph was taken by Alfred Stieglitz

From the outset of the Industrial Revolution, the machine and its products were often seen as agents of a utilitarian ideal inimical to art. Oil painting, stone carving, and bronze casting—these premodern technologies were the appropriate media for artists' defiance of, and escape from, the world created by the Industrial Revolution. In the preface to his novel *Mademoiselle de Maupin* (1835), Théophile Gautier wrote: "There is nothing really beautiful but that which is useless." Variations of that axiom have appeared often in the century and a half since. Of course the artwork's uselessness has its uses, for it frees artists to pursue transcendent aims. Sweeping past the practical concerns of ordinary life, the ambitious work of art ushers its sympathetic audience into the presence of the absolute, which has been defined in modern times as everything from ultimate spiritual truth to the aesthetic purity of the artwork that exists entirely for its own sake. From Gautier's axiom on the uselessness of the beautiful developed the corollary assumption that everything useful is ugly. Thus a chasm separated utilitarian objects from those whose transcendent value qualified them as works of art.

"It seems incomprehensible to the present generation," wrote Gabrielle Buffet-Picabia in 1949, "that the machines which populate the visual world with surprising and spectacular forms, hitherto unknown, could for a long time have remained the victims of a frenzied ostracism in the official world of the arts, that they could have been looked upon as essentially antiplastic, both in substance and in function." Views like that have been revised, says Buffet-Picabia, though she remembers a time when artists turned their backs on the Eiffel Tower in protest against the industrial age it symbolized. She concludes that in the early twentieth century an artist's decision to accept the machine "was in itself a bold, revolutionary act."[6]

The claim is large and yet appears justified. To accept mass-produced objects as the stuff of art was to break violently with the past. Yet, like most revolutions, this one preserved more than it rejected. The barrier that separated paintings and sculptures from other sorts of objects was breached, and many saw this as a cruel desecration; on the other hand, blurred boundaries permitted aesthetic value to flow into regions of the culture from which it had been excluded. In the preface to the *Machine Art* catalogue published by The Museum of Modern Art in 1934, Alfred H. Barr, Jr. spoke of the need to assimilate machines and their products "aesthetically as well as economically."[7]

The campaign to beautify utilitarian works has been successful but is far from complete. In 1915 Duchamp signed a porcelain urinal "R. Mutt" and submitted it to the New York Independents exhibition under the title *Fountain.* Outraged, the hanging committee refused to accept it. Reactions like that are now rare. Nonetheless, a rift still separates transformed objects from artworks made in traditional media. No matter how troubling their

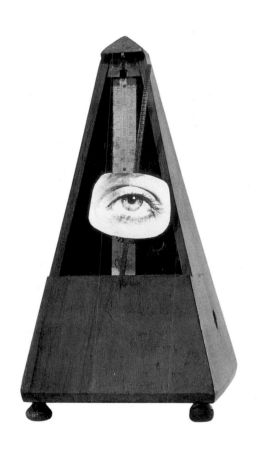

Man Ray
Indestructible Object (or Object to Be Destroyed) 1964
(replica of 1923 original)
metronome with cutout photograph
8⅞ x 4⅜ x 4⅝
Collection The Museum of Modern Art, New York
James Thrall Soby Fund

imagery, paintings and sculptures rest easily in their high-art status. Transformed objects do not, for they make a claim to such status on behalf of forms and materials of mundane origins. Uneasy in their very being, such works are particularly well suited to sustaining Modernism's tradition of challenging settled expectations.

In 1951, the painter Robert Motherwell wrote that Duchamp's *Bottle-Rack*, "a manufactured commercial object from everyday life . . . has a more beautiful form than almost anything made, in 1914, as a sculpture."[8] Some commentators disagree, arguing that only when readymades had entered the Modernist canon did they take on the beauty we ascribe to works of art. Motherwell seems to be closer to the mark. From 1910 to the present, artists have usually favored the most elegant of the machine's products. Though *Bottle-Rack* is an intricate form, its details gain clarity from their quickly deciphered rhythm. The contours of Duchamp's *Fountain* have the smooth organic fullness of Jean Arp's biomorphic marble sculptures. Only on occasion does the transformation of the object lead an artist away from perspicuous form. Kurt Schwitters made art from scraps of paper, wood, and metal. His deliberate clutter might bewilder an eye unfamiliar with Cubism, the style of painting Schwitters took as his starting point. Similarly, a knowledge of Abstract Expressionist painting helps us decipher the rough, even chaotic work that goes by the name of Assemblage. For the most part, however, the artist's eye plunges into the mass-produced flux of contemporary life in search of uncluttered forms.

In 1922 Man Ray cut an eye from a photograph of a woman and attached it to the pendulum of a metronome. A machine for measuring time became a symbol of the pulse animating the body. Later, on the reverse of a drawing related to this work, Man Ray inscribed a note that clarifies its title, *Object to Be Destroyed.* First, the artist advises, adjust the metronome "to the tempo desired;" then, "with a hammer well-aimed, try to destroy the whole with a single blow."[9] The violence of those instructions puts Man Ray at the center of the Dada movement, which loosed a carefully cultivated spirit of anarchy against traditional assumptions about art's proper media and meanings—and against the belief that a work of art should aspire to eternity. *Object to Be Destroyed* was, in theory, disposable, yet its disposability was not that of a gadget fated to become obsolete. Instead, as a symbol of "one who is loved but is not seen any more,"[10] this humanized metronome served as the prospective target of an enraged vengeance.

Object to Be Destroyed confronts us with a restless stare. Man Ray's *The Enigma of Isadore Ducasse* (1920), no longer extant, was a sewing machine shrouded in cloth—a presence with its gaze veiled. The following year he glued a row of metal tacks, points outward, to the lower surface of a flatiron, converting this humble object into a work named *Gift.* The

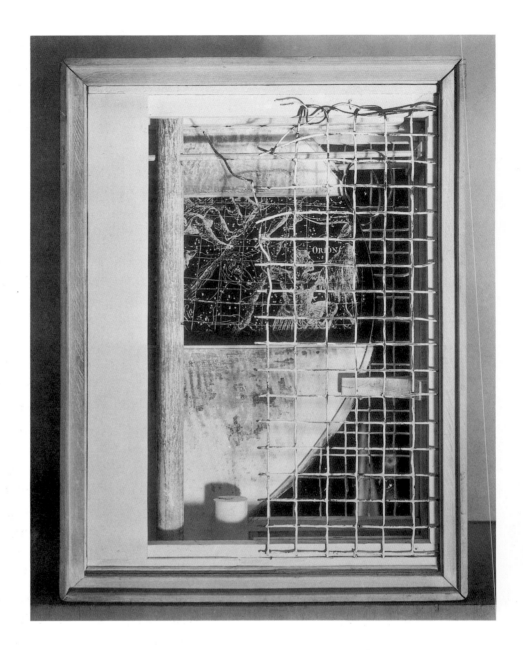

Joseph Cornell
Central Park Carrousel,
in Memoriam 1950
wood, mirror, wire netting, paper
20¼ x 14½ x 6¾
Collection The Museum of Modern Art,
New York
Katharine Cornell Fund

tacks deprive the iron of all its utilitarian virtue, turning it into an emblem of a domestic nightmare. *Gift* asserts itself with an appeal—or a threat—to the hand, rather than an attempt to return our gaze. *Object* (1936), a fur-covered cup, saucer, and spoon by the Surrealist Meret Oppenheim solicits our imaginations with the promise of a peculiar caress. *My Governess* (1936) is a pair of women's shoes bound with twine and presented on a platter. To their high heels Oppenheim attached ruffled paper decorations of the kind usually reserved for crown roasts of lamb. Since governesses routinely administer corporal punishment, these shoes take on life as victims of retaliation. The symbolic nature of the shoes and ruffles enabled the artist to propose cannibalism.

As Dada absurdism became Surrealist obsession, the found object assumed the look of paraphernalia for a cult of one. With its stuffed bird and framed mannequin leg resting on a pedestal for a derby hat, Miró's

Poetic Object looks like a totem commemorating the fragments of a dream. Presumably the artist was able to work his way back, in memory, from this elegant jumble of objects to some coherent meaning. Perhaps others are able to do the same, but of course their memories cannot follow the same paths as Miró's. Such Surrealist objects often isolate viewers in the irreducible particularity of individual experience. Mass-produced objects, by contrast, promise to bring us close to one another by standardizing our lives. They have fulfilled their promise, but only superficially. Transformed by artists, ordinary products can take us beneath the surface of a shared consumerism to zones where each imagination must fend for itself. The art of Joseph Cornell suggests how deeply private are the meanings that lurk in the flow of throwaway objects and images.

Though Cornell admired the Surrealists, he didn't share their revolutionary passions. His were nostalgic, though indifferent to preindustrial crafts. Far from undermining authenticity in Cornell's eyes, mechanical production—and reproduction—made objects and images real for him. Thus he felt no missionary call to redeem the repetitious output of industry and the media. Feeling alone and possibly damned, he called upon the past's accumulation of consumable goods to redeem him. A fantasy of the tropics entered his art by way of parrots clipped from picture books. Pages torn from Baedeker, turn-of-the-century luggage labels, and engravings of early nineteenth-century Italian ballerinas represented European culture. Sepia photogravures of Hedy Lamarr, Bronzino portraits in full color reproduction, marbles, charts of the galaxies, clay pipes, the innards of watches, and many, many other things appear in arrangements that recall, by turns, the cabinets of a relentless hoarder and the altars of a secret religion.

An artist can transform an object simply by selecting it to be a part of his oeuvre. Such choices might be seen as conceptual gestures. Though most transformations are physical and thus require the artist to lay hands on an object, evidence of this engagement is often difficult to find. One must look very closely to detect the seams in Cornell's passages of pasted paper, and even when found these breaks in the image give no sense of the artist's hand. Transformed objects sometimes appear to be the work of some aesthetic ghost in the machinery of mass production. Abstract Expressionism showed signs of impatience with that ghostliness. Each painterly painter of the New York School wanted to impress his canvas with immediately legible, undeniably personal traces of his own hand. Many succeeded. It would be difficult to mistake, say, Willem de Kooning's touch for Philip Guston's. Unintentionally, the Abstract Expressionists also produced a generic image of painterliness, which some younger artists rather uncritically imitated. But one of them, Jasper Johns, treated this New York School style as if it were an object he could appropriate in a Duchampian spirit.

Meret Oppenheim
Object (Le Déjeuner en fourrure)   1936
fur-covered cup, saucer, and spoon
cup, 4⅜ diam.
saucer, 9⅜ diam.
spoon, 8 long
2⅞ overall height
Collection The Museum of Modern Art, New York
Purchase

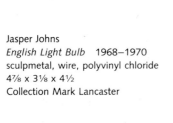

Jasper Johns
English Light Bulb   1968–1970
sculpmetal, wire, polyvinyl chloride
4⁷⁄₈ x 3⅛ x 4½
Collection Mark Lancaster

Johns's version of Abstract Expressionist brushwork is the product of an observation: no matter how passionately deployed, a style is a cluster of conventions subject to analysis and adaptation to new purposes. While Johns was learning to paint in an Abstract Expressionist manner, without the usual emotionally heated, self-revelation of that movement, he borrowed a style of ready-made lettering from stencils used on crates; he took images from the public domain—the American flag, the concentric circles of a target, a map of the United States. He made common objects into sculptures; casting a light bulb in bronze, Johns changed it from a radiant presence to an opaque thing that reflects the light dully. Instead of opening space to vision, the Johnsian light bulb absorbs the viewer's gaze; space becomes a matter of indifference as vision gives way to thought. Johns turns the viewer into a thinker groping through a labyrinth built from a series of conceptual reversals.

Johns's *Painted Bronze* (1960) presents two casts of ale cans side by side, each bearing a Ballantine label meticulously rendered in oils. In their transition from commercial tin to bronze, a high-art material, the ale cans represent two states of verisimilitude—for one is hollow (empty) and the other is not (filled). Yet this hardly matters to vision, which takes the two cans as twins. The difference between them counts chiefly in the realm of concept. In rescuing utilitarian objects from their ordinary uses, Johns turned them into emblems of paradox—the most elusive, ungraspable sort of thought. Yet there is paradox even here, for Johns's transformations

Robert Rauschenberg
Bed 1955
painted bed
75¼ x 31½ x 6½
Collection Mr. Leo Castelli

often give an object a weight, a substantiality, that it didn't have when he found it.

Duchamp haunts Johns's art as a model of wit to be outwitted. Robert Rauschenberg's Duchamp is a different artist, a source of immediate pleasure. In a recent interview, Rauschenberg said that when he first saw Duchamp's *Bicycle Wheel*, "I thought it was the most fantastic sculpture I had ever seen."[11] Rauschenberg was then making paintings with collage elements. As these became bulkier, he had difficulty attaching them to the canvas. His jerry-built solutions produced a hybrid genre, the amalgamation of traditional painting and wall relief he calls "combine painting." In one of his best-known combines, *Bed* (1955), Rauschenberg sent a torrent of virtuosic brushwork spilling over the sheet, pillow, and quilt that take the place of stretched canvas. Here Abstract Expressionism's free-floating imagery soaks deep into familiar surfaces. Though the violence of the style remains ambiguous (does the artist turn it inward or outward or both?), it is suddenly more intimate. Rauschenberg dismisses the decision to paint on bedclothes as a necessity forced upon him by a shortage of canvas, and he underplays his inventiveness in building stuffed animals into his art—as in *Monogram* (1957), a long-haired angora goat ringed by an automobile tire—yet few artists have pursued Surrealist tactics of juxtaposition with Rauschenberg's verve.

Where the Surrealists sought an evocative illogic Breton called "poetic," Rauschenberg's combines and constructions have a declamatory, theatrical feel. Their impact is always visceral, often sexual. But even when they stand free of the wall, they have the air of uncontainable collages that only imply theater. Edward Kienholz assembles ready-made objects in works with a close resemblance to stage sets. And whereas Rauschenberg's ennoblement of the ordinary is cheerful, Kienholz's is elegiac. His tableaux of battered furniture, broken appliances, and chunks of vernacular architecture argue that art cannot redeem modernity, only deepen our sense of its unredeemable nature. Here the found object heightens melancholy, as it does when surrounded by the awkward figures George Segal casts from plaster.

In an essay for the catalogue *The Art of Assemblage,* an exhibition he organized in 1961, William C. Seitz wrote that "assemblage marks a change from a subjective, fluidly abstract art toward a revised association with environment."[12] During this period, artists and commentators alike displayed a particularly clear awareness of what had always been at issue when artists retrieve objects from the world beyond art: the border our culture draws between its aesthetic and non-aesthetic sectors. Intent on obscuring this boundary line, Rauschenberg supplied the catalogue with his well-known remark about trying "to act in the gap" between art and life. The poet Alain Jouffroy was quoted to similar effect on the subject of Daniel Spoerri's "snare pictures:" Assemblages that freeze the contents of an after-dinner table or a cluttered desk in a permanent configuration. These works, said Jouffroy, "are situated at the intersection of art and life, at the point where contradictions cancel each other out."[13]

Objects transformed by artists stand like landmarks at the outer edges of territory newly claimed for art. Commenting on Richard Stankiewicz's scrap-metal Assemblages, the painter and critic Fairfield Porter exchanged the image of a cultural map for an evocation of the life cycle. Made from materials once "mechanical and functional" and now discarded, wrote Porter, Stankiewicz's junk sculpture "is a creation of life out of death, the new life being of quite a different nature than the old one that was decaying on the junk pile, on the sidewalk, on the used-car lot."[14] This talk of resurrection takes its plausibility from the hints of human anatomy and conversational gesture that Stankiewicz built into his works.

Much Assemblage directed harsh questions at the utilitarian culture that had supplied this art with its battered and rusted materials. Is functionalism truly functional? Do aesthetic impulses actually have the power to redeem the debris-filled world created by industrial technology? It is difficult not to read the hapless, defeated air of much Assemblage as a

Edward Kienholz and Nancy Reddin Kienholz
Portrait of a Mother with Past Affixed Also   1980–1981
mixed media environment
99⅞ x 94⅝ x 81
Collection Walker Art Center
Walker Special Purchase Fund, 1985

negative response to such questions. When Pop Art appeared, early criticism tried to interpret it too as a critique of mass-produced culture. By the mid-1960s, few commentators still took this tack. With the exception of James Rosenquist, whose paintings reflect the image-barrage to which the media subject us, the Pop artists borrowed from life with a deadpan insouciance. In any case, Andy Warhol, Roy Lichtenstein, and others were more interested in found images than in found objects.

In recent years Pop artist Claes Oldenburg has enlarged and simplified the forms of such objects as baseball bats and garden trowels with results that are, literally, monumental. During the 1960s, his objects held to a human scale. Made of vinyl or canvas duck and stuffed with kapok, these Oldenburgian washbasins, Eskimo Pies, and drum sets have eerily human presences. Like bodies, they are soft; propped up in a corner or hung from a ceiling or wall, they stretch out or slouch in postures with which one inevitably empathizes. Though Oldenburg came to critical notice in the company of the Pop artists, his sculpture has its closest affinities with the Surrealist dream.

Oldenburg is generally conceded to be the preeminent Pop sculptor, though Andy Warhol's *Brillo Boxes* (1964) extended the tactics of his early canvases to three dimensions; and during the 1960s, the painter Tom Wesselmann built a series of tableaux as glossy as Kienholz's are tarnished. Incorporating hardware and household products straight off the shelf—plumbing fixtures, towel racks, towels, shower curtains— Wesselmann's Assemblages offer a summary of consumerist desires. Transposed in pristine condition from the marketplace to his tableaux, these objects address us as blankly as the eyeless faces of the "great American nudes" that so often appear at the center of these works.

Wesselmann made it difficult for critics to see Pop Art as an assault on the emptiness of mass-produced culture, for he appeared to delight in the formal traits—the bright colors, the lush but uncomplicated out-lines, the sleek textures—of consumer products. An object transported across the border from ordinary life to the realm of art usually takes on an aesthetic value it lacked in its native land. In Wesselmann's art, the opposite occurs: traces of a high-art tradition take on the aura of supermarket products. Within a framework of pictorial devices borrowed chiefly from Matisse, Wesselmann reverses a procedure first employed by Duchamp to redeem mass-produced objects from their banality.

One sees a similar reversal in the work of such artists of the 1980s as Jeff Koons, Haim Steinbach, and other practitioners of "appropriation art," as it is called. The announced purpose of "appropriative" tactics is to render the viewer conscious of the process by which even works of art fall prey to the consumerist imperatives so powerful in contemporary life. For instance, Koons's *Rabbit* (1985), an inflated plastic rabbit cast in chrome-plated steel, reenacts the drama of adding aesthetic value to a

Tom Wesselmann
Bathtub Collage 1963
mixed media
48 x 60 x 6
Collection Museum für Moderne Kunst,
Frankfurt

throw-away item by transposing it to the art world and giving it sculptural
weight. Offered as a critique of the process that produces stylish art-world
commodities, this chrome bunny has become precisely that—a stylish
art-world commodity. Appropriation art often provides the most
convincing examples of the commodification it purports to question.

On shelves designed in a mock-Minimalist style, Haim Steinbach
assembles readymades with an eye to formal affinities. In *vinyl that already
looks wet* (1986), for example, rows of lava lamps, reddish and bluish,
offer a counterpoint to two stacks of ice chests, one stack bright red and
the other a clear blue. Such arrangements invite the viewer to see how
readily consumer products can become occasions for easy delectation and
to wonder if such delectation is not a form of consumerism in disguise.
Finally, though, Steinbach's critique of the artwork-as-commodity
resembles that of Koons; it applies most powerfully to Steinbach's own
work, which glows with the allure of a shop window or merchandise
counter. From the time of Wesselmann's tableaux to the present, a few
artists have deflected the Duchampian tradition of the readymade
from its main path. Rather than charge ordinary things with transcendent
value, they use those objects as the means of transporting ordinary
values into the realm of art. Nonetheless, the line that begins with
Duchamp's *Bicycle Wheel* has continued unbroken into the present.

Yet readymades presented in a consumerist spirit threaten to obscure
the value of the Duchampian tradition, and this is not the only threat that
this tradition has faced. A common object becomes a work of art when
metaphor raises it above its original purpose. During the 1960s, Minimalism

proscribed all metaphorical readings in favor of physical facts directly perceived. Though this proscription was widely respected, Robert Rauschenberg and the Assemblagists defied the ban with juxtapositions that gave found objects the air of human figures, secular totems, ritual objects, and more. This was the decade when Jean Tinguely built anthropomorphic machines from the ruins of ordinary ones, and Lucas Samaras revised the Surrealists' "physics of poetry" for his own, violently idiosyncratic purposes. Metaphor carried on its transforming work during the Minimalist period and, as *Sculpture Inside Outside* shows, ordinary objects have continued to undergo profound transformations at artists' hands.

Breton pointed out that "the overpowering repetition" of ordinary objects dulls us and deprives them of all but utilitarian value. To redeem the common object, to make it the vehicle of transcendent meanings, was for decades a process of releasing it from its sameness. Artists transformed the object to make it singular, to give it the aura of individuality, either in isolation or as part of an aesthetically charged ensemble. Then came Jasper Johns's repetitive images—his gridded series of numbers and alphabets, the concentric circles of his targets and the stripes of his flags. Johns's cultivation of sameness pointed in two directions: toward Pop Art's reiterations, particularly those of Andy Warhol's silk-screened paintings; and toward the Minimalist seriality that made an early appearance in Frank Stella's striped canvases. Repetition had taken on aesthetic value.

Donald Lipski may have found in Pop Art or in Minimalism a precedent for multiplying a single object within a single work. On one hand, he employs products like metal buckets and ballpoint pens, which recall Pop imagery; on the other, he tends to choose hard-edged objects which, in crisp alignment, form patterns of Minimalist clarity. In any case, Lipski's art reaches beyond these formal precedents, for his patterns do not claim geometric self-sufficiency, as Minimalist sculpture does; nor does his choice of objects generate an atmosphere of Warholian irony, much less Wesselmannian celebration.

Free Reef (1987) is a ring of fifteen galvanized steel buckets, each disgorging broken glass. The neatness of the ring suggests the compulsion of ritual; and though shards of glass imply accident, they too are swept into a rather tidy pattern. Ritual order seems to have conquered random violence or at least contained it. In *Building Steam #252* (1984), the ammunition in a cartridge belt has radiated into ballpoint pens. Pursuing resemblances between two sorts of pointed objects—bullets and pens—the artist has disarmed instruments of violence. By detaching serial form from its Minimalist sources, Lipski sensitizes it to the flicker of wit that has played around transformed objects from the time of Duchamp's *Bicycle Wheel*. Lipski's patterns suggest that he sees the industrialized environment as a rebus to be worked out by arranging mass-produced objects in configurations which were until now unknown. His results have the clarity and self-assurance of solutions to puzzles, of jumbles set right. It is up to the viewer to decipher both question and answer. No less than the "poetic" objects of Surrealists, Lipski's works give evidence of obsession without revealing its precise nature. Thus he leaves the way clear for our own obsessions to come to the fore and, perhaps, to evolve into intuitions about mass production, the world it creates, and our place in it.

Unlike Lipski, Walter Martin remakes what he finds. In *A Capital Idea* (1982) he perches the miniaturized ruins of a Greek temple atop a pillar cast from countless toy cars. Faced by a symbol of Western antiquity teetering on a heap of industrial culture's most familiar emblems, one senses Martin's concern for the precariousness of our historical imagination. Can our culture remain whole when present and past are linked by such fragmentary means? Yet this Acropolis of scrap metal also confronts one with a figurative presence, like the Surrealist object, which often has the look of a bodily fragment. Martin's towering form returns the body to wholeness and gives it a heroic stature, as if to suggest that only a tragic sense—rather, a tragi-comic sense—of the past can sustain our history. His choice of objects for transformation also preserves the feel for the absurd that has traditionally attended the metamorphosis of ordinary objects into works of art.

Old Fleece Preaching to the Sharks (1985–1986) sets a dramatic scene without marking off, even sketchily, the boundaries of a stage. As "Old Fleece" (in this incarnation a headless dog) silently addresses a corner piled high with plaster bones, the work drifts free of its gallery setting; seemingly at home in boundlessness, one can imagine no limits on the range of possible meanings in his sermon. Martin invites the imagination to play at the daunting scale of the sublime. Recasting Romanticism's absolutes in latter-day terms, he encourages us to wonder, in an age when so much we prize as natural comes to us in facsimile form, precisely what difference separates organism from machine, and death from growing obsolete.

Like Schwitters, Jin Soo Kim gathers materials from the city's refuse, deploys them with a subtle regard for details of shape and texture, and sustains that subtlety with an energy that produces artworks large enough for the viewer to enter. Kim's environments recall the three versions of Schwitters's *Merzbau.* But such comparisons have limits. Beneath the incipient chaos of Schwitters's *Merz*-surfaces stood the solid architecture of traditional composition. His building block was the wood scrap, with its random, attenuated references not only to the geometry of buildings but to that of the picture frame. By contrast, the most salient element in Kim's work is the metal chain, an object that defies the urban impulse to right angles. Her bits and pieces of wire and fabric show the same indifference to geometry's rationalizing influences.

The *Merzbau* was a Dada house. Kim builds caves. The interiors of her environments have the curving roofs, the jagged forms, one finds in the earth's interior. Yet the proliferation of detail that defines these spaces denies them closure. Their upper surfaces suggest skies as readily as they do the roofs of caves. Like Jackson Pollock's skeins of dripped paint, Kim's intricately tangled materials immerse the eye in textures implying boundlessness; and so, by another route, she brings us to the sublime, the expansive region where Martin spins grand, elusive tales from enigmatic figures. Martin's juxtapositions charge form with narrative. Kim generates a narrative atmosphere from the proliferation of form. Both cultivate a sense of endlessness, the temporal counterpart of infinite space.

Other artists transform the object with the intent to focus our vision rather than expand it. Robert Gober borrows the forms of a familiar object—a sink, a playpen—then reconstructs that object accurately enough for his sculptures to succeed as impersonations. The white enamel covering his *Subconscious Sink* (1985) has the industrial sheen of porcelain over cast iron. This finish looks familiar but the shape does not. Gober's sculptures require us to re-imagine the possibilities for formal evolution. *Subconscious Sink* makes a dramatic self-assertion of an individuality that may have begun as a marginal difference from a standard sink. On the other hand, evolution may have flowed the other way, from a primordial Y-shape that at one extremity developed a resemblance to a sink. If so, a kind of protective adaptation is at work in Gober's art, an impulse for homeless, unanchored forms to take on the familiarity of manufactured objects.

Surrealist poetics rescued materials from functionality by defying the expectations of ordinary life. Such tactics often left an object unchanged. Gober departs from this procedure in two ways: he revises the shapes of things, and in doing so leaves them at least potentially functional; a sink with a Goberian design could be made to operate in the usual way. For Gober, usefulness shades into the artwork's aestheticized condition in an unbroken continuum. Thus his works blend opposites, a tactic that makes them symbols of all-inclusiveness. His forms may express a utopian hope of reconciling our practical and transcendental impulses and thus rendering the user of a functional object indistinguishable from the viewer of an artwork. That would put us at one with ourselves. Why not go on to make up our differences with objects? Such questions lead one to interpret Gober's aesthetic as an extension of Breton's optimistic "revolution of the object." Nonetheless, Gober may deny utopian yearnings. After all, the encompassing nature of their enigmas renders his forms self-sufficient; rather than encourage unity, these objects could support our yearnings for absolute personal autonomy.

Richard Artschwager sometimes blends a demotic shape—that of a table, a chair, a cabinet—with a geometric form like a cube or a parallelogram. Robert Therrien goes further in this direction. He tries, with an ironic sense of futility equal to Artschwager's, to extract from particular things the quality of thingness itself. This would look like a Minimalist revival if Therrien's forms, monochrome and smoothly finished, were not haunted by the ghosts of the ordinary objects that appear to be their ancestors. In the mid-1960s, Robert Morris designed gray boxes to stand on the floor like axioms of geometry made palpable. Therrien has built an untitled piece (1982) that looks like a Morris box. Yet it also recalls a small bench. When the artist focuses his transforming powers on the Minimalist object, he charges it with the sense of history that Minimalism tried to suppress with the dream of a pure art descended, fully formed, from a Euclidean heaven.

On other occasions, Therrien's transformations stress the geometric clarities lurking in ordinary things. An untitled flat red wall piece from 1983 seems to have begun as an image of a steepled church. But as Therrien simplifies outline, scale grows slippery. Couldn't we trace this work to some small, spouted object of a kind we might find in a still life by a Precisionist painter like Charles Sheeler? If so, transformation would be a reduction rather than an enlargement in size. Both possibilities are equally convincing, and that fact stymies conclusions about scale. Generic in its simplicity, this object looks as if it could assume any size and maintain its integrity. Though Therrien makes it impossible to say what his forms take as their starting points, he always ensures that the question comes up. Seen in isolation, *Blue Oval* (1983) could be mistaken for the work of an abstract artist. In the company of Therrien's other works, it looks like an emblem, a form embodying a meaning. But what meaning, precisely? If we knew how *Blue Oval* arrived at its present state, we might be able to say. This sculpture invites interpretation and, with the finesse of a Surrealist object crossbred with Minimalist geometry, eludes it. Therrien's emblems emblematize the unresolved state of our negotiations with the objects that constitute our world—and our art.

With a pneumatic hammer and sheets of aluminum, Robert Lobe takes the imprint of tree trunks, roots, and boulders. The resulting works are large, with rough angles and, where they reproduce the sweeping curve of a heavy branch, they have an imposing span. Nonetheless, Lobe's sculptures have a delicate and, at their edges, almost feathery quality. Lobe stays as close to the form and texture of rock and bark as his thick sheets of metal and mechanized chisel permit him. He achieves a surprising degree of accuracy, yet he doesn't so much transform natural objects as produce after-images of them. Despite their responsibility to literal fact and their evident weight, these works have the feel of startlingly enlarged details from Romantic landscape painting. They seem to be shot through with a spiritualizing vision.

The works of art descended from Duchamp's *Bicycle Wheel* transpose ordinary objects from their usual places to the realm of art—though, as Therrien's sculpture shows, it is not always possible to say what that ordinary object was. This "revolution of the object" broke with tradition for the sake of sustaining that tradition's underlying values. By extending the possibility of aesthetic meaning to objects thought to be incapable of it, the transformed object strengthened those meanings. As ordinary objects entered the realm of art, that realm expanded; and the definition of the natural grew larger, for the products of the machine joined the roster of candidates, like human nature and the preindustrial landscape, worthy of the artist's attention. The "revolution of the object" sought to unify a world divided between nature and the unnatural, the manufactured. Though the division persists, artists have made it possible to imagine its disappearance. By turning a found process, a factory procedure, on objects considered natural in the old sense, Lobe brings the history of the transformed object full circle. Yet his doing so imposes no closure, no end of an aesthetic line. Quite the opposite. Lobe's transformations open the way for a new round of reconciliations between the world we have inherited and the world we have made.

1. Pierre Cabanne, *Dialogues with Marcel Duchamp,* trans. Ron Padgett (New York: Viking Press, 1971), p. 47.

2. André Breton, "Crisis of the Object" in Patrick Waldberg, *Surrealism* (New York: McGraw-Hill, 1966), p. 86.

3. Ibid., p. 85.

4. Ibid.

5. Ibid., p. 86.

6. Gabrielle Buffet-Picabia, "Some Memories of Pre-Dada: Picabia and Duchamp" in *The Dada Painters and Poets,* ed. Robert Motherwell (New York: Wittenborn, Schultz, 1951), p. 257.

7. Alfred H. Barr, Jr., "Introduction," in The Museum of Modern Art, New York, *Machine Art,* exh. cat., 1934, n.p.

8. Robert Motherwell, in *The Dada Painters and Poets,* p. xvii.

9. Man Ray, inscription on the reverse of a 1932 drawing related to *Object to Be Destroyed* (1923), quoted in Pontus Hulten, The Museum of Modern Art, New York, *The Machine as Seen at the End of the Mechanical Age,* exh. cat., 1968, p. 153.

10. Ibid.

11. Robert Rauschenberg, interview in Barbara Rose, *Rauschenberg* (New York: Vintage Books, 1987), p. 87.

12. William C. Seitz, The Museum of Modern Art, New York, *The Art of Assemblage,* exh. cat., 1961, p. 87.

13. Ibid., p. 132.

14. Fairfield Porter, quoted in *The School of New York,* ed. B.H. Friedman (New York: Grove Press, 1959), pp. 72, 76.

Organic Inflections

Douglas Dreishpoon

Form is both deeply material and highly spiritual. It cannot exist without a material support; it cannot be properly expressed without invoking some supra-material principle. Form poses a problem which appeals to the utmost resources of our intelligence, and it affords the means which charm our sensibility and even entice us to the verge of frenzy. Form is never trivial or indifferent; it is the magic of the world.—Albert M. Dalcq[1]

The most fundamental aspect of organic abstraction is its connectedness to nature. And, as object makers, abstract sculptors can always defer, as Theodore Roszak did in 1949, to nature as the ultimate form-giver:

I have yet to see any work [of art], however 'abstract,' that has not already had its counterpart in nature. . . . The most rigid geometry in contemporary art pales when we take time to explore geometric formulations in mineral and other crystalline structures. Microscopic observation reveals a world of geometric and amorphic structures that dispels at a glance the myth that abstract art bears no indebtedness to nature.[2]

Roszak's "microscopic observation" is but one way of looking at the relationship between abstract art and nature. In another sense, the term "organic" implies art that relates to living things and encompasses a wide range of natural motifs that derive from, or imply, internal and external aspects of the human body, landscape, and biological and botanical systems in a perpetual state of growth and decay. "Organic" also denotes, by extension, levels of existence beyond those inferred from obvious natural forms; such "organicism" implies a synthetic model, where every element (natural or man-made) has a homeostatic relationship to the whole.

In tracing the historical convolutions of organic abstraction, it would be misleading to impose narrow stylistic criteria based on formal considerations alone. Compare an amorphic blob with a perfect sphere. Though strikingly different, the forms are topological equivalents and both issue from nature. A concretion by Jean Arp is just as organic as one of Richard Long's circles conceived within landscape, while the work of Constantin Brancusi offers a paradigm that unites organic and geometric principles.

Over the course of about seven decades, organic abstraction has assumed various guises. Some sculptors offered their own explanations for what they did. Arp referred to his work as "concrete." Henry Moore

Jene Highstein
Untitled (detail)   1987–1988
three elements
granite
108 x 48 x 28
75 x 61 x 43
30 x 90 x 51
Commissioned with Lannan Foundation
support for the exhibition
Sculpture Inside Outside
Courtesy the artist and Michael Klein, Inc.,
New York

Theodore Roszak
Golden Bough 1949–1950
steel brazed with brass and copper
18 x 13½
Collection estate of the artist

Constantin Brancusi
Sculpture for the Blind 1916
marble: 12 long
plaster base: 10 high
Collection Philadelphia Museum of Art
Louise and Walter Arensberg Collection

Jean Arp
Aquatique 1953
marble
13½ x 25⁵⁄₁₆ x 9³⁄₁₆
Collection Walker Art Center
Gift of the T.B. Walker Foundation, 1955

proposed Vitalism as a philosophical handle. While the material and ideological underpinnings of the sensibility have changed dramatically over time, certain fundamental characteristics remain constant: the sculptor's position as maker and synthesizer; faith in process and intuition (tempered by intellection); a receptiveness to strange and unfamiliar images; a willingness to experiment with new materials; a strong affinity for the body and landscape; and the object's import as metaphor, symbol, and an index of form-generating principles.

When pondering organic abstraction, Jean Arp's biomorphism immediately comes to mind.[3] Such an association is inevitable given the sculptor's prolific output and his impact on subsequent generations of sculptors. Believing that "art is a fruit that grows in man, like a fruit on a plant, or a child in its mother's womb,"[4] Arp searched for ways to suggest nature's complexity and underlying unity. As early as 1915 he began to investigate the characteristics of natural form in drawings he made of branches, roots, grass, and stones. His *concrétions humaines,* or "stones produced by human hand," developed out of these early drawings as did his Dada woodcuts and reliefs executed during the 1910s and 1920s. Described by the artist as objects that "fit naturally into nature," these concretions extended his preoccupation with organic growth and morphology. Arp's notion of concrete, a term he and Wassily Kandinsky rescued from Theo van Doesburg's earlier—formalist—definition, united aspects of geometric abstraction and Surrealism. Arp was skeptical of art that imposed stylistic limitations and proposed definitive answers to spiritual questions. Concrete art was his way of hedging dogmatic assertions, humoring the unknown, and reaffirming man's vital connection to nature.

Arp's relationship to Parisian Surrealism during the 1920s and 1930s, however, was peripheral. Though he questioned the Surrealists' emphasis on automatism and psycho-sexual themes, the mysterious nature of dreams, a poetic interpretation of objects, and the metamorphosis of matter remained germane to his sensibility. His fascination with undifferentiated form in nature, form without precise definition or distinguishing characteristics, has an affinity to Georges Bataille's concept of the *informe.*[5] As an ideological construct, *informe* signified the collapse of classification. Its task was to undo meaning. Although Bataille's coupling of *informe* with aspects of brutality, mutilation, and putrefaction was antithetical to Arp's optimism, his status as an outsider—a dissident Surrealist—would have encouraged Arp, who never relinquished his own position on the fringe.

Arp's biomorphs are poetic equivalents for natural forms that imply simultaneously everything and nothing. Each object was an empirical investigation of material—plaster, marble, granite—that developed heuristically into organic configurations. His interest in cellular morphology and undifferentiated levels of animal development was not only compatible with a vanguard reductivist aesthetic, but also reflected his deeper search

50

for universal generative principles.[6] What began in 1932 as personal experimentation with abstract forms in the round subsequently spawned a generic school of sculptural abstraction. If less-inspired sculptors have unsuccessfully mimicked Arp's biomorphic imagery, his belief in intuition, poetics, and the fluid manipulation of material has provided a viable procedural approach.

Receptive to Arp's heuristic approach, Henry Moore began to investigate, during the 1930s, the inherent forms and configurations of organic material. Although he was for the most part a figurative sculptor, during that time he pushed his work toward abstraction. As a founding member of Unit One, an association of progressive English architects and painters informed by European Surrealism and Constructivism, Moore developed very definite views about what sculpture should be. He shared his ideas with art historian Herbert Read, who formulated a theory of Vitalism.[7] An elusive concept colored by the earlier writings of Henri Bergson (particularly his notion of life force, or *élan vital*), D'Arcy Thompson's *On Growth and Form* (1917), and Henri Focillon's *La vie des formes* (1934), Vitalism came to embody a poetic, philosophical stance that elevated artistic intuition above scientific rationalism. It stressed an empirical approach to making and forming objects and sought to animate the sculptural object, to infuse life into inanimate material. This quasi-religious overtone, traceable to Rodin, Brancusi, and Arp, gradually evolved into a universal reverence for nature. In this respect, the work of Michael Lekakis represents a contemporary extension of Vitalism. Lekakis, who began making sculpture in the 1930s, always preferred wood as his primary material and sought to maintain a "neutrality" when probing for intrinsic forms. For him, "neutrality" embodied a procedural attitude that relied more on experimentation and self-discovery than on a priori conventions. Working within a tradition established by Brancusi and Arp, Lekakis investigated universal geometrical shapes: variations on the sphere, spiral, tetrahedron, and cube, which he often combined with more amorphic forms. In his best sculpture he realized the full potential of his material by balancing intuition and technical finesse.

Isamu Noguchi's earliest childhood experiences in Japan, followed by his association with Brancusi in Paris in 1926–1927, extensive world travel, and study of ethnographic art, set the stage for a profusion of stylistically diverse objects. Yet his fundamental conception of sculpture has always centered around natural laws of growth and balance:

> The essence of sculpture is for me the perception of space, the continuum of our existence. . . . Since our experiences of space are, however, limited to momentary segments of time, growth must be the core of existence. . . . If I say that growth is the constant transfusion of human meaning into the encroaching void, then how great is our need today when our knowledge of the universe has filled space with energy, driving us towards a greater chaos and new equilibriums.[8]

51

Noguchi's preference for stone and wood (though he has also worked in various metals) is due to their "natural" qualities. He has spoken about his material's connectedness to the earth, to which he "returns recurrently . . . to escape fragmentation with a new synthesis, within the sculpture and related to spaces." Never trite or inconsequential, Noguchi's sculpture—carved, modeled, cast, and fabricated—affirms the totality of existence.

Nature has always provided Louise Bourgeois with a wellspring of ideas. Investigating a variety of materials—marble, wood, plaster, aluminum, bronze, and latex—she has consistently transposed her insights, fears, and obsessions into sculptural equivalents. In this respect, her sustained interest in biomorphic form, initially stimulated by Surrealism, is related as much to the form's psycho-sexual implications as it is to topology.[9]

Early on, Bourgeois investigated biomorphic form on many levels. If nature has provided her with an endless array of organic images, its embodiment in landscape also has been a central inspiration. Not only has she conceived a series of pieces around this theme, but many of the forms in her drawings issue out of nondescript terrains. In her mind, landscape has a strong connection to the human body. Referring to the Landscape series of 1967, she commented:

> . . . they are anthropomorphic and they are landscape also, since our body could be considered from a topographical point of view, as a land with mounds and valleys and caves and holes. It seems rather evident to me that our body is a figuration that appears in Mother Earth.[10]

The work of Lee Bontecou and Eva Hesse, along with that of Bourgeois, underscores a persistent preoccupation with aspects of order and disorder, growth and dissolution, gender and sexual innuendo, and obsessive detail that transforms and animates the object. Though Bontecou and Hesse came to sculpture from different backgrounds, both made work that is highly anthropomorphic. Each deals with serial repetition and emphasizes process. Their compulsion to repeat centers around a formal strategy whose materialization assumes a fetishistic quality. Their works exist in the gap between painting and sculpture; both experiment with materials that require hands-on involvement with the object.

Described by critics as "extinct volcanoes," "craters," and "carapaces," Bontecou's earliest steel and canvas reliefs have a decisively topographical demeanor. Though initially conceived without ideological polemic, these singular images, constructed between 1959 and 1965, were appropriated later by Donald Judd as exemplars of a Minimalist sensibility.[11] The constructional simplicity of Bontecou's assemblages belied their fertile associations.

Deeply impressed by Bontecou's work, Hesse wrote in her diary (sometime in December 1965):

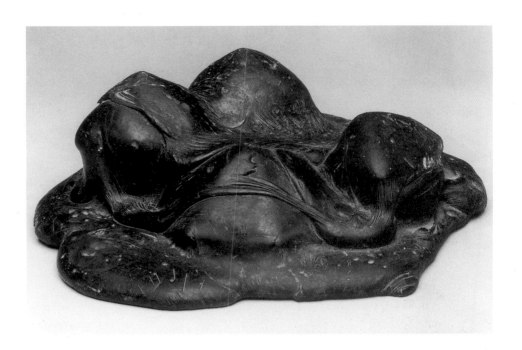

Louise Bourgeois
Soft Landscape 1963
latex
15⅜ x 12⅜ x 4⅛
Courtesy Robert Miller Gallery, New York

(opposite)
Henry Moore
Two Forms 1934
Pynkado wood
11 x 17¾ on irregular oak base, 21 x 12½
Collection The Museum of Modern Art,
New York
Sir Michael Sadler Fund

Isamu Noguchi
Woman with Child 1958
marble
44 high
Contemporary Collection of
The Cleveland Museum of Art

I am amazed at what that woman can do. Actually the work involved is what impressed me so. The artistic results I have seen. This was the unveiling to me of what can be done, what I must learn, what there is to do. The complexity of her structures, what is involved absolutely floored me.[12]

Hesse consciously navigated within the formal boundaries of Minimalism but veered toward extremes that transfigured the object. Within Minimalism's orthodox ranks she was an aberration. She not only warped its formalism, but she embraced the possibilities of anthropomorphism and association at a time when many abstract sculptors masked all signs of them. The strange fragility that permeates Hesse's work is both a reflection of her choice of materials—fiberglass, string and yarn, cheesecloth, rubber tubing, papier-mâché, and wood shavings—and of the way her pieces extend themselves physically and emotionally. As an insider, Hesse extended Minimalism by investing her objects with tension and life.

Though one would not ordinarily consider David Smith an organic sculptor, a certain aspect of his work has a direct bearing on the theme. Between 1945 and 1951, while living in the bucolic environs of Bolton Landing in Lake George, New York, Smith developed a series of about twenty sculptural landscapes.[13] With this work, as with related works by Bourgeois and Bontecou, landscape alludes to or symbolizes human anatomy, dream states, destruction and devastation, history, and mankind's essential bond with nature. Smith made verbal free associations when contemplating the landscape; his words conjure up images of primeval struggle, vanquished civilizations, and atavistic nightmares:

The Landscape

I have never looked at a landscape without seeing other landscapes
I have never seen a landscape without visions of things I desire and despise

lower landscapes have crusts of heat—raw epidermis and the
choke of vines
the separate lines of salt errors—monadnocks of fungus
the balance of stone—with gestures to grow
the lost posts of manmaid boundaries—in molten shade a petrified
paperhanger who shot the duck
a landscape is a still life of Chaldean history
it has faces I do not know
its mountains are always sobbing females
it is bags of melons and prickle pears
its woods are sawed to boards
its black hills bristle with maiden fern
its stones are assyrian fragments
it flows the bogside beauty of the river Liffey
it is colored by Indiana gas green
it is steeped in veritable indian yellow
it is the place I've traveled to and never found
it is somehow veiled to vision by pious bastards and the lord of Varu
the nobleman from Gascogne
in the distance it seems threatened by the destruction of gold[14]

Beginning in the 1940s and 1950s, landscape, which up until that
time had been the exclusive domain of painters, was adapted, in abstracted
form, as a sculptural motif. For many sculptors it functioned as both a
universal metaphor and as a personal symbol.

For Theodore Roszak, nature harbored generative and destructive
forces. To his mind, the bombings of Hiroshima and Nagasaki in 1945
symbolized the devastative collision of these forces and a world desperately
out of balance. In the aftermath of these events, Roszak rejected
streamlined, hard-edged Precisionism—a sign of his disillusionment with
utopian Constructivist principles and of his great uncertainty about the
future of the earth. Doubt and disquiet provoked a severe change of
aesthetic attitude and material process. The polished chrome surfaces of
his machine-tooled constructions were superseded by welded steel
assemblages brazed with coarse and pitted surfaces. Roszak felt that science
and technology had failed in their mission to prolong and enrich life. His
tough objects were "meant to be blunt reminders of primordial strife and
struggle, reminiscent of those brute forces that not only produced life, but
in turn threatened to destroy it."[15] Among a concerned group of artists,
philosophers, and humanists an "all-consuming rage against forces blind
to the primacy of life-giving values" generated a desire to relocate the
"essence of being" through mythology, archetypal imagery, and atavistic
recapitulation.[16]

An urge to combat the "reduction of man's personality to a docile
and convenient cipher" led Roszak to create "proto-images that cut across

time."[17] Strange prehistoric birds of prey, totemic invocations, and natural forms transfigured by spiky projections and encrusted skins represented some of his surreal equivalents for death and destruction. His exploration of form with universal implications had an affinity to Arp's concerns. Like Arp, Roszak set out to deflate man's arrogance and omniscience through images that transcended history and ego; he probed the future by mining the past. If science and technology offered insights that dovetailed with creative pursuits, these were assimilated into the aesthetic program. But within this program, skepticism provided the essential buffer between past and future.

Skepticism, disorder, and history were fundamental features of Robert Smithson's worldview. He courted entropy the way most people presuppose order in their lives. In his mind, entropic systems triumphed over utopian dreams of a mechanistic order; dissolution and degradation were natural agents of perpetual change. Mining the past for insights to the present was a poignant endeavor for Smithson, who viewed the earth's crust as a vast, jumbled museum. His ultimate decision to move beyond the restricted boundaries of the Minimalist object (and the art system) into landscape was precipitated as much by his search for sculptural alternatives as by a desire to ground his work within the unified strata of the earth's history.

In the 1960s, Minimalism entered the art scene like some great purge. As a reaction against the histrionics of Abstract Expressionism, Minimalism posed aloof and impersonal objects. But in spite of its austere facade, Minimalism had its internal eccentricities. Hesse, already cited, pursued more fertile investigations of content within a Minimalist discourse. Even

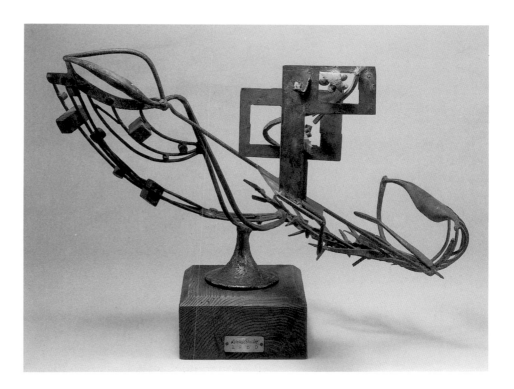

David Smith
Song of a Landscape 1950
iron, bronze
19 x 32 x 19½
Collection Muriel Kallis Newman

Richard Long
Walking A Circle in Ladakh
16,460 Ft. Pingdon LA
Northern India   1984
Courtesy the artist

now, years after her premature death in 1970, many contemporary sculptors, reacting to Minimalism from a distance, continue to do the same.

Today, it is convenient to see Minimalism as a monolithic development, a conceptual foil against which work by contemporary sculptors can be measured and compared. Given its historical proximity, such a perception is understandable but is nevertheless exaggerated within the greater lineage of sculptural abstraction. Organic abstraction signals a sensibility that incorporates aspects of Minimalism—its unitary wholeness, formal simplicity, and conceptual rigor—but historically both precedes and supersedes it. Within this organic sensibility, the biomorph represents a quintessential motif, just as rectangles, squares, and circles constitute the fundamental forms of orthodox Minimalism. But biomorphism has many historical implications, and its formal character within a contemporary sculptural context warrants clarification. Within Surrealist terminology, the biomorph purportedly issued spontaneously from the dark recesses of the subconscious and evoked a host of biological associations. As such, it functioned as a metaphor for reality unbound. We now know that the proliferation of biomorphic imagery in vanguard art between 1920 and 1940 was informed by advances in microscopy, the biological sciences, topology, and by mathematical models.[18] Deformation and warpage may have fantastic overtones, but as sculptural equivalents they also refer to the formative processes by which straight lines become complex curves and perfect spheres become amorphous blobs. Far from materializing spontaneously, sculpture is deliberately mapped out to elicit association. This is an important point, because it revamps our traditional notions of the biomorph as being an exclusively intuitive entity, and illuminates contemporary, post-Minimalist developments.

Consciously constructing, casting, or carving form to enhance levels of association and meaning is pertinent to a growing number of contemporary sculptors who have moved beyond the primary forms of Minimalism. Martin Puryear has acknowledged the impact of the unitary Minimalist object on his own development and has emphasized the importance of "contradiction" and "emotional tension" in his present work. Tom Butter has spoken about opening up all possibilities for new investigations of form: "I want to do everything in my sculpture. I want it to look like it's wet and dry, alive and dead, geometric and organic; I want it to have everything at once."[19] And John Newman has described his own relationship to Minimalism:

> Minimalism squeezed out most aspects of reference and allusion. . . . I feel very close to Minimalism's basic principles of purity and wholeness . . . but with a twist. . . . The twisting, stretching, bending, folding, and knotting of form intimate something more emotive and suggestive . . . it necessitates a wider possibility for response.[20]

In addition to maintaining a rapport with Minimalism, contemporary abstract sculptors continue to interact with nature on various levels—physically, psychologically, and philosophically. Richard Long: "The source of my work is nature. . . . I use materials, ideas, movement and time to express a whole view of my art in the world. I hope to make images and ideas which resonate in the imagination, which mark the earth and the mind. . . . My work has become a simple metaphor of life."[21] Long is acknowledging his place within an existential continuum extending back to the first marks made by Paleolithic shamans. His log circles, rock groupings, and walks into the landscape all over the world are mythical and archetypal symbols—affirmations of presence. But these signs of his having been somewhere are destined to disappear. The notion of permanence, so ingrained in our Western conception of art, is ludicrous within a greater cosmological order.

Within the natural world nothing is entirely stable; all matter exists in a constant state of flux and transformation. A certain humility accompanies this realization. When Michael Singer remarked that, "in order to experience and learn from the natural environment, I felt the need to yield to it, respect it, to observe, learn and work with it," he was consciously removing his presence from the work, and "accepting his role in the environment as no more than an observer, manager, researcher."[22] His extended Ritual series belongs in nature. The works are as much an homage to one man's belief in transcendence, his humble stance before the unknowable, as they are to the resonance of a particular place. Their transposition from a Vermont glade to a gallery is unsettling, because their wholeness within the landscape is ruptured.

How does one define a sensibility whose sculptural manifestations are equivalents for elusive conditions, a sensibility that pokes holes in reason by accepting the primacy of absurdity, and courting the unknown? Ultimately, the objects that characterize organic abstraction affirm an open-ended investigation of form. And the creative invention of form, crucial to the future of any sculptural undertaking, helps to explain the historical persistence and contemporary resurgence of this sensibility. As an extended group, these objects pose more questions than they answer. As analogues for a host of subliminal images and emotions, they are often ambivalent and mysterious; they are quirky and humorous; they baffle at the same time that they illuminate; they are deeply personal and yet suggest the universal; they can be introverted and yet extend aggressively; they may appear primitive and tough, elegant and sophisticated; they incorporate aspects of science and technology for poetic ends; finally, they may appear unitary and simple from the outside but internally they reveal subtle complexities and tensions. That many of these objects imply aspects of anatomy and biology, and function within the greater coordinates of natural systems, is not surprising; an organic sensibility attempts to relocate the center of something that has become fragmented and diffuse by reaffirming what is essential and basic.

Given the eschatological implications of this quest, it is no wonder that nature continues to inform the work of many sculptors. Nature has become a poignant symbol of continuity and wholeness. Today, we regard nature nostalgically, as though it were an old, displaced friend, or something we have lost touch with. A complex system that has silently withstood the unsettling transformations of our technological age, nature has come to signify a transcendent condition. The word "organic" has comforting connotations, because it implies a condition that is healthy, pure, and grounded. In its manifold expressions, "organic" signifies life. And within a world where perception is jockeyed by an endless collision of fleeting impressions, where continuity is superseded by uncertainty, the creation of sculpture that confirms our fundamental connectedness to nature is not only inevitable but consoling.

1. Albert M. Dalcq, "Form and Modern Embryology," in *Aspects of Form: A Symposium on Form in Nature and Art*, ed. Lancelot Law Whyte (London: Percy Lund Humphries & Co., 1951), p. 91.

2. Theodore J. Roszak, "Some Problems of Modern Sculpture," *Magazine of Art*, vol. 42 (February 1949), pp. 55, 56.

3. There are earlier precedents for the theme of organic abstraction. Some of the first abstract sculptural objects were modeled by the painters Georgia O'Keeffe and Max Weber. O'Keeffe modeled two sculptures during her lifetime. Conceptually inseparable from her earlier paintings and works on paper, both objects were derived from landscape and correspond to natural forms. Whereas O'Keeffe's sculptures issued from landscape, many of the objects Weber cast and modeled during 1915 operated on a more metaphysical level, as analogues for consciousness, and speculations on the fourth dimension and space-time mechanics. Though outside the mainstream development of organic abstraction, both O'Keeffe's and Weber's objects are among the earliest prototypes for sculpture that functions as an abstract equivalent for natural forms and spiritual states.

4. Arp, "Art Is a Fruit," *Arp on Arp: Poems, Essays, Memories*, ed. Marcel Jean (New York: Viking Press, 1972), p. 241.

5. For an introduction to this concept in Surrealist photography, see Rosalind Krauss, "Corpus Delicti," *October*, no. 33 (Summer 1985), pp. 31–72. Another version of this essay appears in Krauss and Jane Livingston, *L'Amour Fou: Surrealism and Photography* (New York: Abbeville Press, 1985), pp. 57–112.

6. Harriet Watts, "Arp, Kandinsky, and the Legacy of Jakob Bohme," in Los Angeles County Museum of Art, *The Spiritual in Art: Abstract Painting, 1890–1985*, exh. cat., 1986, pp. 239–255.

7. Herbert Read, "The Vital Image," in *A Concise History of Modern Sculpture* (New York: Praeger Publishers, 1964), pp. 163–228.

8. Quoted in "Isamu Noguchi," ed. Dorothy C. Miller, The Museum of Modern Art, New York, *Fourteen Americans*, exh. cat., 1946, p. 39.

9. Robert Storr, "Louise Bourgeois: Gender & Possession," *Art in America*, vol. 71 (April 1983), p. 137. In a footnote, Storr mentions Bourgeois's early interest in topology and mathematical models.

10. Quoted in Deborah Wye, The Museum of Modern Art, New York, *Louise Bourgeois*, exh. cat., 1982, p. 25.

11. Donald Judd, "Lee Bontecou," *Arts Magazine*, vol. 39 (April 1965), pp. 16–21.

12. Quoted in "Order and Chaos: From the Diaries of Eva Hesse," ed. Ellen H. Johnson, *Art in America*, vol. 71 (Summer 1983), p. 115.

13. Joan Pachner has addressed this aspect of Smith's work within a broader analysis that compares his work with that of Theodore Roszak; see "Theodore Roszak and David Smith: A Question of Balance," *Arts Magazine*, vol. 58 (February 1984), pp. 102–114.

14. Quoted in *David Smith*, ed. Garnett McCoy (New York: Praeger Publishers, 1973), pp. 198, 199. Smith wrote this passage in about 1947. Reprinted here by permission of Candida and Rebecca Smith.

15. Quoted in "Theodore Roszak," *The New Sculpture: A Symposium*, 12 February 1952, ms. transcript, Archives, The Museum of Modern Art, New York, p. 11; reprinted (in part) in Theodore Roszak, "In Pursuit of an Image," *Quadrum*, no. 2 (November 1956), p. 54.

16. For the primitivistic aspects of the New York School during the 1940s and 1950s, see Kirk Varnedoe, "Abstract Expressionism," in The Museum of Modern Art, New York, *"Primitivism" in 20th Century Art*, exh. cat., 1984, II, pp. 615–659, and Jeffrey Weiss, "Science and Primitivism: A Fearful Symmetry in the Early New York School," *Arts Magazine*, vol. 57 (March 1983), pp. 81–87.

17. Quoted in Peter Selz, "Theodore Roszak," The Museum of Modern Art, New York, *New Images of Man*, exh. cat., 1959, p. 134.

18. For a general discussion of this development, see Jennifer Mundy, "Form and Creation: The Impact of the Biological Sciences on Modern Art," in National Gallery of Modern Art, Edinburgh, *Creation: Modern Art and Nature*, exh. cat., 1984, pp. 16–23. The investigation of non-Euclidean geometry in the form of sculptural models was undertaken as early as the 1880s by the French mathematician and physicist Jules Poincaré. During his lifetime, Poincaré made significant contributions to the field of topology and toward the end of his life he constructed models out of wood, metal, plaster, and wire to illustrate his ideas. After his death, these were stored at the Institut Poincaré, then neglected until the early 1930s, when they were found by Max Ernst. Following their discovery, Man Ray was commissioned by Christian Zervos to photograph the objects. Twelve of these pictures were published in *Cahiers d'Art* in 1936; see Laurance Wieder, "Solid Geometry," *Camera Arts*, vol. 3 (July 1983), pp. 30–37, 77.

19. Quoted in Wade Saunders, "Talking Objects: Interviews with Ten Younger Sculptors," *Art in America*, vol. 73 (November 1985), p. 112.

20. Interview with the artist, 10 June 1986.

21. Richard Long, "From Words after the Fact" (1982), quoted in The Solomon R. Guggenheim Museum, *Richard Long*, exh. cat., 1986, p. 236.

22. Quoted in Diane Waldman, The Solomon R. Guggenheim Museum, *Michael Singer*, exh. cat., 1984, p. 17.

Architectural Art

Nancy Princenthal

The visual arts constitute a curiously ordered family, in which architecture counts as both offspring and progenitor. One convention calls it the mother art, while another considers architecture a disadvantaged stepsister to such siblings as painting and sculpture, which are innocent of the problems of utility. Moreover, ambiguities in the distinction between architecture and sculpture can be found in some of our oldest surviving monuments—historians are hard pressed to decide whether Stonehenge, for instance, or the dolmen at Carnac in Brittany, are one or the other. This semantic (and archaeological) heritage has renewed meaning for a growing group of artists creating sculpture that acts like architecture, and also for a number of architects who behave like artists.

The term architectural art, as used here, embraces a great variety of work. There is sculpture that assumes the traditional responsibilities of architecture or design, including the enclosure of space, the provision of shelter, and the creation of seating, tables, paving, wall patterning, lighting, and other amenities for public and private use, and there is also work done by artists at architectural scale, using architecture's construction methods and materials, which, though sometimes placed in public space, is not always functional. Architectural art also includes sculpture with architectural references, and Performance and Conceptual Art that investigate architectural issues. These categories inscribe an enormous and diverse body of work, some of which retreats into a recovered "natural" landscape, others progress toward a utopian, technocentric metropolis. Although cohering more firmly at some points than at others, architectural art sustains overall a susceptibility to architecture's own ideology: the formal history of functional structures, the social history of changes in the functions that architects and designers serve, and the reflexive interactions between these two cultural narratives are potent stimuli for many contemporary sculptors.

The Neolithic monuments at Stonehenge and Carnac serve imaginatively as entryways to our culture. Like the mysterious earth markings of South America, they are spiritual in nature; they are heroic efforts to appease, understand, articulate, and ultimately, dominate the natural environment. The awe of nature they reflect, and their sheer scope and authority, remain powerful sources of reference—and nostalgia—for

Meg Webster
Glen (detail) 1988
earth, steel, plants, fieldstone
142 x 504 x 510
Commissioned with Lannan Foundation
support for the exhibition
Sculpture Inside Outside
Courtesy the artist and Barbara
Gladstone Gallery, New York

Mary Miss
Field Rotation 1981
wood, steel, gravel, earth
4-acre site
central well: 720 x 720 x 84
Collection Governors State University,
University Park, Illinois

artists working in the landscape. While cultural communities have long since evolved from congregants to consumers, both artists and architects still regret the loss of a unified, reverential relationship with nature.

A model of this relationship can be found not just in prehistoric structures, but also in such non-Western vernacular architecture as that illustrated in Bernard Rudofsky's influential 1964 exhibition and catalogue, *Architecture Without Architects.* Rudofsky says of "non-pedigreed" architecture that its "great builders draw no line between sculpture and architecture. With them, sculpture is not 'commissioned' as an afterthought or budgetary dole. Neither is so-called landscaping. The three are inseparable."[1] Just as this encomium has become a battle cry for many artists, the examples Rudofsky cites, mostly remote geographically or no longer in existence, provide a wealth of imagery for sculptors whose work explores architectural reference. Rudofsky himself saw the significance of non-Western vernacular architecture for contemporary art, observing that certain Chinese cemeteries bring to mind Isamu Noguchi's "contoured playgrounds." Similarities also exist, for instance, between the remarkable underground villages he documents in northern China—home to ten million inhabitants—and below-grade chambers in the work of Alice Aycock, Mary Miss, and Andrea Blum. Terraced mountaintops, again in China, are suggested by Athena Tacha's stepped and contoured plazas; and African villages with streets that "run erratically, like raindrops on a windowpane," are evoked in Charles Simonds's miniature metropolises.

Rich as the assortment of structures Rudofsky compared is, he presented them merely as images; apart from his idealizing claim that anonymous builders "rarely subordinate the general welfare to the pursuit of profit and progress," these structures are not given social or cultural profiles. Contemporary artists involved with vernacular architecture, many of whom have undertaken extensive independent research into non-Western design and also into such domestic sources as Shaker and American Indian work, for the most part sustain Rudofsky's ahistorical attitude. Formal invention, flexible responses to the demands of use and site, and, to some extent, subordination of individual to communal expressive impulses are what these artists bring to their work, rather than a responsibility to archaeological or ethnographic sources.

Pedigreed history, however, also has its place among the referents of architectural art. The Parthenon and St. Peter's remain obligatory reference points in some public art discussions, and their formal precedents are certainly implicit throughout the built environment of the West. But it is the many historical revisions of these ideals, including the Romantic English garden and French visionary Neoclassicism, that have proven more directly suggestive to contemporary artists. First epitomized in the designs of William Kent and Charles Bridgeman and in the writings of Joseph Addison and Alexander Pope, and popularized by Lancelot "Capability" Brown, the English garden offered an arcadian vision of antiquity. With deftly placed mock ruins, follies, grottoes, sculptures, and other occasional structures of diverse period references, and above all with the subtle manipulation of the landscape to enhance its "natural," or picturesque, characteristics, such undertakings as Stourhead Park, designed between 1744 and 1765 by the Kentians Henry Flitcroft and Henry Hoare, replaced the regular geometry of earlier gardens with complexity, irregularity, and concealment.

The Romanticism expressed in these gardens survives, and with it the longing for a naively submissive relationship to nature and the use of the Classical past as an object of nostalgic reverie more than aesthetic authority. It recurs not only in landscape design but also in the bucolic fantasies of such artists as Ian Hamilton Finlay, whose Stonypath garden in Scotland is a particularly faithful—albeit rather abstruse—homage to its Neoclassical prototypes. Other less literal responses abound. Richard Long's walks, photographs, and salvages of rocks and twigs share a documentary approach with Alan Sonfist's acts of commemoration, preservation, and stimulation of organic processes, from microbial growth to the maturation of forests; each artist suggests that the natural environment has become an artifact. The sensitivity of Michael Singer's frail and fugitive outdoor sculpture to its environment is profound, and sometimes agonizingly deferential—one piece in the early Situation Balance Series, involving the rearrangement of wind-felled trees, took three years to complete. Meg Webster's work, which ranges from reductive sculptures made of organic materials to quasi-performance installations, indoors and out, is less elegiac—in one particularly irreverent gesture she filled a gallery with barnyard animals—but it sustains, nevertheless, a kind of neo-Transcendentalist fascination with nature, and our still problematic domestication of it.

Along with the English garden, the eighteenth century's other crucial legacies to architectural sculpture are the rigorously unsentimental Neoclassicism of Claude-Nicolas Ledoux's most radical designs, especially the remarkably reductive geometry he conceived for the ideal city of Chaux, and the colossal historicizing extravaganzas envisioned by Étienne-Louis Boullée. The severe formal clarity of their work, and its social idealism, have had repercussions in both reactionary and avant-garde circles, from the Third Reich to the Bauhaus. The energetic and inevitably futile attempt of Bauhaus designers to forge, through geometry, an inviolable unity of form with function is central to the culture of our century. Equally fundamental is the utopianism the Bauhaus shared with Constructivism and De Stijl. The Constructivist Tatlin's unrealized *Monument to the Third International* (1920), a spiraling tower of three separately revolving chambers that at 1,300 feet would have constituted the world's tallest building, is a demonstration piece of early modernist utopian projects; conceived in celebration of the new socialist state, it suggested an affinity between social egalitarianism and a dynamic, machine-age aesthetic purged of retrograde historical reference. Tatlin's *Monument* also anticipated the exhortation of Walter Gropius, director of the Bauhaus: "The ultimate if distant aim of the Bauhaus is the *collective* work of art—the Building—where there is no distinction between structural and decorative art."[2] In addition to proposing architecture as a unifying practice—as had the English Arts and Crafts Movement and its Jugendstil and Deutscher Werkbund successors—the Bauhaus, along with Constructivism and De Stijl, offered formal principles that have had an inescapable influence on contemporary architectural art: Scott Burton's celebrations of Gerrit Rietveld and Marcel Breuer, Andrea Blum's De Stijl-inspired seating and paving designs, and the neo-Constructivism of Dennis Adams's politically charged bus shelters, are just a few among countless examples. As all of these artists would acknowledge, however, the link between simple geometry and exemplary functionalism—the existence of an absolute style, independent of cultural conditions and answerable only to the demands of use—remains a matter of faith.

Of course, Postmodern designers have long since questioned this faith, embracing a variety of styles and reaffirming the value of decoration. With the 1966 publication of *Complexity and Contradiction in Architecture*, Robert Venturi released what became a manifesto of liberation from the strictures of an increasingly vitiated Minimalist aesthetic. Though his own work represents a cautious approach to historicism and to decoration generally, Venturi's theories opened floodgates to historically referenced, highly pictorial design. While the eclectically historical designs of Michael Graves, Robert A.M. Stern, Charles Moore, and their colleagues are not inherently more hospitable to art than those of their predecessors, these architects have common cause with sculptors, painters, and other artists who have also liberally appropriated elements of their visual heritage. And the open-ended referentiality of Postmodernism has certainly enlarged the ground on which the several disciplines of the visual arts can meet.

Architects have never laid exclusive claim to the creation of expressive, enclosed spaces, and throughout the twentieth century a variety of other artists have taken up the challenge, with considerable effect on contemporary architectural art. Noguchi's pioneering designs for playgrounds, parks, and monuments, proposed from the 1930s on (though realized only after World War II), established a new license for sculptors concerned with the urban landscape. Through his extensive study and residence in Japan, Noguchi was also instrumental in bringing the lessons of Eastern architecture and landscape design to this country. Japanese design, particularly that of gardens, has had considerable influence on the works of artists ranging from Mary Miss, whose compositions reveal her interest in the Japanese garden's "borrowed views" of distant, framed landscapes, to Michael Singer, whose ritualistic working methods, choice of materials (including a reliance on reed and bamboo), and scrupulous deference to the forms and rhythms of nature are closely related to Eastern thought and artistic practice.

Theater design has also attracted many twentieth-century sculptors, perhaps because it is concerned with spaces both alienated and perceptually enhanced by their artificiality—a peculiarly Modernist kind of architecture. Noguchi was a pioneer in this respect as well, having started to design sets for the Martha Graham Dance Company in 1935, but such earlier works as Malevich's sets for the 1913 Futurist opera *Victory over the Sun* have also had enduring influence. When a few radical artists, notably Louise Nevelson, Louise Bourgeois, and Herbert Ferber, began in the late 1940s to create sculptural environments that framed—or staged—the viewer's experience, theater design was surely an inspiration. Bourgeois's 1949 Peridot Gallery installation of totemic figures, like Nevelson's dimly lit, densely packed *Moon Garden + One* exhibition nine years later, extended the Surrealist vocabulary into quasi-architectural space. At the same time, both artists suggested the wealth of subconscious associations with which domestic interiors and their furnishings are imbued. Ferber's 1961 *Sculpture as Environment* installation wholly engulfed the viewer, creating an organic, expressive room closely related to the fluid, "endless" spaces conceived by maverick architect Frederick Kiesler.

Other anomalous incidents in modern sculpture that enriched the heritage of architectural art include Duchamp's anarchic gesture in the 1938 *International Exhibition of Surrealism* with the ceiling-hung *1,200 Bags of Coal*, and his similarly unrestrained use of string in the 1942 *First Papers of Surrealism* exhibition; the claustrophobically personal spaces of Kurt Schwitters's *Merzbau* (ongoing from 1923); and the equally rich atmosphere of Joseph Cornell's miniaturized architecture. Duchamp's peremptory use of space and Schwitters's architecture by accumulation reappear in work as various as the theme park interiors of the collaborative group TODT and Brower Hatcher's delicately drawn figurative structures of wire mesh and found objects.

The intimate scale and evocative presence of Bourgeois's and Nevelson's environments and the expressionism that characterized the postwar generation of American sculptors with whom they were grouped found an antithetical reaction in the heroic outdoor undertakings of the late 1960s and early 1970s. Michael Heizer, Walter de Maria, Robert Smithson, Robert Morris, and Nancy Holt went into the remote Western landscape in part to confound traditional commercial and civic art institutions, but primarily to transform the viewer's understanding of space. Purging art both of psychology and aestheticism, they aimed for an art of purely perceptual content, apprehension of which would involve not just vision but the viewer's whole physical being. The Earthwork artists were also interested in enhancing the sense of place—in heightening sensitivity to the deserts, lake beds, and grass fields in which they realized their dauntingly ambitious projects. Heizer's *Double Negative* of 1969–1970 and Morris's *Observatory* of 1971 necessitated the removal and repositioning of formidable quantities of earth, resulting in the reformation of the visible, and physically accessible, terrain. Appreciation— and orientation—required an integrated visual and bodily response.

Phenomenology, which offered a conceptual framework for an art without discrete objects, became a philosophical lodestone for Earthworks artists. Describing "the powerful imbrication of the visual with the physical"[3] in Richard Serra's sculpture, Rosalind Krauss says that "the generation of the 1960s encountered in Merleau-Ponty's text the analysis of a 'spatiality without things.'"[4] Merleau-Ponty's investigation of visibility, in which he rejected "the age-old assumptions that put the body in the world and the seer in the body,"[5] helped these artists formulate their demonstrations that perception was susceptible to the vagaries of context and the predispositions of the viewer. Robert Irwin is among those interested in perception's more flexible parameters, and his work with scrim, wire fencing, and (most recently) tinted glass represents his investigation into the conditional nature of the aesthetic response. Richard Fleischner also accomplishes subtle alterations of rural and urban visual fields through the use of plantings, built geometric elements, fencing, and paving stones—alterations undertaken more and more often in collaboration with architects and designers. Similarly, George Trakas's carefully placed and modestly constructed walkways and resting places, often involving delicate negotiations between water's edge and land's end, direct the viewer's experience of the environment, as do James Ford's designs of paths and occasional structures for rural estates as well as his urban proposals.

George Trakas
Berth Haven 1983
steel, wood
approx. 80 ft long x 8 ft deep
Collection National Oceanic and
Atmospheric Administration
Western Regional Center, Seattle,
Washington

Gordon Matta-Clark
House Splitting (Englewood,
New Jersey) 1974
color photograph
29¾ x 39½
Collection Holly Solomon

Siah Armajani
*Dictionary for Building: Back Porch
with Picnic Table* 1985
painted wood, stain, bronze screen
168 x 216 x 288
Courtesy Max Protetch Gallery, New York

Gaston Bachelard's phenomenology is of a more lyrical and less abstract variety than Merleau-Ponty's, and his gnomic observations, particularly his suggestion that "there is ground for taking the house as a *tool for analysis* of the human soul,"[6] have been especially fertile for artists investigating the nature of the built environment. Bachelard's study of man's dominion in nature, of the "passionate liaison of our bodies . . . with an unforgettable house"[7] and of the transcendence of inhabited over "geometrical" space, proceeds mainly by citation of poetic examples. Nevertheless, the imagery of which he writes finds visual expression in, for instance, Alice Aycock's allusive, eccentric wooden structures and the fragmentary dwellings of Mary Miss's carpentered outdoor work. Bachelard's fascination with well-remembered attics, cellars, and secret passages is also shared by Siah Armajani, as can be seen in the irregular passages of Armajani's superficially straightforward constructions. The breathtaking slices that Gordon Matta-Clark made through entire facades and floors, returning a personal—if ravished—presence to otherwise unforthcoming structures, constituted a particularly commanding use of the allusive power of ordinary, abandoned houses and commercial buildings. And Michael Singer's recent sculptures in slate, granite, and fieldstone, which evoke dormant cities as devoid of human interaction as Giacometti's plazas, also draw on architecture's subjective associations.

The sense of place, which Bachelard develops so closely, was also given shape by Heidegger's influential text "Building Dwelling Thinking"[8] (Armajani has often cited it), in which building is related reciprocally—and etymologically—to an enriched concept of dwelling. "Location" for Heidegger is called into being by building, a notion shared by most artists involved with site work, from Smithson on. The particularities that Smithson was concerned with, however, go beyond the abstraction of designating a subjective location. His sustained interest in geology was as important as his opposition to referential sculpture; of the *Spiral Jetty*, for instance, he wrote that its form echoed the molecular lattice of the individual salt crystals that saturated the surrounding water.[9]

Not only the geological composition of a particular site, but that site's position with respect to its own context has been of interest to many artists working in the landscape. Like their Neolithic forebears, Nancy Holt, James Turrell, and others have created work that measures and dramatizes astronomical phenomena. The four nine-foot-high concrete pipes of Holt's *Sun Tunnels* (1973–1976) are aligned to the summer and winter solstices, and their upper surfaces have perforations that match major constellations, offering the viewer a vivid image of the relationship between the Earth, its star, and the others in the galaxy. Similarly, Turrell's ongoing Roden Crater project, in which an extinct volcano in Arizona is being carved into an enormous astronomical instrument, will afford visitors an unusually direct understanding of the planet's position in space.

Minimalism also has its place in a survey of architectural sculpture, if only for its influence over—and ultimately, identification with—a generation of corporate plaza art. But more significantly, Minimalism's ban on relational composition and all representationalism, its concern with its own irreducible factuality, and its observations on basic physical structure set it on a parallel course with contemporary architecture. Moreover, Sol LeWitt's built white grids and Donald Judd's boxes simply look inescapably architectural. These high Minimalist works could be likened (though the comparison does violence to artistic intention) to Anthony Caro's welded I-beam and metal grating sculptures and Mark di Suvero's similar use of such industrial materials as steel beams, timber, and hardware. While the intellectual positions and stylistic attitudes of these artists differ greatly, they share a reliance on methods of composition and construction commonly related to architecture and, by extension, they believe that such architectural practices can refresh the consideration of sculptural form.

At the same time that the Minimalist and Earthwork artists were reconfiguring the urban and Western landscape, a different artistic application of the scale, materials, and forms of architecture and design, and a different kind of purge of aestheticism and psychology, were being carried out by Pop sculptors. Claes Oldenburg's visionary structures and Richard Artschwager's laminated plastic furniture, both begun in the mid-1960s, bring the questions provoked by Dada into the realm of public art. Oldenburg's proposals for skyscrapers, bridges, temples, museums, and monuments combine the imagery of (generously inflated) readymades with utilitarianism, performing a kind of Möbius twist on Duchamp's subversion of the quotidian object. Like the other Pop artists, Oldenburg defied conventional sanctions against the representation of consumer goods and of middle-class regalia generally. But he combined defiance with pragmatism, enlisting commonplace objects—screws, lollipops,

Richard Artschwager
Portrait II 1964
Formica on wood frame
68 x 26 x 13
Private collection

electric plugs—in the wholly dutiful, if cross-disciplinary, service of conventional architectural uses. Artschwager's laminated plastic and Celotex dressers, tables, chairs, lecterns, and confessionals are similarly deadpan perversions of pedestrian objects. But Artschwager has not proposed a practical application for his work; rather, he questions the utility of sculpture by disengaging the concept from its common metaphorical application.

The proposition made by Oldenburg, Artschwager, and their colleagues that lowbrow material culture be taken seriously as subject matter has, of course, continued to compel interest. Consumerism—its objects of desire and the pressures it exerts against the boundaries that separate art from other manufactured goods—is a central issue to many young sculptors, an issue that sustains, often ambivalently, the legacy of Pop and Dada. Availing themselves of the products of industrial and interior design, R.M. Fischer, Jeff Koons, Haim Steinbach, John Armleder, and others direct their attention, often in admiration, to contemporary material culture. Koons works with the iconography of brand-name goods, enshrining vacuum cleaners, basketballs, and liquor dispensers in sculptures that have had the immediate, widely broadcast appeal of a successful advertising campaign. In Steinbach's artistic instatement of lava lamps and running shoes, as in Koons's work, cynicism and enchantment operate in equal measure. Similarly, Armleder joins furniture and artlike elements—an unprepossessing hat rack cum umbrella stand is emblazoned with a Malevich-inspired painting, a dressing table mirror is replaced with a gray "Color Field" painting.

While such Pop-related sculpture trades on the mundane palpability of design objects, there is much recent art with architectural ties that studiously avoids the tangible. Like Earthworks, the Performance work that proliferated in the late 1960s was partly conceived in defiance of traditional institutional presentations. And a great deal of it has also been concerned with the experience of architectural space. In his career-long investigation of how various behaviors modify spatial perception, Vito Acconci looks to both architecture and design. Recently, he has made seating ensembles of cheerfully non-functional forms—mirrored surfaces, cartoonlike configurations, and potted plants are among their features. In other works he thwarts functionalism with such prankish assemblages as aluminum rowboats laden with tinted water and fish and an overstuffed Naugahyde armchair embedded in concrete. His well-known early performance pieces, however, dogged architecture's steps, distorting various commercial and "found" spaces, as well as public thoroughfares, with sometimes coercive, often voyeuristic actions and commands. By following randomly selected people down the street, luring an invited audience with the promise of secrets to a threateningly debilitated building, and, most memorably, masturbating under a platform in a gallery, Acconci psychologized these spaces and the physical relationships among people in them, dramatizing the behavioral factors with which all designers of space contend.

Dennis Oppenheim, Scott Burton, and Richard Serra also experimented in the late 1960s and early 1970s with performance, film, and video work, all centered on routine gestures and postures, which supported (and anticipated, in Burton's case) their sculptural investigations of architectural problems. The ossification of ordinary movement in Burton's Behavior Tableaux; Serra's filmed enactment of a hand catching a piece of lead, defying gravity as his sculpture labored to do; and Oppenheim's submission to, and illustration of, standard physical stress (as when he slung his body between two parallel brick walls), together propose a rudimentary vocabulary for the operation of bodies in space—a fluid vocabulary analogous to the static one with which architects work. Several contemporary performance artists have also focused on behavioral definitions of space. Tehching Hsieh's yearlong exercises in self-denial (he has lived in the streets of New York, been confined to a cell, and been tethered to co-performer Linda Montano) explore issues also framed by architectural theory—the roles of psychology (or, as Hsieh would have it, ritualized discipline) and metaphysics in the understanding of space.

Indeed, impermanence is considered a virtue by many architects as well as sculptors; architectural historian Kenneth Frampton has spoken of the symbolic value of the ephemeral, opposing what he calls "the archaic tradition of inscribing memory in the earth," which he believes is characterized in the work of Smithson and Heizer, to "the paradoxical monumentality of the aerial," as seen in the work, for instance, of performer-sculptors Otto Peine and Christo.[10] The latter's work, Frampton believes, speaks for the "talismanic" rather than the "tragic," for the eternal return rather than the myth of progress. These values, of transience and charm, of the intellectual and the spiritual, of shifting perspectives and temporal dislocation, are sustained throughout the history of visionary architecture, from Piranesi's prisons to Sant'Elia's Futurist cities to Ambasz's half-buried meditation chambers. Such variously unbuildable, impractical, and unconventional projects have clear points of intersection with sculpture and performance, though the confrontation is not always congenial. Similarly, the recently renewed enthusiasm of architects for furniture, often whimsical and highly sculptural (for instance, Robert Venturi's chairs and Frank Gehry's fish lamps) and in any event less permanent than building, brings architects into territory increasingly occupied by sculptors. And just as stage sets allow artists to design a pretense of real habitation, the many recent world's fairs have allowed architects to dally with the fictive, creating structures—e.g. the undulating highway by SITE Projects, Inc. for the 1986 World Exposition in Vancouver, or Charles Moore's decorative "Wonderwall" for the Louisiana World Exposition in 1984—which, though real enough, pretend to be imaginary.

SITE Projects, Inc.
Highway '86—Processional 1986
World Exposition, Vancouver, B.C.
Courtesy the artists

For that matter, there are those who believe that the physical reality of all architecture has begun to give way under the pressures of post-industrial society; long beleaguered in other disciplines, objecthood is now seen to be weakening in one of its most unassailable strongholds. Ten years ago, Paul Virilio wrote that the significant units of military control and political power in the modern world are not structures but thoroughfares, that "the city is but a stopover, a point on the synoptic path of a trajectory . . . there is only *habitable circulation*."[11] More recently, he said that neither buildings nor cities still have proper facades: "the opacity of construction materials is virtually being eliminated," he wrote, by the use of glass and plastic, just as the screen interface of a computer-linked society redefines traditional interpersonal, interurban, and international relationships.[12]

Assaults on the ontology of the built environment notwithstanding, a growing number of artists are engaging themselves not just in the critique, but also in the practice of architecture and design. Adams, Armajani, Burton, Blum, Ford, Holt, Miss, and Trakas are just a few among dozens of artists working either alone or in collaboration with architects in the design of art projects that are also functional amenities. Pragmatically, these projects present daunting challenges and commensurate rewards— access to a much larger audience than that usually generated by contemporary art being primary among the gratifications. But the politics of these projects is notoriously complex. Kate Linker claims that they are born, at least in part, in cynicism. "The amenities strategies currently used in innumerable American cities," she wrote in 1981, "spring from the realization, recent and widespread, that life's quality can be strategically improved through culture, to the benefit of economic return."[13] It is precisely because such strategies may require compromises with public taste that many architects have given up practice for theory. Will Insley, trained as an architect but engaged exclusively in theoretical work, writes: "One of the prime differences between art and architecture is morality. Architecture, operating in the functional social world, must serve the dictates of this world's morality. Art, operating outside functional restrictions, is free of such obligation."[14]

Though Scott Burton has spoken to just this question, insisting on the moral responsibilities of public art and welcoming the freedom such responsibilities offer from the limitations of autobiography, suspicion lingers between architects and artists. Architect Bernard Tschumi argues that much of the recent interdisciplinary activity is fundamentally misguided. "To envy architecture's 'usefulness' or, reciprocally, to envy artists' 'freedom' shows in both cases naivete and misunderstanding of the work. . . . Buildings may be about usefulness, architecture is not necessarily so."[15] In guarding the prerogative of architects to design artfully as well as functionally, and in insisting, regretfully, on the inherent limitations of pure art, Tschumi is

Andrea Blum
Rotational Shift 1988
cast concrete, plant material
approx. 6 x 75 x 125 ft
Computer Science Building Plaza
University of Wisconsin at Madison
Wisconsin State Arts Board Commission
and University of Wisconsin

joined by Peter Eisenman, who again argues, as do most architects, for a central distinction: "Building is about serving function: Architecture is about serving art. The difficulty for artists and sculptors . . . is [that] they do not have a distinction between building and architecture."[16] But it is precisely the ineffable "artistic" quality defended by Eisenman and others as architecture's true distinction that many artists consider spurious. "Public art's basic aim is to demystify the concept of creativity," Siah Armajani has written. "Public art is non-monumental. It is low, common and near to the people."[17]

The arguments some public artists have with the traditions of their field are less ideological. Alice Aycock complained in a 1984 panel discussion about the obstacles that inevitably arise from committee situations: "I sometimes feel that the only way I can survive is by cultivating a few supportive, eccentric patrons."[18] Admittedly, Aycock's concern is more with fantasy than utility. Though she claimed that public art distinguishes itself from mainstream, mainly "symbolic," contemporary art by dealing "with real time and real space," she is willing in extremity to give up realizing her proposals. "If all I get to do is just draw the thing and never get to build it, I wouldn't care,"[19] she concluded. Her comments were countered by Mary Miss: "I deal with committee situations because I don't want to build things out in the middle of some special preserve set aside for culture. I want to build things in context." Miss's concern with activating public spaces, particularly those brutalized ones typical of urban plazas, places her, she says, "at the other end of the spectrum from somebody like Duchamp or the traditional avant-garde position which is about negating everyone else's stance."

Though the field of public amenities, perhaps now the liveliest in the realm of architectural art, is formidably large and heterodox, it can also—and Miss's comment points the way—be seen as dichotomous. On the one hand, it appears to offer a way out of formalist self-referentiality while also silencing the problem of expressionism; crises of emotional and intellectual authenticity, which provide a primary dynamic of Postmodernism (though they are hardly original to it), are seldom occasioned by useful objects. On the other hand, sculpture that presents itself in the form of a granite park bench, a concrete bridge, or a steel and glass bus shelter offers, in Arthur Danto's term, a new "transfiguration of the commonplace,"[20] a readymade made better. As elsewhere, and despite the clamorous successes of Postmodernism, the problems of Modernism are not quite disposed of.

The effects of the public artists' trespasses are undeniably felt in the field of architecture proper—witness the mixture of antagonism, conventional and newly articulated, that such ventures elicit, and the genuine enthusiasm with which they are increasingly welcomed. But the effects are also felt, surely most strongly, in the realm of art. In his extended examination of the Dada and Pop problem of how distinctions can be made between two outwardly identical objects, one of which is an artwork and the other not (the concluding case is Warhol's Brillo boxes), Danto argues that all artwork is metaphorical, and all appreciation of it is grounded in interpretation. Sculpture that looks indistinguishably like architecture, and even functions as such, nevertheless remains within art's critical range, provoking reconsiderations of all the questions of expression, formal resolution, and conceptual position that vex fellow artists. At the same time, such art submits itself to evaluation by architectural standards. Its utility and its response to the history of built forms are thus subject to judgment by two tribunals. This rigorous trial results, it seems clear, in work of unusual clarity and vitality.

1. Bernard Rudofsky, The Museum of Modern Art, New York, *Architecture Without Architects*, exh. cat., 1964, n.p.

2. Walter Gropius, "Idee und Aufbau des Staatlichen Bauhauses, Weimar," in *Staatliches Bauhaus Weimar, 1919–1923* (Weimar and Munich, 1923), p. 9, translated in George Heard Hamilton, *Painting and Sculpture in Europe 1880–1940* (Middlesex, England: Penguin Books, 1975), p. 332.

3. Rosalind Krauss, The Museum of Modern Art, New York, *Richard Serra: Sculpture*, exh. cat., 1986, p. 28.

4. Ibid., p. 29. The text Krauss refers to is Merleau-Ponty's *Phenomenology of Perception*, translated into English in 1962.

5. Maurice Merleau-Ponty, *The Visible and the Invisible, Followed by Working Notes* (Evanston, Illinois: Northwestern University Press, 1968), p. 138.

6. Gaston Bachelard, *The Poetics of Space* (Boston: Beacon Press, 1969), p. xxxiii.

7. Ibid., p. 15.

8. Published in Martin Heidegger, *Poetry, Language, Thought* (New York: Harper & Row, 1971).

9. *The Writings of Robert Smithson: Essays with Illustrations*, ed. Nancy Holt (New York: New York University Press, 1979), p. 112.

10. Kenneth Frampton, "Intimations of Tactility: Excerpts from a Fragmentary Polemic," *Artforum*, vol. 19 (March 1981), p. 57.

11. Paul Virilio, *Speed and Politics: An Essay on Dromology* (New York: Semiotext[e], 1986), pp. 5, 6.

12. Paul Virilio, "The Overexposed City," *Zone*, no. 1–2 (1986), p. 17.

13. Kate Linker, "Public Sculpture: The Pursuit of the Pleasurable and Profitable Paradise," *Artforum*, vol. 19 (March 1981), p. 67.

14. Statement in *Site: The Meaning of Place in Art and Architecture, Design Quarterly 122*, published by the MIT Press, Cambridge, Massachusetts, and London, England, for the Walker Art Center, Minneapolis, 1983, p. 12.

15. Bernard Tschumi, "Architecture and Limits," *Artforum*, vol. 19 (December 1980), p. 36.

16. Statement in *Design Quarterly 122*, p. 16.

17. Introduction to Kunsthalle Basel and Stedelijk Museum, Amsterdam, *Siah Armajani*, exh. cat., 1987, n.p.

18. Roundtable discussions between Alice Aycock, Richard Fleischner, Mary Miss, George Trakas, Hugh Davies, and Ronald Onorato, published in Davies and Onorato, La Jolla Museum of Contemporary Art, *Sitings*, exh. cat., 1986, p. 109.

19. Ibid., p. 111.

20. The title of Danto's 1981 book (Cambridge, Massachusetts: Harvard University Press). He acknowledges in the preface that the term is borrowed from Muriel Spark.

Profiles of the Artists

Peter W. Boswell
Donna Harkavy

Phoebe Adams	Donald Lipski	Peter Shelton
Tom Butter	Robert Lobe	Michael Singer
Robert Gober	Walter Martin	Robert Therrien
Brower Hatcher	John Newman	Meg Webster
Jene Highstein	Martin Puryear	Steven Woodward
Jin Soo Kim	Judith Shea	

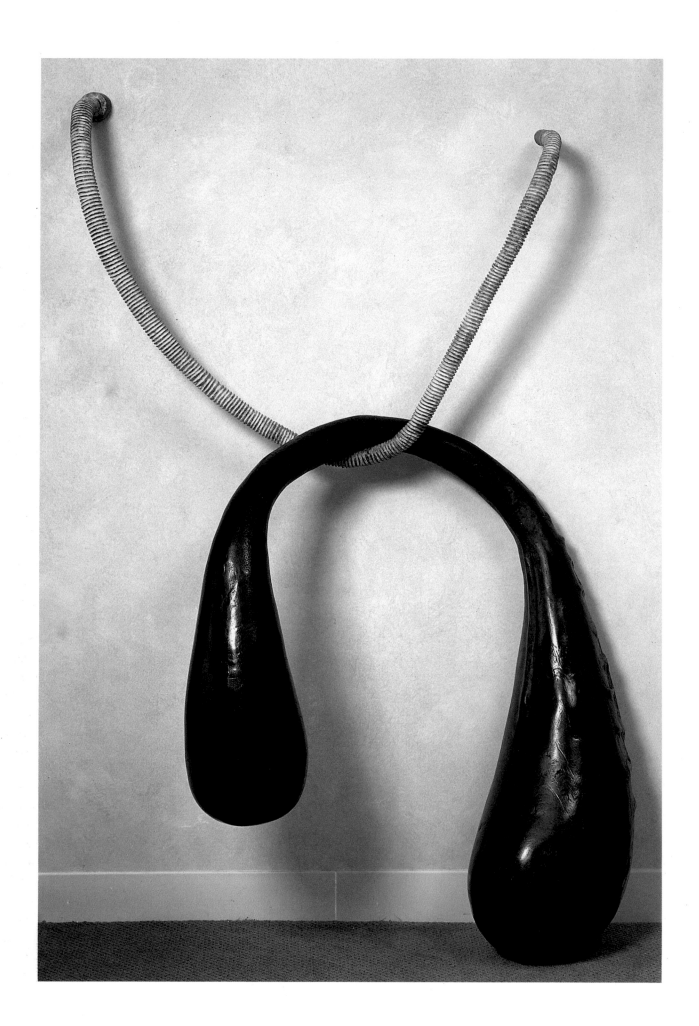

Phoebe Adams

Phoebe Adams's sculpture is within the tradition of biomorphism pioneered by such artists as Jean Arp, Joan Miró, and more recently, Louise Bourgeois. Like them, she has chosen to employ the imagery of organic growth and transformation as a metaphor for the psychic process: the manner in which ideas grow, turn in on themselves, transform, and give birth to new thoughts. But Adams brings a unique sculptural sensibility to her work. Hanging precariously from the wall and spilling over each other in tenuous connection, her forms are ripe with the possibility of metamorphosis. They are isolated moments in an implied continuum of change. "I like things that can be something else," she says, "things that hold inside of themselves motion and change."[1]

In the early 1980s, Adams began using cloth stiffened with wax to create ribbonlike forms that were then cast in bronze and assembled into compositions that suggested species of attenuated sea life undulating in the tide. More recently, she has moved away from such direct organic imagery to what she terms the "memory" of the organic: "I have taken the memory of the way things attach, the surface of things, the way things grow." Combining forms taken from drapery, found objects, and geometric shapes, she creates ensembles which evoke the spirit of nature while still retaining the individual identities of the component parts. In the process, her work has moved from the literal to the metaphoric. Her goal, she explains, is to evoke in the viewer a sense of intuitive recognition: "You know what

it is, you have an experience of it, but you don't have a name for it." She likens the sensation to peripheral vision, in which presences can be felt but not identified.

Her 1985 work *Sleep,* for example, appears at first to be a primitive aquatic organism, but the presence of the stovepipe and the modeled spine renders the allusion more enigmatic. Recalling the origin of the piece, she says, "I was thinking that my brain is like a stovepipe, everything—the smoke and cinders—is just coming out while I'm sleeping." Thus the biological merges with the psychological, the ocean melds into the subconscious, the sea creature into unconscious thoughts.

Although Adams's sculptures are wall-mounted, they are far from conventional reliefs. By allowing them to touch the wall only at selected points, she liberates her pieces from the wall plane and invests them with a deceptive sense of weightlessness. Rather than treating the room's architecture as a neutral entity, she engages it in an active dialogue. Her pieces seem to float off the wall or billow forth from within it; they nestle in corners and hang to the ground.

In *Bilge,* a work from 1987, a cast hose looks as if it passes through the plane of the wall and continues behind it. A pair of bulbous forms is draped over the hose. The larger hangs pendulously to within a fraction of an inch from the ground. Adams has added a subtle note of deception: although the sacklike form appears to be suspended from the hose, she has discreetly attached it to the wall; the impression of suspended weight is

Bilge 1987
bronze
62 x 42 x 20
Collection Art Berliner and Anita Ettinger

77

The Waste That Is Ours   1987
bronze
78 x 31 x 13
Collection Mr. and Mrs. Harry W. Anderson

Sleep 1985
bronze
44½ x 53¼ x 32½
Collection Solomon R. Guggenheim
Museum, New York
Exxon Corporation Purchase Award,
1985

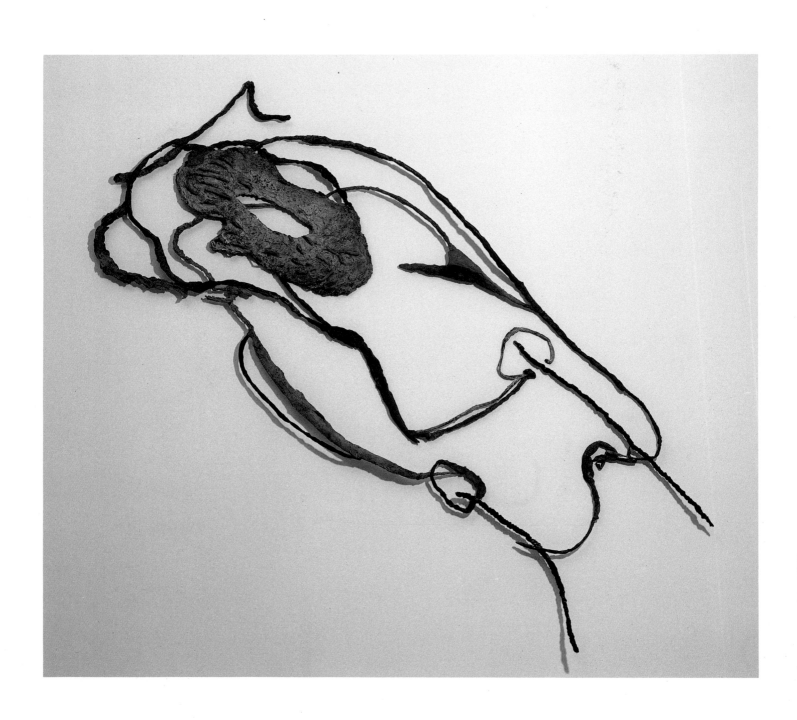

Nerve Cell   1984
bronze
54 x 64 x 3
Collection the artist

It Goes Both Ways   1986
bronze
50 x 31 x 20
Collection Walker Art Center
Clinton and Della Walker Acquisition Fund,
1986

Which Way?   1986
bronze
39 x 59 x 25
Collection Storm King Art Center,
Mountainville, New York
Gift of Cynthia Hazen Polsky

Collusion   1986
bronze
95½ x 23½ x 60½
Collection Dr. and Mrs. Louis E. Rossman

Phoebe Adams fabricating and installing
Away from Stasis

(opposite)
Away from Stasis   1988
concrete, bronze, brass, stainless steel
100 x 78 x 45
Commissioned with Lannan Foundation
support for the exhibition
Sculpture Inside Outside
Courtesy the artist

completely illusory.

The individual components within each of Adams's pieces often scarcely touch one another, thus imparting to her work a sense of fragility. In *Collusion* (1986), she locates the work in a corner, each of its two elements connected to a different wall. But Adams focuses the viewer's attention on the point where the forms barely touch. The result is a composition that emphasizes contig-uousness without union.

Adams has found bronze to be the ideal vehicle for her sculpture. The casting process allows her to create forms that are at once delicate, sinuous, and sturdy. She casts the diverse elements of her compositions individually and then pieces them together, joining them at isolated points to provide the work with the tenuity she prizes. A wide variety of textures can be duplicated in bronze, allowing Adams to differentiate the surfaces of the elements in her sculpture. In recent years, she has become particularly adept at using transparent dyes and patinas to color her work. In so doing, she arrives at color that looks as if it comes from within the bronze itself. "I don't want it to look like something that was made," she explains, "but something that is found, something that *is*."

Nonetheless, Adams's handling of bronze is quite unconventional. She disdains the traditional practice of casting bronze sculptures in editions, preferring to achieve qualities of form and surface that can be attained only in unique casts. Her absorption with intricacies of texture, form, and color imbues her work with a sensual delicacy that subtly counter-balances the solidity of the bronze. She has taken a material prized for its durability and created something that is intimate, fragile, and ephemeral in feeling.

For the exhibition *Sculpture Inside Outside*, Adams has made her first outdoor sculpture. Set before a gently curved wall, a bronze sphere is held in perplexing equilibrium by a taut steel cable and a delicate sheet of cast drapery. Titled *Away from Stasis,* the piece reflects Adams's continuing interest in creating paradoxical situations that appear unstable and yet are forever frozen in place.

P.W.B.

1. All quotations are taken from a conversation with the artist, 1 July 1987.

Phoebe Adams

1953
Born in Greenwich, Connecticut
1976
B.F.A., Philadelphia College of Art
1977
Skowhegan School of Painting and Sculpture
1978
M.A., State University of New York, Albany

Lives in Philadelphia

Solo Exhibitions

1981
Nexus Gallery, Foundation for Today's Art, Philadelphia
1984
Lawrence Oliver Gallery, Philadelphia
1985
Grace Borgenicht Gallery, New York
1986
Lawrence Oliver Gallery, Philadelphia
1987
Curt Marcus Gallery, New York
1988
Pence Gallery, Santa Monica (with Tom Butter)

Selected Group Exhibitions

1979
Art in Boxes, Philadelphia Art Alliance (catalogue)
1980
Sculpture 1980, Maryland Institute, College of Art, Baltimore (catalogue)
Opens Friday, Moore College of Art Gallery, Philadelphia
1981
Regional Trends in Sculpture, Stockton State College, Pomona, New Jersey, in conjunction with Marion Locks Gallery, Philadelphia
1982
S/300, Philadelphia Art Alliance (catalogue)
1983
Sophia's House, Morris Gallery, Pennsylvania Academy of the Fine Arts, Philadelphia (catalogue)
1984
Made in Philadelphia 6, Institute of Contemporary Art, University of Pennsylvania, Philadelphia (catalogue)
Small Scale Sculpture, Mathews Hamilton Gallery, Philadelphia
1985
Faculty Exhibition, Tyler School of Art, Temple University, Philadelphia
New Horizons in Contemporary Art, 1985 Exxon National Invitational, Solomon R. Guggenheim Museum, New York (catalogue)
1986
Skowhegan, A Ten-Year Retrospective, Leo Castelli Gallery, New York
Sculpture on the Wall, The Aldrich Museum of Contemporary Art, Ridgefield, Connecticut (catalogue)
Inaugural Exhibition, Curt Marcus Gallery, New York
1987
Alternative Supports: Contemporary Sculpture on the Wall, David Winton Bell Gallery, List Art Center, Brown University, Providence, Rhode Island (catalogue)
Perspectives From Pennsylvania, Carnegie-Mellon University Art Gallery, Pittsburgh (brochure)
Bronze, Plaster and Polyester, The Goldie Paley Gallery, Moore College of Art, Philadelphia (brochure)
Emerging Artists 1978–1986: Selections from the Exxon Series, Solomon R. Guggenheim Museum, New York (catalogue)
1988
Four Sculptors, Nina Freudenheim Gallery, Buffalo, New York

Selected Bibliography

Sozanski, Edward J. "Art: More New Talent at the I.C.A.," The Philadelphia Inquirer, 13 March 1984.
_____. Exhibition review, The Philadelphia Inquirer, 27 September 1984.
Siedel, Miriam. Exhibition review, The New Art Examiner, Vol. 12, February 1985.
Brenson, Michael. "Art: New Horizons at the Guggenheim," The New York Times, 20 September 1985.
Sozanski, Edward J. "A Show of Sculpture with an Eye toward the Imaginary," The Philadelphia Inquirer, 6 November 1986.
Marincola, Paula. Exhibition review, Artforum, Vol. 25, January 1987.

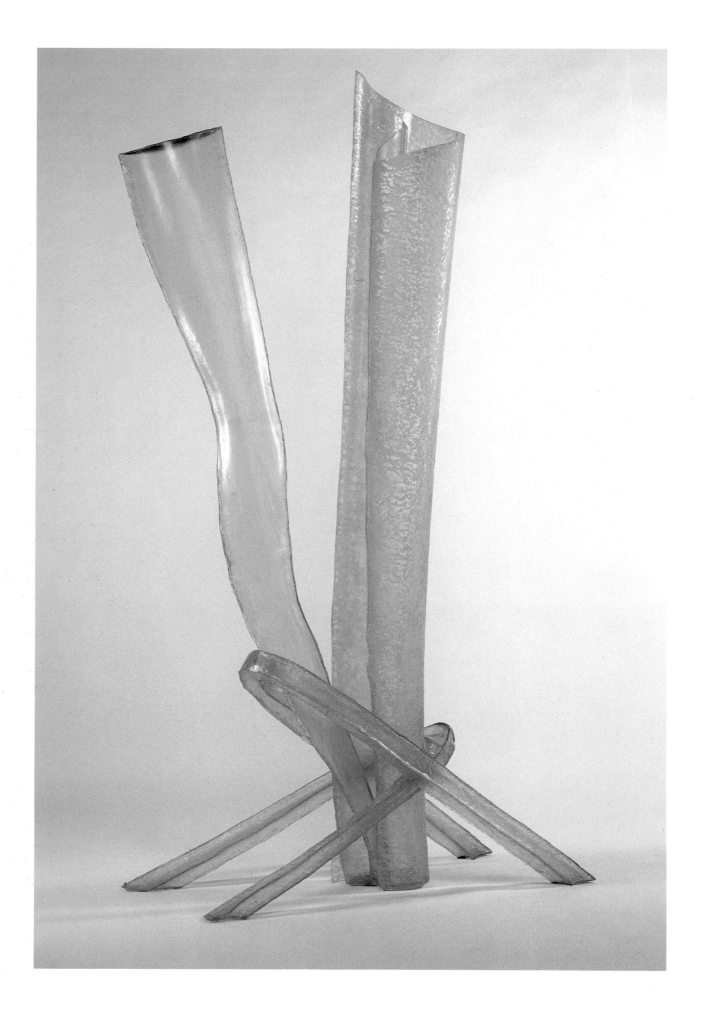

Tom Butter

S.C. 1985
fiberglass, resin
92 x 40 x 23
Collection The Pennsylvania Academy
of the Fine Arts, Philadelphia
Contemporary Arts Purchase Fund and
Henry D. Gilpin Fund

Over the past ten years, Tom Butter's sculptures have undergone a significant metamorphosis, moving from striking, brightly colored evocations of organic growth to subtle, even understated, manipulations of the structural properties of materials. Throughout this period, Butter has worked principally in fiberglass, skillfully exploiting its unique properties of fluidity, rigidity, and translucence to create works that are both sensuous and rigorous.

Butter first became familiar with fiberglass during his youth on Long Island when, as an avid sailor, he used it to make repairs and modifications on the hulls of his boats. Primarily a printmaker during his art school years, Butter turned increasingly to sculpture while a graduate student at Washington University, St. Louis, in the mid-1970s. There he produced a series of cardboard and tracing paper constructions that established a dialogue between solid, structural planes and glowing planes of light.

But it was not until Butter moved to New York in 1977 that he began to use fiberglass in his art. At the time, he was intrigued by the sculptures of Eva Hesse, particularly her *Repetition Nineteen III*, from 1968. In this piece, nineteen irregular fiberglass cylinders rise some three feet from the ground, their simple forms seeming to writhe with a lively organicism. Taking his cue from this work and from Brancusi's 1918 *Endless Column*, with its implication of continuous vertical extension, Butter created in the early 1980s a series of eight-foot-tall tubular fiberglass forms saturated with rich, translucent colors. In making these pieces,

he imposed two sets of conditions on himself: to employ only fiberglass, using gravity rather than molds to shape the limp material into forms that became self-supporting once they cured; and to make them simple enough that they were instantly comprehensible from any vantage point.

It was not only the structural and conceptual challenges posed by Hesse and Brancusi that attracted Butter; he was also intrigued by the balance they had achieved in their sculpture between allusive and formal concerns. In his sculptures from 1982 to 1985, Butter increasingly employed organic imagery to strike a similar balance between structural invention and personal expression. He modified his earlier fiberglass columns by thinning them down, squaring them off, or giving them bulging, podlike configurations. These forms were often supported by thin tubes of fiberglass that twisted, spiraled, folded, or coiled around them. In *A.A.*, from 1985, one of these pod shapes is combined with a saw-toothed element, reminiscent of the repeated indentations of Brancusi's column, which adds an aggressive dynamism to the work.

Butter's sculptures from this period are highly evocative of biological forms. In part this is due to his method of manufacture. Because he constructed his pieces without the use of molds, gravity and air pressure influenced the final configurations in much the same way as they do in natural forms. His hollow pods and tubes were inflated with an air pump to give them their shape, much as gases

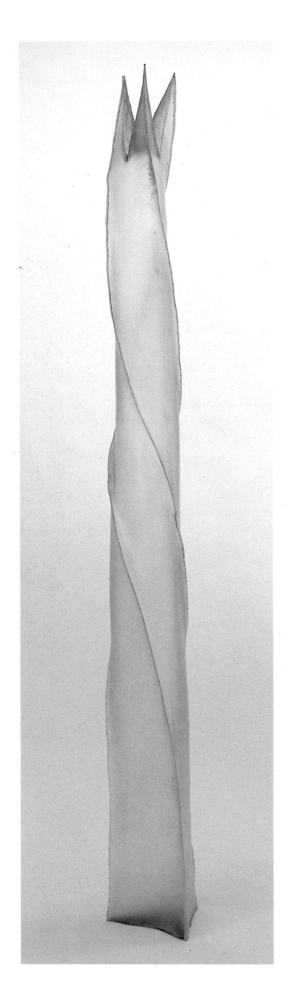

Fleece 1987
fiberglass, resin, wire, wire lath
73 x 43 x 23
Susan and Leland David Collection

(opposite, left)
G.B. 1982
fiberglass, resin
100 x 12 x 10
Collection Robert M. Kaye

(opposite, right)
A.A. 1985
fiberglass, resin, paint
88¼ x 28 x 24
Collection Walker Art Center
Gift of Grace Borgenicht Brandt, 1986

Orbit 1986
fiberglass, resin
91 high, 12 diam.
Courtesy Curt Marcus Gallery, New York

In Irons 1986
fiberglass, resin, wood
84 x 39 x 20
Collection Mr. and Mrs. Harry W. Anderson

will inflate a seed pod. In a work such as *G.B.* (1982), Butter achieved a sense of vertical growth by fabricating the piece upside-down; once it was righted, it appeared to be pushing upward, defying gravity. The organic quality of these sculptures was accentuated by the wet, membranous look of the fiberglass and the bright, limpid colors he employed, including blood reds, grass greens, milk whites, and sunny yellows. With each component given a distinct color and gesture, the sculptures were suggestive of a variety of life forms, from congregations of exotic, intertwined vegetation to submicroscopic molecular clusters.

Given their scale and vertical orientation, works such as *G.B.* and *A.A.* also carry distinctly figural associations, a fact underscored by Butter's practice of naming his pieces with the initials of friends, artists, musicians, and others he admires. Toward the middle of the decade, Butter accentuated this figural aspect by seeking to infuse his sculpture with what he refers to as a "kinesthetic sense; that is, a relationship to the body. When it works, it seems you translate the piece into a certain kind of body motion or body language."[1] The impression that a work such as *S.C.* (1985) gives a viewer has less to do with imagery than with physical sensation. Accordingly, Butter began to make his titles more descriptive of the body and its functions—*Pulse, Lifting Body, Hand, Heel.*

In his work since 1986, Butter has abandoned his earlier, self-imposed restrictions. In addition to fiberglass, his recent sculptures have incorporated wood, wire, sheet metal, and aluminum. He has also opened up his vertical forms to create a contrast between inside space and exterior surface. As a result of these changes in both materials and form, the work is no longer immediately comprehensible at a single glance; the viewer must walk around it to take it all in. In his piece *In Irons* (1986), a sheet of laminated wood curls to form a shell around a tall sheet of fiberglass, holding it upright. From one side, the viewer sees only two contrasting surfaces: the smooth, opaque curve of the wood and the flat, glistening sheet of fiberglass. From the opposite side, however, it is the sense of enclosed space and the means by which the fiberglass is held aloft by the wood that predominates. "The basic shift has been away from a 'one-shot' presence to a 'situation,'" says Butter. "With a situation comes a slower reading, because the situation unfolds in time: you can't see one side from another, so you have to go around and add up the experiences."

The introduction of wood and metal into the new works coincides with Butter's move away from the organic imagery of his earlier work, though echoes of nature are still perceptible in the uncoiling curves, reminiscent of leaves emerging from their buds. In these recent works, Butter has also forsaken saturated colors, employing instead more muted tones or, in many cases, a completely clear resin. Since one's experience of the work unfolds more slowly than before, Butter felt that "the color had to slow down as well." The neutral tones render his pieces more sensitive to ambient light, allowing the sculptures to interact with their surroundings rather than standing abruptly out from them, as the earlier work had. The net result of these changes is that Butter's current work is less allusive and more rigorously formal than before, lively animation giving way to a more austere, though no less alluring vision.

P.W.B.

1. All quotations are from a conversation with the artist, 4 July 1987.

Tom Butter

1952
Born in Amityville, New York
1975
B.F.A., Philadelphia College of Art
1977
M.F.A., Washington University,
St. Louis

Lives in New York

Solo Exhibitions

1981
Grace Borgenicht Gallery, New York
(with Paul Burlin)
1983
Grace Borgenicht Gallery, New York
Hammerskjold Plaza Sculpture Garden,
New York
Lawrence Oliver Gallery, Philadelphia
1984
Grace Borgenicht Gallery, New York
Lawrence Oliver Gallery, Philadelphia
1985
Morris Gallery, Pennsylvania Academy
of the Fine Arts, Philadelphia (brochure)
Lawrence Oliver Gallery, Philadelphia
1986
Curt Marcus Gallery, New York
Lawrence Oliver Gallery, Philadelphia
1987
John Berggruen Gallery, San Francisco
Nina Freudenheim Gallery, Buffalo,
New York
1988
Pence Gallery, Santa Monica, California
(with Phoebe Adams)

Selected Group Exhibitions

1980
Art for the Eighties, Galerie Durban,
Caracas, Venezuela (catalogue)
1981
Color, Light and Mass: Ten Sculptors,
Hallwalls, Buffalo, New York
(catalogue)
1982
American Abstraction Now, The
Institute of Contemporary Art, Virginia
Museum of Fine Arts, Richmond
(catalogue)
Art Across the Park, Central Park,
New York
Critical Perspectives, P.S. 1, The
Institute for Art and Urban Resources,
Inc., Long Island City, New York

Energie New York, ELAC, Lyon, France
New Work/New York, The New
Museum of Contemporary Art,
New York (catalogue)
Summer Exhibition, Lawrence Oliver
Gallery, Philadelphia
1983
Lifesigns, 55 Mercer, New York
New Sculpture: Icon and Environment,
Independent Curators, Inc., New York
(catalogue)
Language, Drama, Source, and Vision,
The New Museum of Contemporary
Art, New York
1984
A Growing American Treasure: Recent
Acquisitions and Highlights from the
Permanent Collection, Pennsylvania
Academy of the Fine Arts, Philadelphia
(catalogue)
Twentieth Century Sculpture:
Selections from the Metropolitan
Museum of Art, Storm King Art Center,
Mountainville, New York (catalogue)
Painting and Sculpture Today,
Indianapolis Museum of Art, Indiana
(catalogue)
Transformation of the Minimal Style,
Sculpture Center, New York
Totem, Bonnier Gallery, New York
1985
New York Art Now: Correspondences,
Laforet Museum, Tokyo
Affiliations: Recent Sculpture and its
Antecedents, Whitney Museum of
American Art, Fairfield County,
Stamford, Connecticut (catalogue)
Contemporary Issues II, Holman
Gallery, Trenton State College,
New Jersey
Translucid, Public Art Trust,
Washington Square, Washington, D.C.
Chromatics, Modern Art Consultants,
New York
1986
Sculpture on the Wall, The Aldrich
Museum of Contemporary Art,
Ridgefield, Connecticut
Inaugural Exhibition, Curt Marcus
Gallery, New York
1987
Perspectives from Pennsylvania,
Carnegie-Mellon University Art
Gallery, Pittsburgh (brochure)
Synthesis, Fuller Goldeen Gallery,
San Francisco
1988
Four Sculptors, Nina Freudenheim
Gallery, Buffalo, New York

Selected Bibliography

Cohen, Ronny H. "Energism: An
Attitude," Artforum, Vol. 19,
September 1980.
Raynor, Vivien. "Butter, Burlin," The New
York Times, 11 September 1981.
Silverthorne, Jeanne. Exhibition review,
Artforum, Vol. 20, December 1981.
Russell, John. Exhibition Review, The New
York Times, 19 March 1982.
Lichtenstein, Therese. Exhibition review,
Arts Magazine, Vol. 57, March 1983.
Donahoe, Victoria. Exhibition review, The
Philadelphia Inquirer, 18 March 1983.
Saunders, Wade. Exhibition review, Art in
America, Vol. 71, April 1983.
Brenson, Michael. "Critics' Choices," The
New York Times, 21 August 1983.
Linker, Kate. Exhibition Review, Artforum,
Vol. 22, November 1983.
Kramer, Kathryn. "Lifesigns," Arts
Magazine, Vol. 58, February 1984.
Raynor, Vivien. Exhibition review, The
New York Times, 17 February 1984.
Donahoe, Victoria. Exhibition review, The
Philadelphia Inquirer, 14 April 1984.
Martin, Richard. "Tom Butter," Arts
Magazine, Vol. 59, November 1984.
Raynor, Vivien. Exhibition review, The
New York Times, 18 November 1984.
Saunders, Wade. "Talking Objects:
Interviews with Ten Younger
Sculptors," Art in America, Vol. 73,
November 1985.
Sozanski, Edward J. "Art Concerning
Different Ideas About Sculpture," The
Philadelphia Inquirer, 21 November
1985.
Madoff, Steven Henry. "Sculpture
Unbound," ARTnews, Vol. 85, April
1986.
Jarmusch, Ann. Exhibition review,
ARTnews, Vol. 85, April 1986.
Dreishpoon, Douglas. "Tom Butter," Arts
Magazine, Vol. 61, January 1987.
Rubinstein, Meyer Raphael, and Daniel
Wiener. "Sites and Sights:
Considerations on Walter De Maria,
Jeff Koons, and Tom Butter," Arts
Magazine, Vol. 61, March 1987.
Baker, Kenneth. Exhibition review, San
Francisco Chronicle, 24 December
1987.
Porges, Maria F. "A Lesson On Beauty,"
Artweek, Vol. 18, 26 December 1987.

Robert Gober

Robert Gober's sculpture exists in an unsettling state between intimacy and impersonality. His re-creations of outmoded domestic objects are rendered with a matter-of-fact simplicity reminiscent of the naiveté of childhood perception. But beneath the unadorned surfaces of these beds, sinks, chairs, and cribs are intimations of loss, frustration, and despair so subtly injected that only slowly do they seep into the viewer's consciousness.

Gober studied painting at Middlebury College in Vermont and subsequently moved to New York City, where he painted intimate scenes of urban life. He made his first sculptures of plaster in the early 1980s: a crouching man, a dog lying splay-legged on its back, and a small church decorated with painted scenes of city life. But it was in 1985 that he first attracted public attention with a series of sink sculptures that managed to be at once idiosyncratic, common, mysterious, disturbing, and humorous. The sink motif inevitably invited comparison to Marcel Duchamp's notorious 1917 *Fountain,* an ordinary porcelain urinal laid on its back and signed with the artist's pseudonym, R. Mutt. Through such perverse utilizations of common objects, Duchamp asserted that any object could be a work of art if the artist declared it so, an attitude that has informed the work of subsequent artists from Robert Rauschenberg to Jeff Koons.

Gober's work, however, is as much personal as conceptual. Unlike Duchamp's urinal, the sinks are not found objects, but handcrafted sculptures made from wood, wire, and plaster, the slight imperfections in their smooth white surfaces subtly betraying the presence of the artist's hand. "Most of my sculptures have been memories remade, recombined, and filtered through my current experiences," he recalls. "Looking back now at why I built sculptures of sinks, I can remember sinks that I knew as a child, a recurring dream of a roomful of sinks with water flowing through them, the fact that a friend was dying of AIDS. But when I was making them, my considerations were for the most part sculptural and formal ones."[1] In an ironic twist, Gober's sculptured sinks are devoid of plumbing; the holes where faucets and drains would fit are left open. In their uselessness these sinks become emblems of a frustrated desire for purification. "What do you do when you stand in front of a sink?" asks Gober. "You clean yourself; but you can't with these sinks."

Though the early works in the series were straightforward representations of common cast-iron wall sinks, Gober soon began modifying them, some becoming distinctly anthropomorphic while others were geometricized and abstracted almost beyond recognition. His craftsmanship is decidedly understated: the smooth, simple forms are coated with layers of glossy white enamel paint which all but obliterate the evidence of their making. When hung as they generally are against a white wall, these sinks are perversely reticent, seeming to disappear into their environment rather than stand out from it.

Such understatement hints at the influence of Minimalist Art, in which the activation of space is as important as the

X-Crib 1987
wood, enamel paint
44 x 50½ x 33¾
The Oliver-Hoffmann Collection

Untitled Dog   1982
plaster, wire lath
14 x 35 x 18
Collection James Mulvihill

Crouching Man   1982
plaster, wood, wire
24 x 24 x 18
Collection George H. Waterman, III

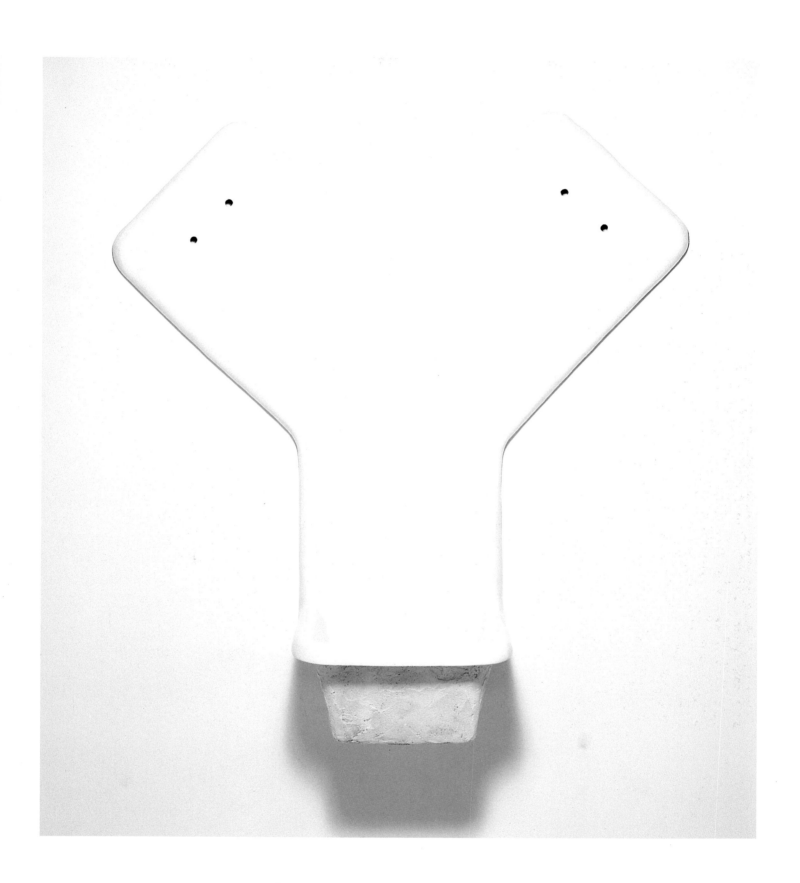

The Subconscious Sink 1985
plaster, wood, wire lath, enamel paint
90 x 83 x 28
Collection Walker Art Center
Clinton and Della Walker Acquisition
Fund and Jerome Foundation Purchase
Fund for Emerging Artists, 1985

Two Partially Buried Sinks   1987
cast iron, enamel paint, earth, grass, wood
39 x 120 x 72
Private collection

(opposite)
The Ascending Sink   1985
plaster, wood, wire lath, enamel paint
30 x 33 x 27 each
Private collection

Slipcovered Armchair 1986–1987
plaster, wire lath, wood,
linen, fabric paint, enamel paint
31½ x 30½ x 29
Collection the artist

Untitled   1986
wood, cotton, down, wool, enamel paint
36½ x 43 x 77
Collection Elaine Werner Dannheisser

created object. As a student in the mid-1970s Gober had found Minimalism oppressively dogmatic, but he is now more receptive to its concerns. His 1985 *Ascending Sink,* consisting of two sinks hung one above the other, recalls Donald Judd's stacked and cantilevered wall pieces, while at the same time suggesting the unlikely ascension of a decidedly earthbound object. Gober speaks of "taking the forms of a more minimal vocabulary and infusing them with an emotional, biographical, hallucinatory quality."

Through such evocative concerns, Gober endows his sinks with a curiously animate quality. With their paired, eyelike spigot holes, they resemble cartoon ghosts, though they remain disquieting. This anthropomorphism is underscored by Gober's titles, which repeatedly allude to conditions of the psyche or spirit. *Subconscious Sink* (1985), with its split, elongated splashboard and two sets of wide-eyed spigot holes, evokes a sense of profound psychological schism. In 1987, Gober finally "put the sinks to rest" with *Two Partially Buried Sinks,* a pair of splashboards rising up from the ground like tombstones.

"From the beginning," says Gober, "my subject matter was always symbolic and domestic." Since abandoning the sink, he has worked with a number of what he terms "domestically nondescript" motifs—beds, cribs, playpens, upholstered chairs, dog beds—all of which deal with questions of intimacy and childhood recollections. Like his first sinks, Gober's untitled bed of 1986 is modeled after beds he remembers from his childhood. Despite this, he has made the bed with such an unassuming simplicity that it is distinctly impersonal. Its impassive stolidity is relieved only by a slight slump in the mattress, as if it had been worn down by a body. This subtle touch endows the work with a paradoxical sense both of human presence and absence.

Recently, Gober has been working on a series of variations on cribs and playpens, which he refers to as being "like childhood cages." As with the sinks, the earliest of these are quite straightforward while later versions become more distorted. *X-Crib* (1987), with its converging sides, projects a disquieting sense of constriction or restraint. To Gober such pieces are "emblems of emotional predicaments I find myself in."

The unadorned simplicity, predominant rectilinearity, and anonymity of manufacture of Gober's beds, cribs, and playpens inevitably recall the Minimalist boxes of Robert Morris and Donald Judd. Even in the distorted cribs and playpens, the parallel lines of the bars accentuate the essential geometry of the work. By emphasizing the formal properties of his domestic objects, Gober effectively counterbalances the potent emotional and associational implications of his imagery.

P.W.B.

1. All quotations are from a conversation with the artist, 26 June 1987.

Robert Gober

1954
Born in Wallingford, Connecticut
1973–1974
Tyler School of Art, Rome
1976
B.A., Middlebury College, Middlebury, Vermont

Lives in New York

Solo Exhibitions

1984
Slides of a Changing Painting, Paula Cooper Gallery, New York
1985
Daniel Weinberg Gallery, Los Angeles
Paula Cooper Gallery, New York
1986
Daniel Weinberg Gallery, Los Angeles
1987
Galerie Jean Bernier, Athens
Paula Cooper Gallery, New York
1988
Tyler School of Art, Temple University, Philadelphia (brochure)

Selected Group Exhibitions

1979
112 Greene Street Workshop, New York
1981
Three Look into American Home Life, Ian Berstedt Gallery, New York
1982
Paula Cooper Gallery, New York
1983
New York Work, Studio 10, Chur, Switzerland
1984
P.S. 122 Gallery, New York
Jus de Pomme Gallery, New York
1985
Scapes, University Art Museum, Santa Barbara, California (catalogue)
1986
Robert Gober, Jeff Koons, Peter Nadin, Meyer Vaisman, Jay Gorney Modern Art, New York
Objects from the Modern World: Richard Artschwager, R.M. Fischer, Robert Gober, Jeff Koons, Daniel Weinberg Gallery, Los Angeles
Robert Gober and Kevin Larmon: An Installation, Nature Morte, New York

New Sculpture: Robert Gober, Jeff Koons, Haim Steinbach, The Renaissance Society at The University of Chicago (catalogue)
Robert Gober, Nancy Shaver, Alan Turner, Meg Webster (organized by Robert Gober), Cable, New York
Works from the Paula Cooper Gallery, John Berggruen Gallery, San Francisco (catalogue)
Art on Paper Exhibition, Weatherspoon Art Gallery, University of North Carolina at Greensboro (catalogue)
Max Hetzler Gallery, Cologne, West Germany (catalogue)
Art for Young Collectors, The Renaissance Society at The University of Chicago (catalogue)
Art and Its Double: Recent Developments in New York Art, La Fundacio Caixa de Pensiones, Barcelona (catalogue)
1976–1986: Ten Years of Collecting Contemporary Art (Selections from the Edward R. Downe, Jr. Collection), The Wellesley College Museum, Massachusetts (catalogue)
1987
Artists from Paula Cooper Gallery, Galeria Emi Valentim de Carvalho, Lisbon (catalogue)
Extreme Order, Lia Rumma, Naples (catalogue)
New York Art Now: The Saatchi Collection, The Saatchi Collection, London (catalogue)
Avant-Garde in the Eighties, Los Angeles County Museum of Art, California (catalogue)
1988
Laurie Rubin Gallery, New York
Utopia Post Utopia, The Institute of Contemporary Art, Boston
Artschwager, His Peers and Persuasion 1963–1988, Daniel Weinberg Gallery, Los Angeles (catalogue)

Selected Bibliography

Russell, John. Exhibition review, *The New York Times*, 4 October 1985.
Decter, Joshua. "Robert Gober," *Arts Magazine*, Vol. 60, December 1985.
Rinder, Larry. "Kevin Larmon and Robert Gober," *Flash Art*, No. 128, May–June 1986.
Collins, Tricia, and Richard Milazzo. "Robert Gober: The Subliminal Function of Sinks," *Kunstforum*, Vol. 84, June–August 1986.
Cone, Michele. "Ready-Mades on the Couch," *Artscribe*, Vol. 58, June–July 1986.
Juarez, Roberto. "Selected Similarities," *Bomb*, No. 18, Winter 1987.
Kaplan, Steven. "Head, Heart, and Hands," *Artfinder*, Spring 1987.
Power, Kevin. "Art and Its Double," *Flash Art*, No. 132, February–March 1987.
Nickas, Robert. "Art and Its Double," *Flash Art*, No. 132, February–March 1987.
Beyer, Lucie. Exhibition review, *Flash Art*, No. 132, February–March 1987.
Koether, Jutta. Exhibition review, *Artscribe*, Vol. 62, March–April 1987.
Cameron, Dan. "Art and Its Double: A New York Perspective," *Flash Art*, No. 134, May 1987.
Princenthal, Nancy. Exhibition review, *Art in America*, Vol. 75, December 1987.

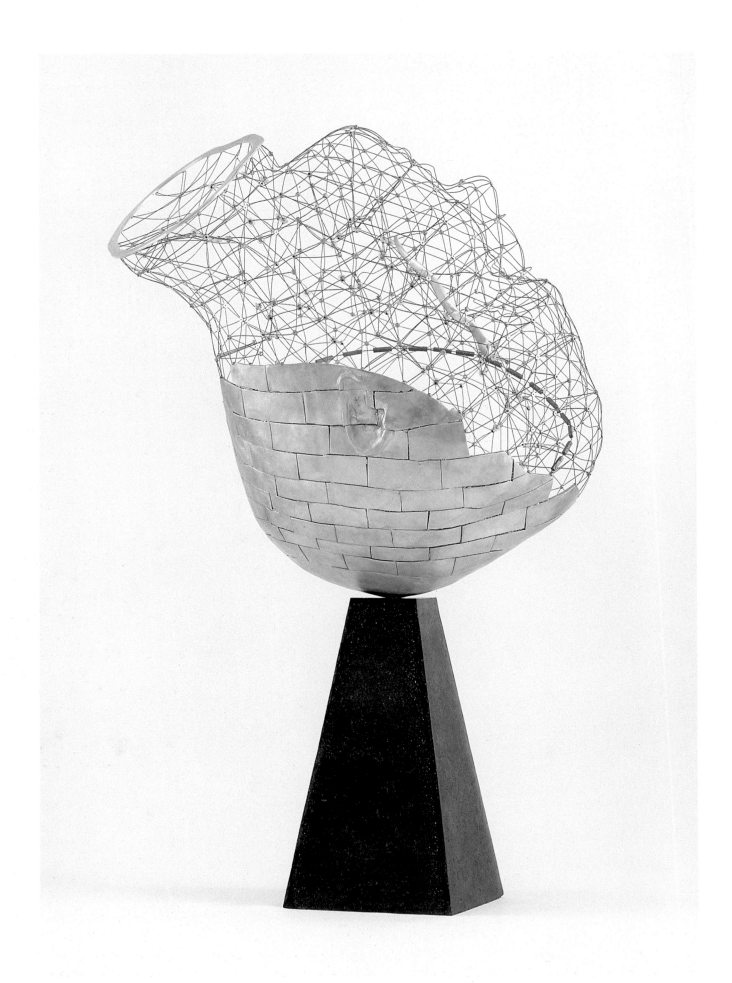

Brower Hatcher

For as long as he can remember, Brower Hatcher has been a builder and a maker of things, so it is fitting that he now makes sculptures that are a cross between sophisticated spatial puzzles and visionary architecture. Based on an elaborate system of interlocking polyhedrons, his stainless steel mesh structures filled with floating objects are at once whimsical and high-tech in character. As a student at Vanderbilt University in the early 1960s, Hatcher pursued studies in engineering. After two years at Vanderbilt, however, he decided that engineering was too limited a field for his aspirations and in 1963 he moved to New York where he enrolled at Pratt Institute to pursue a degree in industrial design. On completion of his studies at Pratt, he went to London where he studied sculpture and later taught at St. Martin's School of Art. That institution provided an especially lively atmosphere during Hatcher's residency from 1967 to 1972. On the one hand the classical modernist orthodoxy espoused by the sculptor Anthony Caro, who taught there at the time, continued to be influential; on the other hand, a new generation of artists studying there, including the conceptualists Hamish Fulton, Gilbert and George, and Richard Long, was beginning to challenge Caro's formalist aesthetic.

It was in this fertile environment that Hatcher began making his first significant sculptures. These consisted of masses of colored wire ordered in layers and sequences that roughly resembled geometric bushes. Hatcher regarded his constructions, with their elusive tonality, as sculptural analogues to Color Field painting. In his view, as transparent and luminous structures, they represented a sharp departure from the Constructivist-oriented ideas underlying the formalist sculpture of the preceding generation. Often, Hatcher placed his structures in the landscape where natural light dissolved their materiality into shimmering chromatic sequences which created a dialogue with nature and changed character depending on atmospheric conditions and the viewer's position.

Hatcher returned to the United States in 1972 and by 1974 was working on a series of monochrome steel sculptures composed of metal ribbons attached to vertical plates. The opaque plates serve both as a foil to and a framing edge for the animated configurations of twisting lines which resemble spatial calligraphy.

Since 1979, Hatcher has fabricated steel structures composed of hundreds of small polyhedral modules attached to one another at their vertices to form irregular domelike shapes that loosely recall the geodesic structures of Buckminster Fuller. As Hatcher became more adept at manipulating and deforming these geometric configurations, he was able to mold them into figural shapes such as the giant head of *Adirondack Guide Monument*, constructed in 1984.

Embedded within the skeletal structures are a profusion of solid geometric and representational forms that seem to hover in space. In some cases, the artist used objects indigenous to a specific area as in *Adirondack Guide Monument;* these include a wooden backpacker, a guide boat, an adirondack chair, a wooden

Ancient Concept 1987
imitation stone, aluminum, bronze,
glass, stone
77 x 52 x 40
Collection the artist
Courtesy Cava Gallery, Philadelphia

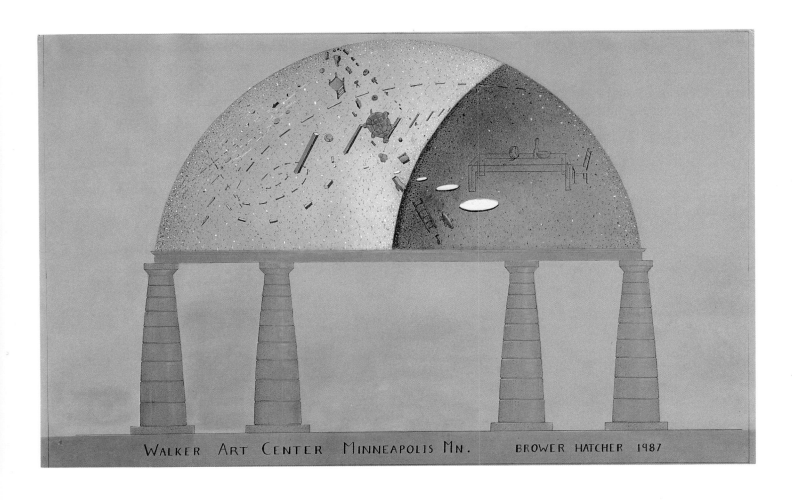

WALKER ART CENTER MINNEAPOLIS MN.   BROWER HATCHER 1987

Study for *Prophecy of the Ancients*   1987
mixed media on Mylar
36 x 60½
Collection Walker Art Center
Acquired with Lannan Foundation
support in conjunction with the
exhibition *Sculpture Inside Outside*,
1988

(opposite)
Astrolab   1980
steel, stainless steel, copper, aluminum, iron
44 x 36 x 32
Collection the artist

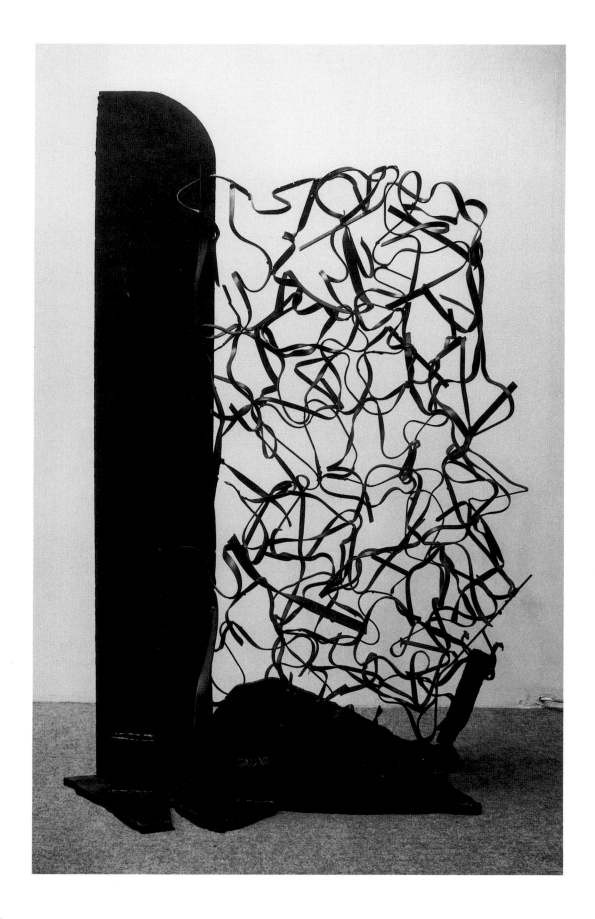

Forecaster 1974
steel
75 x 50 x 18
Collection Dr. Charles and Rose Gibbs

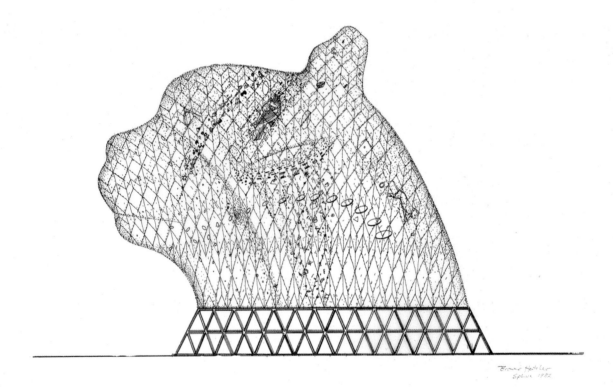

The Riddle of the Sphinx   1982
ink on Mylar
22 x 24
Collection the artist

Adirondack Guide Monument   1984
stainless steel, steel, wood, concrete
456 x 300 x 300
Collection Plattsburgh State Art
Galleries, State University of New York

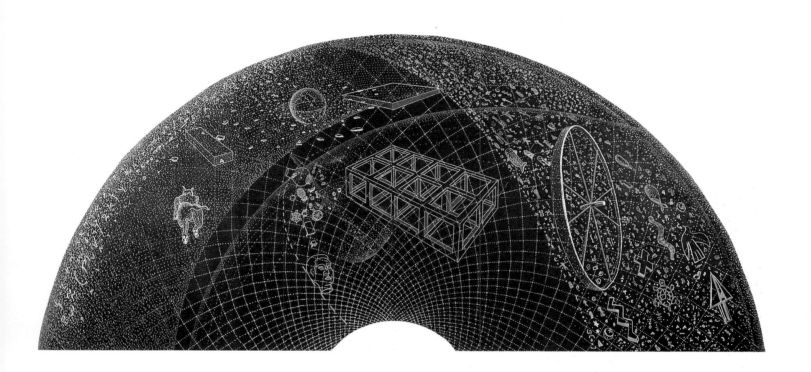

The Manifold of Language 1987
hand-colored photo collage
mounted on six panels
74 x 168
Collection the artist
Courtesy Cava Gallery, Philadelphia

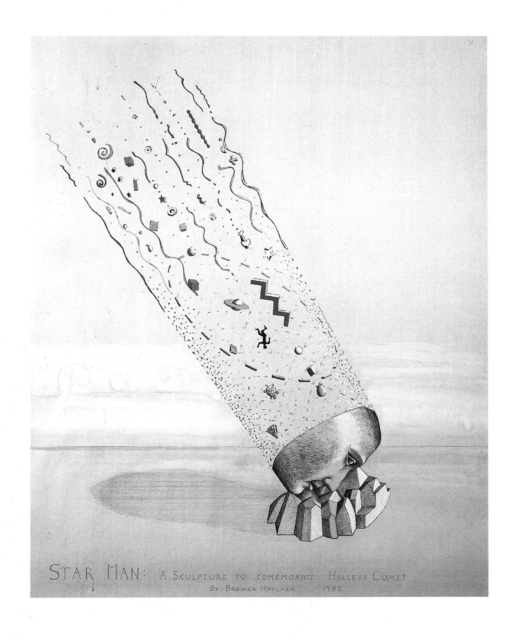

Starman 1985
hand-colored sepia print
45 x 36
Collection the artist

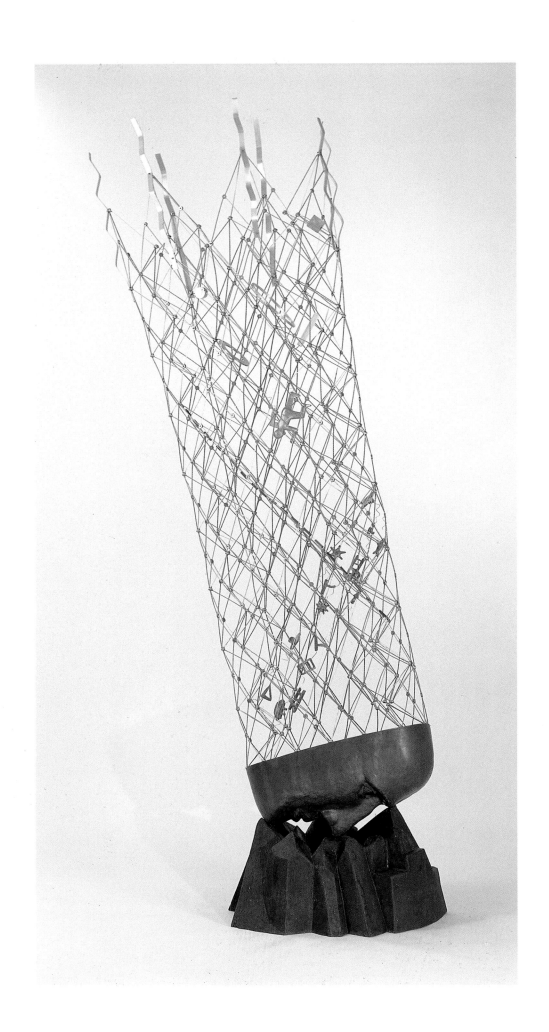

Starman   1985–1988
imitation stone, bronze,
stainless steel, aluminum
144 x 72 x 32
Collection the artist
Courtesy Cava Gallery, Philadelphia

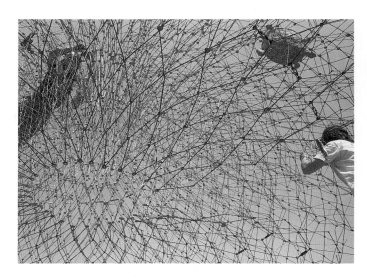

Construction and installation of
Prophecy of the Ancients

Prophecy of the Ancients   1988
cast stone, stainless steel, bronze,
mixed media
202 high, 246 diam.
Commissioned with Lannan Foundation
support for the exhibition
Sculpture Inside Outside
Courtesy the artist and Cava Gallery,
Philadelphia

Collaborating and assisting in
fabrication and installation: Barbara
Owen, Sam Coe, Matt Chinian, Fuller
Cowles, John Hock, and Mike Czuba

loon, and a miniature log cabin. In most of his work, however, he incorporates geometric shapes and re-creations (often in cast metal) of everyday objects that appeal to him. Turtles are ubiquitous in Hatcher's work; their domed shape and gridded shell echo the basic geometry of the metal structures. Other favorites are tables and chairs, ladders, books, boats, and animals. He prefers such ordinary images because, he says, "I'm real interested in the everydayness of things and how one can rupture them from context and enable them to become metaphorical."[1] Within his transparent steel webs, these suspended elements serve as focal points. They also function pictographically as abstract markings that generate meaning.

Hatcher says he is interested in examining the various ways a mark or an image signifies an idea. Moreover, he carefully arranges his objects to establish relationships between them and the sculpture as a whole:

> I'm trying to get to that point where there is an integration between symbol and structure. . . . It has to do with the fundamental nature of language. When you write a sentence, you have words which are fragments, but it's through structure that they work upon one another to generate significance and meaning.

Initially, Hatcher mounted his metal superstructures on simple, geometric forms. More recently, these networks have been supported on bases that refer to historical architectural and sculptural forms, such as columns, pyramids, and figural fragments. In *Starman* (1985–1988), the base consists of a head resting face down in a landscape of prismatic shapes. In this work, the superstructure takes the form of a comet tail streaming from the back of the head. The initial design for this piece was done in 1985, and several models of increasing scale were made. The final forty-foot-high version will be permanently installed in a public plaza in Philadelphia.

Prophecy of the Ancients (1988), commissioned for the Minneapolis Sculpture Garden, contains classical and highly futuristic elements. Its industrial stainless steel dome rests on six "antique" columns. "It occurred to me," Hatcher reflects, "that you can make a historical metaphor by the way you use technology, as a language of the way things are made." By juxtaposing disparate styles and using a variety of techniques to fabricate his work, the artist combines aspects of the past, present, and future within a single sculpture.

Recently, Hatcher has re-introduced color (after an absence of some thirteen years) into some of his work. The internal webbing of the Walker commission is constructed of enamel-coated stainless steel rods, creating a multi-hued spectrum. His use of color transforms the industrial-looking dome into a luminous open grid evoking the twilight sky. Light reflecting hubs and other objects floating, like constellations, within the web reinforce the celestial allusion. The use of pure geometric form in combination with cosmological references links Hatcher's structures to the imaginative designs of such eighteenth-century visionary French architects as Boullée and Lequeu.

Hatcher describes his works as philosophical models. They are metaphorical statements rather than functional forms. "Basically," he says, "I'm trying to build an inclusive model that represents a unification of the diversity of things as we know them; both abstractly through structure and mathematics and figuratively through representation and symbol." In his structures, he synthesizes mechanical and symbolic systems to present a subjective worldview in which fantasy and technology are united.

D.H.

1. Unless otherwise noted, all quotations are from a conversation with the artist, 28 June 1987.

Brower Hatcher

1942
Born in Atlanta, Georgia
1961–1963
Attended Vanderbilt University, Nashville, Tennessee
1967
Bachelor of Industrial Design, Pratt Institute, Brooklyn, New York
1969–1972
Attended St. Martin's School of Art, London

Lives in Diamond Point, New York

Solo Exhibitions

1971
Museum of Modern Art, Oxford, England
1972
Kasmin Ltd., London
1973
Andre Emmerich Gallery, New York
1975
Andre Emmerich Gallery, New York
City University of New York, Graduate Center Mall
1980
Diane Brown Gallery, Washington, D.C.
1982
Diane Brown Gallery, Washington, D.C.
1987
Paul Cava Gallery, Philadelphia

Selected Group Exhibitions

1969
Galleria dell'Ariete, Milan
1970
City Sculpture, Cambridge, England
1972
Objects and Documents, Arts Council of Great Britain, London (catalogue)
1973
American Painting and Sculpture 1973, Krannert Art Museum, University of Illinois, Champaign
1974
Monumenta: A Biennial Exhibition of Outdoor Sculpture, Newport, Rhode Island (catalogue)
1975
The Condition of Sculpture: A Selection of Recent Sculpture by Younger British and Foreign Artists, The Hayward Gallery, Arts Council of Great Britain, London (catalogue)
Sculpture: American Directions 1945–1975, National Collection of Fine Arts, Smithsonian Institution, Washington, D.C. (catalogue)
1976
Artists at Bennington: Visual Arts Faculty, 1932–1976, Bennington College Art Center, Bennington, Vermont (catalogue)
1977
Alexander F. Milliken Gallery, New York
Sculpture Space, Munson-Williams-Proctor Institute Museum of Art, Utica, New York
1978
15 Sculptors Around Bennington, Park McCullough House, North Bennington, Vermont (catalogue)
1979
Prospect Mountain Sculpture Show, Lake George, New York
NY/8, Joe and Emily Lowe Art Gallery, Syracuse University, Syracuse, New York (catalogue)
Diane Brown Sculpture Space, Washington, D.C.
1980
11th International Sculpture Conference Exhibition, International Sculpture Center, Washington, D.C.
Diane Brown Sculpture Space, Washington, D.C.
1981
Tibor de Nagy Gallery, New York
1983
Ice and Air Show, Lake George Arts Project, Bolton Landing, New York
Art on the Beach, Creative Time, Inc., New York
1984
The Houston Festival
1985
Small Monuments, Temple Gallery, Philadelphia
1986
Paul Cava Gallery, Philadelphia

Selected Bibliography

Everett, Anthony. Exhibition review, *Studio International,* Vol. 183, April 1972.

Exhibition review, *Village Voice,* 25 May 1973.

Exhibition review, *The New York Times,* 26 May 1973.

Brooks, Rosetta. Exhibition review, *Studio International,* Vol. 186, December 1973.

Kagan, Andrew. "Optical Continuity: The Sculpture of Brower Hatcher," *Arts Magazine,* Vol. 49, February 1975.

Ashbery, John. "Telling it on the Mountain," *New York Magazine,* 27 August 1979.

Baro, Gene. Exhibition review, *Art International,* Vol. 24, August–September 1981.

Lewis, Jo Ann. Exhibition review, *The Washington Post,* 22 May 1982.

Front page photograph, *The New York Times,* 6 July 1983.

Photo, *Houston Chronicle,* 1 March 1984.

Reilly, Jim. "Sculpture at Lake George: A brand of sophisticated folk art," *The Saratogian,* 16 September 1984.

Johnson, Ken. "Monumentally Sublime or Absurd," *Times Union,* Albany, New York, 14 October 1984.

"Monument to be relocated," *Post-Star,* Glens Falls, New York, 14 November 1984.

Sozanski, Edward J. "Capturing the Cosmos in Earthly Metals," *The Philadelphia Inquirer,* 1 October 1987.

Marincola, Paula. Exhibition review, *Artforum,* Vol. 26, January 1988.

Jene Highstein

Jene Highstein's monolithic sculptures hover in a twilight existence between nature and artifice. Fashioned from a variety of materials—stone, bronze, iron, steel, plaster, cement—their compact, rounded forms are at once resolutely rocklike and clearly shaped by the artist. Simultaneously familiar and enigmatic, they recall totems carved in homage to an animistic universe, or meteoric boulders cast down from the heavens. Highstein infuses his work with a compacted energy and charged presence that seem disproportionate to the blunt simplicity of his forms.

Now in his mid-forties, Highstein is among those artists who were raised on nonobjective art, rather than having come to it from a basis in representation. His father, a Baltimore physician, was a collector of contemporary art who included among his acquaintances the painter Morris Louis. "Pretty much every square inch of the walls of the house were covered with abstract paintings," recalls Highstein, "and that was what I took for granted art was about."[1]

Thus, unlike the great modernist sculptors from earlier in the century—Brancusi, Arp, Moore, Noguchi—all of whom took nature as a point of departure for their art and moved toward a greater abstraction, Highstein has evolved from a non-representational art toward a greater allusion to nature. "The content of my work is not so much nature abstracted," he explains, "but form which is evolved in relation to nature and which carries with it natural associations."[2]

Highstein's earliest sculptures, dating from the late 1960s and early 1970s, were indoor installations designed to heighten the viewer's awareness of the surrounding space. "So in a sense the room was half the sculpture," he says. His *Double Pipe Piece* of 1974, for example, consisted of two lengths of seamless steel pipe that spanned the width of a room at different heights, effectively redefining the architectural space.

In the mid-1970s, Highstein began to create self-contained objects whose impact was determined not so much by their relationship to surrounding architecture, but by their dialogue with the viewer's body. One such piece was *Black Sphere* (1976), a huge ball of black cement hand-troweled over a steel armature. Standing over six feet tall, it was slightly larger than the average human, a size Highstein found at once impressive and assertive without being overwhelming. The absolute simplicity of its geometric form and the starkness of its black surface made it visually comprehensible at a glance, a quality Highstein considers to be the essential lesson of Minimalism.

In this and other pieces from the later 1970s, Highstein's emphasis was largely on silhouette. He describes his sculptures from this period as "icons." "They were primary forms," he says. "They tended to operate as an overall image which could flatten out in your mind. They weren't so much about what was going on within them as about their first impact. You were surprised if you went around the other side and they were different."

Highstein's work began to change in scale and complexity in the late 1970s.

Palm II   1986
palm wood
66½ high, 36 diam.
Collection Joan Sonnabend

Black Sphere 1976
concrete, steel
76 diam.
Collection The University of Chicago
Gift in honor of Mr. and Mrs. Edwin A.
Bergman

Untitled 1987
concrete on wood, wire
114 x 120 x 147
Permanent installation at the Mattress Factory,
Pittsburgh

Untitled   1987
charcoal, graphite on paper
44¾ x 27⅞
Collection Walker Art Center
Acquired with Lannan Foundation
support in conjunction with the
exhibition
Sculpture Inside Outside, 1988

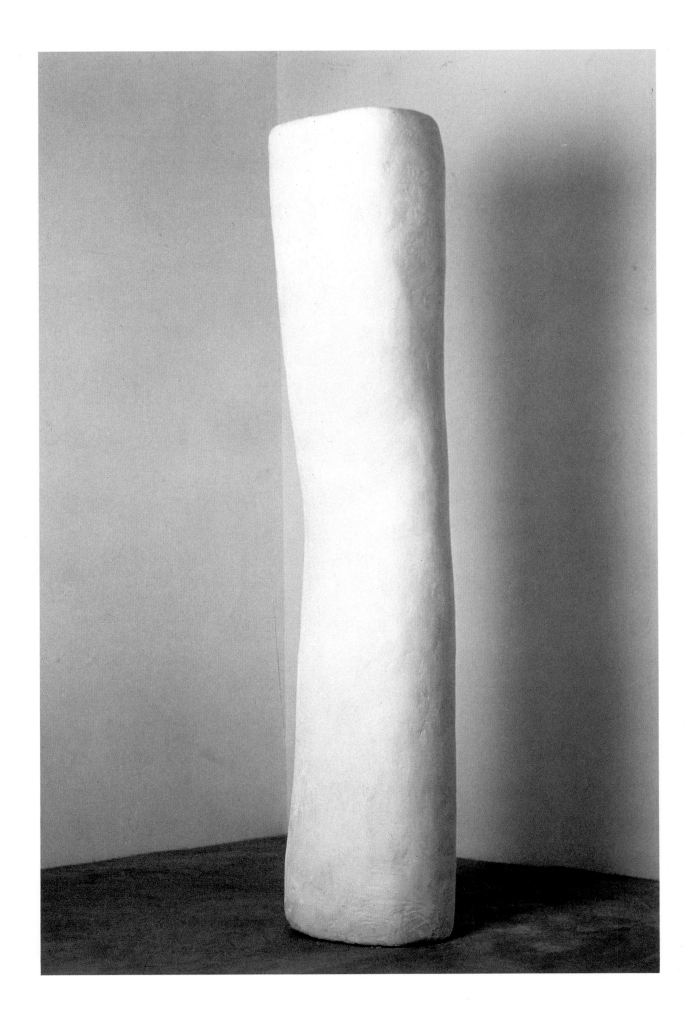

Interferon 1980
solid iron casting
21 x 25½ x 31½
Collection Museum of Contemporary Art,
Chicago
Gift of Mr. and Mrs. Bruce A. Littman

(opposite)
Eolith 1 1986
plaster on styrofoam
86 high, 20 diam.
Courtesy the artist and Michael Klein, Inc.,
New York

Untitled 1986–1987
plaster and paint on metal armature
64 x 96½ x 38
Courtesy the artist and Michael Klein, Inc.,
New York

Untitled 1987
charcoal on paper
64 x 60
Collection Mr. and Mrs. Julius E. Davis

Jene Highstein installing *Untitled*

Untitled   1987–1988
three elements
granite
108 x 48 x 28
75 x 61 x 43
30 x 90 x 51
Commissioned with Lannan Foundation
support for the exhibition
Sculpture Inside Outside
Courtesy the artist and Michael Klein, Inc.,
New York

Untitled (detail)   1987–1988
three elements
granite
108 x 48 x 28
75 x 61 x 43
30 x 90 x 51
Commissioned with Lannan Foundation
support for the exhibition
Sculpture Inside Outside
Courtesy the artist and Michael Klein, Inc.,
New York

"I was trying to figure out a way to make things that were smaller and more practical," he recalls. Working in cast iron and forged steel, Highstein found that physical presence had less to do with size than with mass, density, and weight. "I decided that if I did something smaller, then I would make it very dense. I would make it solid, in iron, so that it would have the impact of a large object, but it would have small dimensions."

As the work diminished in scale and became more accessible to circumambulation, Highstein began to move away from the iconic simplicity he had previously favored. "What I'm doing now is not about the long view, but about the experience of being relatively close to it," he asserts. "At a certain point I shifted to the short view and started making things that were more complex." Complexity is, of course, relative; for Highstein it has principally meant that though his forms remain compact, rounded masses, their silhouettes are rendered more irregular, so that the profiles of the works change as the viewer walks around them.

A significant consequence of this shift has been that Highstein's works from the 1980s tend toward a greater allusion to nature than his earlier pieces. Speaking of works like *Untitled* (1986–1987), with its two snoutlike projections, Highstein says:

> To me, these kinds of forms relate to a whole vocabulary of stuff: to animal forms, to fish forms, to phallic forms, to a whole spectrum of associations. And that's what makes them work. I prefer that they suggest a really broad range of things. If it comes down to one image, then there's something wrong.

Since 1980, Highstein has worked with a variety of materials, among them carved wood and stone. He contends that his carved works are far subtler than his built sculptures. With his earlier works in concrete or plaster, the execution was secondary to the conception. As a result, the works tended to have a sharp, clear,

authoritative presence. On the other hand, in working with wood or stone, Highstein has found that he must be responsive to the inherent properties of the material: its color, its internal structure, its surface quality. In conjunction with the general reduction in scale, this has given Highstein's recent work a new sense of intimacy and sensuousness without diminishing the quality of compacted energy he prizes. Perhaps the most extreme example of this is *Palm II* (1986), in which he simply inverted a palm stump and trimmed its fibrous roots.

Highstein made his first stone pieces in 1980 and 1981. In a sense, he had been working toward the use of stone since the mid-1970s, when he made the transition from creating environments to making discrete objects. He had initially used cement only because at that point in his career stone was too expensive and time-consuming a material to work with. To date, all of his stone works have been outdoor commissions.

Highstein has found that the spatial awareness he had arrived at in his early indoor installations has been crucial to these outdoor stone pieces. For the tripartite work commissioned by the Walker Art Center, the dimensions of the stones were calculated so that the tall, vertical piece and the low, ground-hugging stone would have equal mass. The third piece, intermediate in height, would be the heaviest and serve visually to anchor the work. Once the rough dimensions of each element had been determined, the stones were selected from a quarry in Pennsylvania and shipped to Highstein's farm near Salem, New York. There they were placed in a field and carefully positioned in a triangular arrangement that balanced each stone's "field of influence" against that of the other two. Only then were the pieces chiseled down to their final forms. After the stones had been shaped, Highstein scored their surfaces with a series of parallel lines about an inch apart. This allowed him to

retain a sense of the rough, crystalline structure of the rock without having it look "bruised" by the chisel.

P.W.B.

1. Quoted in Hugh Davies and Lynda Forsha, La Jolla Museum of Contemporary Art, *Jene Highstein*, exh. cat., 1986. Unless otherwise noted, all other quotations are from a conversation with the artist, 25 June 1987.
2. Quoted in Mattress Factory, Pittsburgh, *Installation—Jene Highstein*, exh. broch., 1985.

Jene Highstein

1942
Born in Baltimore, Maryland
1963
B.A., University of Maryland,
College Park
1963–1965
University of Chicago
1966
New York Studio School
1970
Diploma, Royal Academy Schools,
London

Lives in New York

Solo Exhibitions

1970
Lisson Gallery, London
1973
New Sculpture, Coney Island, New York
1974
112 Greene Street Workshop,
New York
Galleria Salvatore Ala, Milan
1975
Galerie Rencontres, Paris
1976
Holly Solomon Gallery, New York
Galleria Salvatore Ala, Milan
1977
Galleria Marilena Bonomo, Bari, Italy
1978
Musée d'Art et d'Industrie,
Saint-Etienne, France (catalogue)
Ugo Ferranti Gallery, Rome
Michele Lachowsky Gallery, Brussels
Mollet-Vieville/Najar Gallery, Paris
(catalogue)
1979
Droll/Kolbert Gallery, New York
1980
Young-Hoffman Gallery, Chicago
The Renaissance Society at The
University of Chicago
LA Louver Gallery, Venice, California
(brochure)
University Art Museum, Berkeley,
California (brochure)
1981
Michele Lachowsky Gallery, Brussels
Ace Gallery, Venice, California
Ugo Ferranti Gallery, Milan
1982
Oscarsson Hood Gallery, New York
Young-Hoffman Gallery, Chicago

1983
Miami-Dade Community College,
Miami
1984
Sheldon Memorial Art Gallery,
University of Nebraska, Lincoln
(catalogue)
Anders Tornberg Gallery, Lund,
Sweden
Rhona Hoffman Gallery, Chicago
1985
Mattress Factory, Pittsburgh
1986
Flow Ace Gallery, Los Angeles
La Jolla Museum of Contemporary Art,
California (catalogue)
1988
Michael Klein, Inc., New York

Selected Group Exhibitions

1968–1969
Pavilions in the Parks, Blackheath Park,
Camden Square, London
1970
Between 11, Kunsthalle, Düsseldorf
Visions, Projects, Proposals, Midland
Group Galleries, Nottingham, England
The Human Presence, Camden Arts
Center, London
1971
Brooklyn Bridge Show, New York
1972
112 Greene Street Workshop,
New York
Six Sculptors—7,000 Square Feet,
10 Bleeker Street, New York
1973
In Spaces, Sarah Lawrence College,
Bronxville, New York
Mass '73, Chicago
Sculpture in the Fields, Storm King Art
Center, Mountainville, New York
*Jene Highstein, Richard Nonas—
Outdoor Sculpture*, University of
Rhode Island, Kingston
1974
Artpark, Lewiston, New York
Front and Center, Paterson College of
New Jersey, Paterson
Discussion/Works, The Clocktower,
The Institute for Art and Urban
Resources, Inc., New York
Anarchitecture Show, 112 Greene
Street Workshop, New York
1975
Collectors of the Seventies, The
Clocktower, The Institute for Art and

Urban Resources, Inc., New York
*Tendences Actuelles de la Nouvelle
Peinture Americaine*, Ninth Paris
Biennial, Musée d'Art Moderne de la
Ville de Paris (catalogue)
Galerie Rencontres, Paris
1976
Sculptors' Drawings, The Fine Arts
Building, New York
Rooms P.S. 1, P.S. 1, The Institute for
Art and Urban Resources, Inc.,
Long Island City, New York (catalogue)
1977
Collection in Progress, Moore College
of Art Gallery, Philadelphia (catalogue)
Recent Acquisitions, Solomon R.
Guggenheim Museum, New York
Customs and Culture, Creative Time,
Inc., New York
Space Windows, David Winton Bell
Gallery, List Art Center, Brown
University, Providence, Rhode Island
(catalogue)
Drawings for Outdoor Sculpture, John
Weber Gallery, New York (catalogue)
1978
Indoor/Outdoor Sculpture, P.S. 1, The
Institute for Art and Urban Resources,
Inc., Long Island City, New York
Drawings for Outdoor Sculpture,
Muehlenberg College Center for the
Arts, Allentown, Pennsylvania
Focus, Centre Culturel du Marais, Paris
1979
A Great Big Drawing Show, P.S. 1, The
Institute for Art and Urban Resources,
Inc., Long Island City, New York
Young-Hoffman Gallery, Chicago
(catalogue)
*Tendencies in American Drawing of
the Seventies*, Stadtische Galerie im
Lenbachhaus, Munich
1981
*Alternatives in Retrospect: An
Historical Overview 1969–1975*, The
New Museum of Contemporary Art,
New York (catalogue)
*Schemes—A Decade of Installation
Drawings*, Elise Meyer Gallery,
New York (catalogue)
*Variants: Drawings by Contemporary
Sculptors*, Sewall Art Gallery, Rice
University, Houston (catalogue)
*The New Spiritualism: Transcendant
Images in Painting and Sculpture*,
Oscarsson Hood Gallery, New York
(catalogue)

1982

The UFO Show, The Queens Museum,
Flushing, New York
Bang, Highstein, Roosen, Sperry,
Stedman Art Gallery, Rutgers
University, Camden, New Jersey
(catalogue)

1983

Monumental Drawings by Sculptors,
Hillwood Art Gallery, C.W. Post Center
of Long Island University, Greenvale,
New York
Iron Cast, Pratt Manhattan Center
Gallery, Pratt Institute, New York
Art on Paper, Weatherspoon Art
Gallery, University of North Carolina at
Greensboro

1984

*An International Survey of Recent
Painting and Sculpture*, The Museum
of Modern Art, New York (catalogue)
*Projects: World's Fairs, Waterfronts,
Parks and Plazas*, Rhona Hoffman
Gallery, Chicago
*Painting, Drawing, and Sculpture:
American and European*, LA Louver
Gallery, Venice, California

1985

*Chicago Sculpture International/Mile
4*, Chicago International Art Exposition
(catalogue)

1986

*American Abstract Artists: 50th
Anniversary Celebration*, The Bronx
Museum of the Arts, New York
(catalogue)
*New Sculpture: James Casebere, Mary
Carlson, Jackie Ferrara, Ian Hamilton
Finlay, Jene Highstein, Michael Klein,
Inc.*, New York

1987

The Success of Failure, Independent
Curators, Inc., New York (catalogue)
Sculptors on Paper: New Work,
Madison Art Center, Wisconsin
(catalogue)

Selected Bibliography

Lusker, Ron. "New York: The Season in
Sculpture," *Craft Horizons*, Vol. 31,
August 1971.

Matthias, Rosemary. "Indoor-Outdoor:
Space and Materials—Six Young
Sculptors," *Arts Magazine*, Vol. 47,
September–October 1972.

Crimp, Douglas. Exhibition review,
ARTnews, Vol. 71, April 1973.

Gilbert-Rolfe, Jeremy. Exhibition review,
Artforum, Vol. 12, December 1973.

Moore, Alan. Exhibition review,
Artforum, Vol. 12, April 1974.

Ratcliff, Carter. "Jene Highstein: Form in
the Active Mode," *Art in America*,
Vol. 62, July–August 1974.

Lippard, Lucy R. "A is for Artpark," *Art
in America*, Vol. 62, November–
December 1974.

Ratcliff, Carter. Exhibition review, *Art
International*, Vol. 20, April–May
1976.

Perreault, John. "P.S. 1, I Love You,"
SoHo Weekly News, 17 June 1976.

Foote, Nancy. "The Apotheosis of the
Crummy Space," *Artforum*, Vol. 15,
October 1976.

Lambarelli, Roberto G. Exhibition review,
Flash Art, No. 86–87, January–
February 1979.

Castle, Ted. "Jene Highstein: A Full
Roundness," *Artforum*, Vol. 18,
November 1979.

Cavaliere, Barbara. Exhibition review,
Arts Magazine, Vol. 54, November
1979.

Bradley, Laurel. Exhibition review, *Arts
Magazine*, Vol. 54, November 1979.

Welish, Marjorie. Exhibition review, *Art
in America*, Vol. 68, January 1980.

Artner, Alan G. "Flying Saucer Ready to
Land on Governors State," *Chicago
Tribune*, 31 August 1980.

Pincus-Witten, Robert. "Jene Highstein
and Sensibility Minimalism: A Tissue of
Happenstance," *Arts Magazine*, Vol.
55, October 1980.

Morris, Robert. "American Quartet," *Art
in America*, Vol. 69, December 1981.

Kirshner, Judith. "Thieves Like Us,"
Artforum, Vol. 21, September 1982.

Schjeldahl, Peter. "Spacey Invaders,"
Village Voice, 14 September 1982.

Seidner, David. "Interview," *Bomb*, No. 6,
1983.

Cotter, Holland. "Jene Highstein," *Arts
Magazine*, Vol. 59, April 1983.

Raynor, Vivien. "Art: Explanations for
'Success of Failure,' " *The New York
Times*, 21 December 1984.

Artner, Alan G. Exhibition review, *Chicago
Tribune*, 25 January 1985.

Castle, Frederick Ted. Exhibition review,
Art in America, Vol. 73, September
1985.

Warren, Reid. "Anti-Matter," *Omni
Magazine*, Vol. 8, May 1986.

Muchnic, Suzanne. Exhibition review,
Los Angeles Times, 13 June 1986.

Pincus, Robert L. "Highstein: Sculptor's
Monumental Works Rise Above His
Minimalist Roots," *The San Diego
Union*, 13 December 1986.

McDonald, Robert. "Highstein's
Retrospective in La Jolla," *Los Angeles
Times*, 20 December 1986.

Muchnic, Suzanne. "Highstein's Primal
Sculptures," *Los Angeles Times*,
20 December 1986.

Pincus, Robert L. "Minimal and Always
Meaningful," *The San Diego Union*,
11 January 1987.

McManus, Michael. "Of Preservation and
Selection," *Artweek*, Vol. 18,
24 January 1987.

Taylor, Robert. "Contemporary Art Roars
into the Los Angeles Fast Lane," *The
Boston Globe*, 25 January 1987.

Gardner, Colin. Exhibition review,
Artforum, Vol. 25, March 1987.

Pincus, Robert L. Exhibition review, *Art in
America*, Vol. 75, May 1987.

Welish, Marjorie. "Jene Highstein at La
Jolla Museum of Contemporary Art,"
New Observations, No. 50, September
1987.

Jin Soo Kim

To walk into one of Jin Soo Kim's astonishing environments is to enter a world that combines high fantasy and mundane reality. Forms drip down from the ceiling, twist through the air, spread across the walls, and sprout up from the ground like lush vegetation in a tropical rainforest, or human viscera magnified to colossal scale. Yet fantastic as these forms are, they are made from the gritty, abandoned debris of the urban landscape. Bedsprings, rubber tubing, plastic pipe, electrical conduit, floor tiles, canvas scraps, molded ceiling squares, wire mesh, cyclone fencing, chicken wire, rope, twine, broken chairs, exhaust manifolds, air filters, headlights, radiators, bicycles, light fixtures, bedspreads, fire hoses, and thick, muscular braids of crumpled brown paper are intertwined into seemingly chaotic assemblages that give new meaning to the term "hobo jungle." Kim transforms the waste of this world into a perversely beautiful wonderland that is at once delicately fragile and resolutely un-precious. Her environmental sculptures are vast metaphors of life, death, and resurrection in which objects degraded and discarded are endowed with new life and dignity.

The cycle of birth, death, and renewal is nothing new to Kim. Her mother had been a midwife in her native Korea and Kim can recall a childhood punctuated by midnight visits, the cries of laboring women, the tense stillness before the howl of a newborn baby, the joy of birth followed by tubs of blood washed down the courtyard drain, and her mother toiling endlessly over soiled sheets to make them clean again.

Social and economic constraints prevented her from studying art in Korea, and Kim spent her college years training to be a nurse, a profession she continues to practice today. Determined to pursue her interest in art, she left Korea for the United States in 1974. Moving at first to Los Angeles, she was appalled by the vast sprawl of the city and the isolation engendered by its freeway culture. After only a few months, she abandoned Los Angeles for its antithesis, the small rural college town of Macomb, Illinois, where she began her graduate studies in art. In 1978, she moved to Chicago, where she now lives, earning her M.F.A. at the School of The Art Institute of Chicago.

Until the early 1980s, Kim worked principally in painting and collage. Upon her move to Chicago, however, she began to haunt the vast empty lots south of the downtown area that had become casual dumping grounds. "I was shocked," she recalls, "when I saw how much was thrown away."[1] She began bringing home cast-off objects that intrigued her, having no intention, at first, of incorporating them into her art. Somewhat timidly, however, she began gluing fragments of tin cans to her paintings to give them added color and texture. Her work subsequently grew steadily more three-dimensional until she was finally creating freestanding sculptures.

Kim did not begin to work on an environmental scale until 1983, when the director of the Randolph Street Gallery, a

untitled 1988
mixed media
156 x 504 x 384
Commissioned with Lannan Foundation
support for the exhibition
Sculpture Inside Outside
Courtesy the artist

untitled   1988
mixed media
156 x 504 x 384
Commissioned with Lannan Foundation
support for the exhibition
Sculpture Inside Outside
Courtesy the artist

Untitled elements for installation
1985–1987
mixed media
Courtesy the artist

Jin Soo Kim installing environment at
Walker Art Center

(opposite, top)
untitled   1988
mixed media
156 x 504 x 384
Commissioned with Lannan Foundation
support for the exhibition
Sculpture Inside Outside
Courtesy the artist

(opposite, bottom)
untitled   1988
(details)

Chicago artists' cooperative, visited her studio and, entranced by the multifarious clutter she found there, invited Kim to create an installation at the gallery. Kim recalls the experience as being immensely liberating. "It was the first time I felt so right. I was consumed with the process of making the installation. I felt so free." Kim has found that working on an environmental scale allows her to become completely absorbed in the process of creation: "When I am making an installation, I am so close to it that I lose sight of it."

Working with such unself-conscious absorption has allowed her to tap into a source of intuited, subconscious imagery often dealing with suppressed memories. "For me, art is experiential," she says, "and in this process, the work seems to explore aspects of my early life that would otherwise remain obscure." The completion of her first installation in 1983, for example, unleashed a flood of long-suppressed memories of her mother's work as a midwife. Much of the organic imagery in her work can be attributed to these childhood memories and to her current work as a hospital nurse.

Given her intuitive approach, Kim has grown accustomed to pursuing a course of action without having a clear idea of where it will eventually lead her. Among the more striking aspects of her installations, for example, are the thick skeins of tightly knotted brown paper that snake through her environments and rise from the ground like armless wraiths. Kim remembers working alone in a studio while in graduate school in 1982 and seeing a two-by-four-inch board and a roll of brown paper nearby. Without much regard to what she was doing, she began wrapping the paper around the wood. As she worked, she found that this simple repetitive act had a remarkably soothing effect. Only later did she realize that this ritual wrapping served to release the suppressed anxiety caused by one of her duties as a nurse: the wrapping of dead bodies in plastic before they leave the hospital. The wrapping of objects has become an increasingly integral part of Kim's work, on the one hand accentuating the distressed nature of these bandaged items, and on the other hand suggesting the process of healing and recovery.

Jin Soo Kim has created ten installations to date, including her environment for the Walker Art Center. Her earliest installation, at the Randolph Street Gallery, was what she has described as a "dimensional painting," essentially filling a wall and building out from it. Subsequent works have grown more fully environmental, filling rooms and corridors so that viewers actually enter into the works. In each piece, Kim recycles the elements used in earlier installations while continually adding new materials. By so doing, she not only prolongs the lives of the objects she uses, but also sees them go through a process of constant renewal. Between commissions, Kim works on individual sculptures that may either stand alone or be incorporated into her next installation.

Each site provides Kim with a new set of challenges and experiences, for "in an installation, the space is the most crucial factor." In her most recent exhibition, at the Krannert Art Museum in 1987, Kim was given a 3,000 square-foot room to work with, roughly three times the size of any of her earlier installations. Lacking the material necessary to fill the entire gallery, she limited her environment to one end of the room, devoting the remaining space to a series of wrapped chairs that she has been working on for the past two years. To separate her environment from the rest of the gallery, Kim used wire mesh to create semi-transparent walls through which she laced materials such as rubber tubes, canvas scraps, and brown paper braids. This allowed viewers to walk around and look into the space before entering it, something that had not been possible in earlier installations, which filled the rooms they were in. The result was an airiness and ethereality quite distinct from the impression given by her previous environments.

A number of wrapped chairs were used in the Krannert environment in addition to those in the space beyond it. Because of their association with the human figure, these decrepit chairs swathed in paper, chicken wire, and old chenille bedspreads were disconcertingly evocative of derelict street people huddled on urban stoops. These presences underscore the connection Kim establishes between humans and the objects they create. As she writes, "I see traces of people in the scattered and forgotten objects I pick up in the margins of the city."[2] For all their air of fantasy, Kim's installations raise the unsettling question of whether, in a society so willing to discard the products of its own manufacture, human beings have also become disposable.

P.W.B.

1. Unless otherwise noted, all quotations are from unpublished written statements by the artist and a conversation with the artist, 27 September 1987.
2. Quoted in Museum of Contemporary Art, Chicago, *Options 24: Jin Soo Kim,* exh. broch., 1985.

Jin Soo Kim

1950
Born in Seoul, South Korea
1973
B.S., Seoul National University
1976–1977
Western Illinois University, Macomb
1983
M.F.A., School of the Art Institute of Chicago

Lives in Chicago

Solo Exhibitions

1977
Green Rose Gallery, Macomb, Illinois
1985
Museum of Contemporary Art, Chicago (brochure)
1986
Simard & Halm Gallery, Los Angeles
1987
Krannert Art Museum, Champaign, Illinois

Group Exhibitions

1970–1972
Shinmoon Hwegwan Gallery, Seoul
1977
Illinois Graduate Students Art Exhibit, Mitchell Museum, Mt. Vernon, Illinois
1981
WPA Preview, WPA Gallery, Chicago
Exchanges, Maryland Institute, College of Art, Baltimore
1982
Young Artists Show, Contemporary Art Workshop, Chicago
1983
Contemporary Art Workshop, Chicago
Randolph Street Gallery, Chicago
International Student Show, School of the Art Institute of Chicago Gallery
1984
Five Installations, Hyde Park Art Center, Chicago
Chicago Heads, Randolph Street Gallery, Chicago
1985
Inaugural Exhibition, State of Illinois Art Gallery, Chicago (catalogue)
Sculpture Chicago '85, South Loop Planning Board, Chicago (catalogue)

1986
Awards in the Visual Arts 5, Southeastern Center for the Visual Arts, Winston-Salem, North Carolina (catalogue)
Showing Off, State of Illinois Art Gallery, Chicago
A New Generation from SAIC, Museum of Contemporary Art, Chicago (catalogue)

Selected Bibliography

Bone, James. "Separate Pieces," *Reader*, Chicago, 3 February 1984.
Lifton, Norma. "Five Installations," *New Art Examiner*, Vol. 11, April 1984.

Donald Lipski

Donald Lipski is filled with an eager, restless energy. He prowls through his spacious studio tinkering with whatever object comes to his attention, wondering what can be done with it to give it new life and identity. He has made a career of combining a few disparate objects into compact, iconic configurations whose internal logic defies the irrationality of their juxtapositions. A crystal ball mounted atop an ancient telephone intercom looks like an instrument for contacting alien civilizations. A pair of open-toed shoes stuffed with red-tipped wooden sticks seems ready to blast off. Lipski invests his idiosyncratic creations with a sense of dynamic potential that makes them appear ready to burst into action.

Lipski began to put his nervous fidgeting to use in his art while a graduate student at the Cranbrook Academy of Art in the early 1970s. Using a cigar box as a container, he collected the casual products of his busy fingers, objects that most people would create but then discard: plastic stir sticks with one end inserted into the other, matches intertwined in their books, toothpicks interlocked in their paper wrappers, pencils bound with rubber bands, and hundreds of other artifacts of marginally motivated agitation. He called his collection *Gathering Dust* and installed it in galleries and museums by distributing his tokens in an even pattern over entire walls.

Twisting, wrapping, accumulating, joining, combining—these activities are the essence of Lipski's art. Though he has gone on to create far more imposing works, the nervous curiosity exhibited in

Gathering Dust underlies all of his art: "I really don't think that there's any difference between this [*Gathering Dust*] and the bigger work that has come since then," says Lipski. "It's all the same impetus, except that this took five minutes and cost nothing and the buoy piece is going to take a year and cost a lot more."[1] The buoy piece in question is an outdoor installation commissioned by the Walker Art Center for *Sculpture Inside Outside.* It consists of fifty-five marine floats stacked in a diamond-shaped pyramid that rises some 22 feet in height. Ironically, Lipski conceived of the piece by piling a handful of ball bearings into a variety of configurations.

The objects in *Gathering Dust* were all small enough to fit into the palm of one's hand. Lipski did not begin using larger materials until 1979, after he had returned from a State Department-sponsored visit to Bulgaria. He had found life in that country to be oppressive in its restrictiveness. "They operate under very stringent rules, lots of dos and don'ts, not just about art but about everything," he recalls. "There was something about that experience that, when I came back, I cast off all my rules. I'm sure I've made new ones along the way, but at that time that's what it felt like."

When he returned to New York, Lipski cleared his studio of all his earlier projects. Beginning with a cast-iron dumbbell that he placed, receiverlike, on his telephone, he began to fill the space with manipulated and transformed objects. "Over the next year I was really driven," he says, "I just kept making stuff

Xalupax 1986–1988
mixed media
dimensions variable
Collection the artist

Passing Time #502   1980
women's shoes, wood, paint
4⅞ x 9⅜ x 10
Collection Lois and Bruce Berry

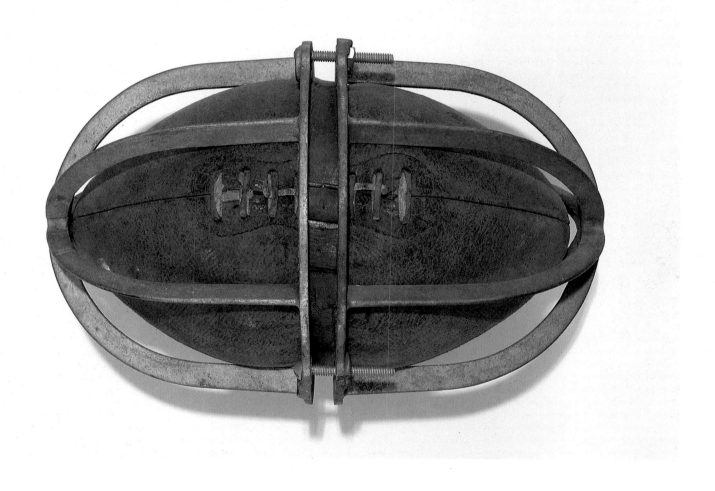

Passing Time #290
(For Arthur Lipski) 1980
football, leather strap, steel cage
8⅜ x 12 x 8⅜
Collection the artist

Building Steam #317   1985
crystal ball, telephone intercom base
9½ x 6 x 5
Collection the artist

(opposite)
Untitled #126   1987
steel hook, glass rings
36 x 19 x 10
Collection Penny and Mike Winton

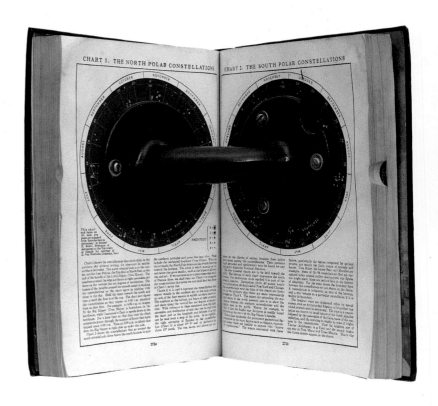

Building Steam #266　1984
light bulb, metal stand, adhesive tape,
rubber, water
15 x 10½ x 6½
Collection Sylvia Lipski

Building Steam #105　1983
book, steel handle
12 x 9 x 10
Collection Mr. and Mrs. Raymond D. Nasher

Untitled (For Martha) 1983
boots, wax, steel rods, electrical cord
13⅛ x 37⅞ x 11½
Collection Lois and Bruce Berry

Untitled #75 1986
birch branch
62 x 57 x 7
Collection the artist

and putting it there on the floor until it felt like I was walking through one of my cigar boxes." He gave the works the collective title *Passing Time,* "Because that's all I really knew then, that I was keeping busy."

Lipski maintains that his primary concern in making his sculpture is strictly formal: "It's about what the object looks like way before what the object is." His selection of what objects to bring together is highly intuitive. As he explains: "It just comes from working. I know something's going to fit; I know something's the right size for something else. So it's like it all goes together in a way that's almost expected." The result is an art that is incongruous and yet perplexingly natural: his objects don't belong together logically, but they look as if they do. A baseball is held fast in a wax-filled ladle. An old football is bound in a steel cage just its size. A buoy is studded with tiny dice.

The flexibility of Lipski's intuitive working method requires that he be able to get his hands quickly on a wide variety of objects. His Brooklyn studio is a vast storehouse of objects of every size. They come from surplus stores, salvage yards, trade fairs, secondhand stores, and bankruptcy sales.

As he insists on an economy of means, Lipski's works tend toward an iconic formal symmetry and rarely involve more than three or four objects joined together. The method of their juncture is also relatively elemental—tying, wrapping, gluing. He credits this simplicity and directness to the influence of Minimalist art during his school years in the early 1970s. But like so many of his generation, Lipski seeks to reinvest his art with a greater allusive resonance than can be found in Minimalism: "I like work to be seductive, to grab you right off the bat, but then I like it to keep giving, to grow over time."

Lipski downplays the importance to his working method of humor, irony, metaphor, or social commentary—qualities that are often ascribed to his work

by others. He contends that he does not worry much about the motives and meaning of his art. "I have more faith in doing than in thinking," he says. "Maybe the work is ironic, or funny, or something, but that's really not my intent. My intent is simpler than that. I love the metaphors, but they're secondary, they come afterwards."

Although Lipski argues that he selects his objects not for their content but for their beauty, he seems to favor objects that imply action. Among them are tools, military equipment, and aerospace hardware, all objects charged with a sense of potential energy. Simple tools like an axe or a pitchfork carry with them the implication of their use: their ability to cut or pierce and the muscle it takes to handle them. Inherent in weaponry—Lipski has used machine gun cartridge belts, bomb parts, armor-piercing shells, and more—is its explosive capacity. Likewise aerospace hardware contains the intention of great speed. Even books, another favorite Lipski material, are an embodiment of mental energy. By using such potent objects, he creates works that bristle with implied activity. Unlike the Assemblage sculptors of the 1950s—Rauschenberg, Kienholz, Conner, and others—Lipski prefers new, unused material to discarded junk; it is not memory that interests him so much as potential.

On two separate occasions in 1986 and 1987, Lipski was given access to the salvage yards of aerospace engineering firms, the Grumman Corporation in Bethpage, New York, and the Boeing Company in Seattle. He was particularly attracted to aerospace hardware because of the remarkable meticulousness that goes into its fabrication. "It has the sort of care and attention lavished on it that's qualitatively different from most other manufactured goods," he has said, "It's high, high tech manufacturing and at the same time, it can be like handicraft."[2] Compressed within each precision-crafted item is the energy that went into its

fabrication: from the power that ran the tools that formed it to the skill and concentration of the technicians who worked on it. For Lipski, the beauty of aerospace hardware lies in the effort that has gone into its making.

The fact that Lipski often negates the utility of his materials only seems to accentuate their active nature. He will cap the tines of a pitchfork with rounded wooden handles, coat an axehead with tar, bolt the pages of a book together, arm a cartridge belt with glass pipettes, strip the bristles off paintbrushes, and ring a nosecone with buckets. By preventing these objects from carrying out the task for which they were intended, Lipski traps their energy inside them.

Not surprisingly, a series of Lipski's objects from the mid-1980s were given the collective title *Building Steam.* The term was in partial homage to the eighteenth-century inventor James Watt, whose steam engine helped launch the Industrial Revolution. In his tension-filled sculptures, Lipski creates an equivalent, paradoxically visible yet intangible, to the compressed energy of trapped steam. He can, perhaps, be regarded as the equivocal laureate of the technological era: taking the finished products of industry as his raw materials, he strips them down and reassembles them into new entities, effectually inventing the useless from the useful.

P.W.B.

1. Unless otherwise noted, all quotations are from a conversation with the artist, 24 June 1987.
2. Quoted in Judy Collischan Van Wagner, Hillwood Art Gallery, C.W. Post Campus, Long Island University, Brookville, New York, *Broken Wings: Donald Lipski at Grumman,* exh. cat., 1987.

Donald Lipski constructing and installing
Balzac #55

Balzac #55   1988
marine buoys
241 x 288 x 468
Commissioned with Lannan Foundation
support for the exhibition
Sculpture Inside Outside
Courtesy the artist and Germans van Eck Gallery,
New York

Donald Lipski

1947
Born in Chicago
1970
B.A., University of Wisconsin, Madison
1973
M.F.A., Cranbrook Academy of Art, Bloomfield Hills, Michigan

Lives in New York

Solo Exhibitions

1974
Contemporary Arts Foundation, Oklahoma City, Oklahoma
1975
Everson Museum of Art, Syracuse, New York (brochure)
OK Harris, New York
1976
Macalester College Galleries, St. Paul, Minnesota
1977
I-35, Moore, Oklahoma, in conjunction with the Oklahoma Highway Commission
1978
Artists Space, New York
Anthology Film Archives, New York
1979
The Museum of Modern Art, New York
Anthology Film Archives, New York
Tangeman Fine Arts Gallery, University of Cincinnati, Ohio
Western Michigan University Gallery, Kalamazoo
1980
Fort Worth Art Museum, Texas (brochure)
Eaton/Shoen Gallery, San Francisco
1981
Braathen-Gallozzi Gallery, New York
Triton Museum of Art, Santa Clara, California
1982
Portland Center for the Visual Arts, Portland, Oregon
Turnbull, Lutjeans, Kogan Gallery, Costa Mesa, California
1983
Germans van Eck, New York (brochure)
Galleriet, Lund, Sweden
1984
Gloria Luria Gallery, Bay Harbor Islands, Florida
Rhona Hoffman Gallery, Chicago

Margo Leavin Gallery, Los Angeles
Thomas Segal Gallery, Boston
P.B. van Voorst van Beest Gallery, The Hague (catalogue)
1985
Piecemaker, University Gallery, University of Delaware, Newark (brochure)
New Orleans Museum of Art
Germans van Eck, New York (catalogue)
Carpenter + Hochman Gallery, Dallas
1986
Rhona Hoffman Gallery, Chicago
Edward Totah Gallery, London
1987
Galerie Pierre Huber, Geneva
Anders Tornberg Gallery, Lund, Sweden
Broken Wings: Donald Lipski at Grumman, Hillwood Art Gallery, C.W. Post Campus, Long Island University, Brookville, New York (catalogue)
Center on Contemporary Art, Seattle (brochure)
Germans van Eck, New York
1988
Germans van Eck, New York (with Roni Horn)
Rhona Hoffman Gallery, Chicago

Selected Group Exhibitions

1972
Michigan Artists, 59th Exhibition, The Detroit Institute of Arts
1974
Non-Coastal Flatlands Sculpture Show, Wichita Art Museum, Kansas
1977
Xth International Encounter on Video, Mexico City (catalogue)
1978
XIth International Encounter on Video, Tokyo (catalogue)
Atlanta Film Festival, The High Museum of Art, Atlanta (catalogue)
1979
Sculptors' Photographs, Hunter College Gallery, New York
1980
Diamond, Liberman, Lipski, Root Art Center, Hamilton College, Clinton, New York (catalogue)
The Artist at Work in America, Varna, Bulgaria, organized by the International Communications Agency, U.S. Department of State

Other Media, Florida International University, Miami (catalogue)
Seven Artists, Neuberger Museum, State University of New York at Purchase (catalogue)
1981
Stay Tuned, The New Museum of Contemporary Art, New York (catalogue)
Art on the Beach, Creative Time, Inc., New York
1982
15 Artists, Cranbrook Academy of Art Museum, Bloomfield Hills, Michigan (catalogue)
1983
Language, Drama, Source and Vision, The New Museum of Contemporary Art, New York (catalogue)
Awards Exhibition, The American Academy of Arts and Letters, Rome
The End of the World: Contemporary Visions of the Apocalypse, The New Museum of Contemporary Art, New York (catalogue)
1984
Awards in the Visual Arts 3, Southeastern Center for Contemporary Art, Winston-Salem, North Carolina (catalogue)
Premio Internacional de Escultura, Museo Orensanz Y Artes Del Serrable, Spain
Twelve on 20 x 24, School of the Museum of Fine Arts, Boston (catalogue)
1985
Wolfgang Amadeus Mozart—Neue Bilder, Galerie Thaddaus Ropac, Salzburg (catalogue)
Working in Brooklyn/Sculpture, The Brooklyn Museum, New York (catalogue)
Selections from the William J. Hokin Collection, Museum of Contemporary Art, Chicago (catalogue)
1986
Joseph Cornell and his Legacy: Part II, ACA Galleries, New York
Donald Lipski, Matt Mullican, Kiki Smith, The Clocktower, The Institute for Art and Urban Resources, Inc., New York
Small Monuments, Tyler School of Art, Temple University, Philadelphia
1987
American Sculpture: Investigations, Davis/McClain Gallery, Houston

Contemporary Assemblage, Germans van Eck, New York (catalogue)
1988
    Real Inventions/Invented Functions, Laurie Rubin Gallery, New York
    Sculpture/Aspen, Aspen Art Museum, Colorado (catalogue)

Selected Bibliography

Cox, Cathy. "Scenes," *Village Voice,* 16 October 1978.

Perlberg, Deborah. Exhibition review, *Artforum,* Vol. 17, April 1979.

Kinz, Lance. "Donald Lipski: Gathering Dust," *Dialog,* Vol. 1, November–December 1979.

Larson, Kay. "Spring Cleaning," *New York Magazine,* 30 March 1980.

Raynor, Vivien. "Two Exceptional Young Talents at Neuberger," *The New York Times,* 2 November 1980.

Levin, Kim. Exhibition review, *Village Voice,* 18 March 1981.

Perreault, John. Exhibition review, *SoHo Weekly News,* 25 March 1981.

Wilson, Judith. "Outside Chances," *Village Voice,* 8 July 1981.

Zimmer, William. "Beached," *SoHo Weekly News,* 15 July 1981.

"An Outdoor Sculpture Safari in the City," *The New York Times,* 7 August 1981.

Blau, Eleanor. "Artistic Video," *The New York Times,* 10 August 1981.

Doubilet, Susan. "Artists on Architecture," *Progressive Architecture,* Vol. 62, September 1981.

Zimmer, William. "Stay Tuned Out," *SoHo Weekly News,* 8 September 1981.

Wooster, Ann-Sargent. Exhibition review, *Art in America,* Vol. 69, October 1981.

Phillips, Deborah. "New Faces in Alternative Spaces," *ARTnews,* Vol. 80, November 1981.

Stofflet, Mary. Exhibition review, *Images and Issues,* Vol. 3, November–December 1982.

Ballatore, Sandy. "Sculpture Conferencing—A Personal Response," *Images and Issues,* Vol. 3, November–December 1982.

Raynor, Vivien. "Lipski's 'Building Steam' Opens SoHo Gallery," *The New York Times,* 30 September 1983.

Smith, Roberta. "Forays," *Village Voice,* 25 October 1983.

Princenthal, Nancy. Exhibition review, *ARTnews,* Vol. 82, December 1983.

Kwinter, Sanford. Exhibition review, *Art in America,* Vol. 72, January 1984.

Cohen, Ronny. Exhibition review, *Artforum,* Vol. 22, January 1984.

Wilson, William. Exhibition review, *Los Angeles Times,* April 1984.

Glueck, Grace. Exhibition review, *The New York Times,* 20 September 1985.

Levin, Kim. Exhibition review, *Village Voice,* 24 September 1985.

Saunders, Wade. "Talking Objects: Interviews with Ten Younger Sculptors," *Art in America,* Vol. 73, November 1985.

Schwabsky, Barry. Exhibition review, *Arts Magazine,* Vol. 60, November 1985.

Heartney, Eleanor. Exhibition review, *ARTnews,* Vol. 84, November 1985.

Brenson, Michael. "A Sculpture Revival All Around Town," *The New York Times,* 1 November 1985.

McEvilley, Thomas. Exhibition review, *Artforum,* Vol. 24, December 1985.

Hapgood, Susan. Exhibition review, *Flash Art,* No. 125, December 1985–January 1986.

Arnason, H.H. *History of Modern Art,* Third Edition. New York: Harry N. Abrams, 1986, p. 685.

Stein, Harvey. *Artists Observed.* New York: Harry N. Abrams, 1986, essay by Elaine King, pp. 38–39.

Gibson, Eric. "Two Sculptors," *The New Criterion,* Vol. 4, January 1986.

Brenson, Michael. Exhibition review, *The New York Times,* 10 January 1986.

McGill, Douglas C. "Art People: Mining the Scrap Heap," interview, *The New York Times,* 24 January 1986.

Plagens, Peter. "I Just Dropped in to See What Condition My Condition Was In . . . ," *Artscribe,* No. 56, February–March 1986.

Schwabsky, Barry. "Donald Lipski's Book of Knowledge," *Artscribe,* No. 57, April–May 1986.

Frank, Nigel. Exhibition review, *Arts Review,* London, Vol. 3, June 1986.

Brenson, Michael. Exhibition review, *The New York Times,* 6 March 1987.

Russell, John. "Turning the Plain Into Fantasy," *The New York Times,* 15 March 1987.

Lipson, Karin. "Sculpture From Scrap," *Newsday,* 17 March 1987.

Smallwood, Lyn. "Expert on inertness juggles junk," *Seattle Post-Intelligencer,* 7 May 1987.

Sofer, Ken. Exhibition review, *ARTnews,* Vol. 86, Summer 1987.

Kimmelman, Michael. Exhibition review, *The New York Times,* 12 February 1988.

Robert Lobe

The aluminum shells that Robert Lobe forms over trees and rocks fix a particular moment in time, transforming nature into ghostly images at once recognizable and distinctly abstract. These reliefs and freestanding simulacra are fabricated by covering trees and rocks with sheets of aluminum, and hammering on them until the forms of the subject matter are impressed in the metal. Later, in his studio, Lobe rivets or welds together the fragments of metal skins he creates in the woods. The results are hollow masses whose expressive surface records the process of their fabrication.

Lobe's sculpture career began in the late 1960s with works that have little connection to the repoussé pieces he makes today. Like many other artists of his generation working in New York, he was looking for alternatives to Minimalism's dominance, and found himself making distribution pieces that consisted of metal, rubber, wood, and rope laid out on the floor. By the early 1970s, he switched to large-scale outdoor works consisting of hollow laminated and carved wooden structures that he allowed to be weathered by the forces of nature.

Lobe was, however, disenchanted with this direction: "I had been mimicking a natural process," he says, "it was even competing with nature in a way—but this now became a very sentimental and use-less idea for me."[1] A breakthrough in subject matter and technique occurred in 1976 when he made his first aluminum sculpture—a series of ten small rocks. "It was based," he recalls, "on a disillusionment with rationality, with geometry, with the intellect. I realized that all the things that really are exciting about art, like accident, discovery and spontaneity, were simply not available to me, given my thinking at that time."[2]

Lobe chose commercially available aluminum because of its artificial and industrial associations; it represented a complete antithesis to wood, and using it allowed him to work outdoors, where in the solitude of the woods he found new freedom. However, he points out that this approach to nature, which he continues today, is decidedly unromantic:

> I'm not trying to use nature's beauty to romanticize my work. I'm trying to do something that's tailor-made to what my life seems to be about and what my environment seems to be about. . . . It really boils down to a way of making sculpture, rather than a way of looking at nature. I see nature as an underlying important message, a theme, the idea to be presented. I feel an obligation to be truthful to my subject in that it's a rock and a tree and it's not surreal. I think of it as a very straightforward thing, the way [George] Segal uses people [in his sculptures].[3]

The particular character of a Lobe sculpture is determined by the site where it was begun. The large 1985 relief *Killer Hill C.W.* was made at Chesterwood, the Massachusetts home and studio of Daniel Chester French, the celebrated creator of the Lincoln Memorial. Its title describes the place where it was made, a knoll dubbed "Killer Hill" by the local children. Lobe fabricated it on a large shale boulder

Killer Hill C.W. 1985
anodized hammered aluminum
100 x 192 x 27
Collection Walker Art Center
Justin Smith Purchase Fund, 1986

White Lake 1987
anodized hammered aluminum
57⅞ x 48⅛ x 26¼
Collection Michael Egan

(opposite)
Life by Strangulation 1981
hammered anodized aluminum
90 x 38 x 40
Collection Steven and Cecile Biltekoff

Robert Lobe fabricating *Harmony Ridge No. 19*

Harmony Ridge No. 19   1987–1988
hammered aluminum
76 x 101 x 76
Commissioned with Lannan Foundation
support for the exhibition
Sculpture Inside Outside
Courtesy the artist and Blum Helman Gallery,
New York

bordered by a fir and a maple. Not only did the artist record the expansive surface of the rock and trees, but by his treatment of the theme, he paid particular attention to the confluence of the elements. In a manner of speaking, his imagery, which generally contains stone and tree shapes, is a commentary on the relationship between nature's inorganic and organic forms.

Rocks have always been of interest to Lobe: their surfaces, he says, are like that of the Rosetta Stone, except that the information they impart is about the rock's mass and structure. Pairing rocks and trees, Lobe generates an impressive array of compositional situations. The rocks in his sculptures are generally horizontal, swelling forms, while the trees are vertical and linear.

For large pieces, such as *Killer Hill C.W.*, Lobe uses power tools and varies the hammering to create rich surface textures. At times, he pounds the metal to such an extent that parts of it are virtually worn through. Power tools enable him to work rapidly and to incorporate chance occurrences into the work, a fluid process that the artist compares to Pollock's drip technique or to manipulating clay. By no means are his reliefs line for line copies of what underlies them; he selects, modifies, and improvises as he goes along. The shape of the pneumatic tool head determines the final texture of the work. In *Killer Hill C.W.*, he carefully chiseled the surface of the aluminum in striations in order not to destroy the soft shale underneath; to render the trees he systematically hammered the surface so that the heavily textured metal would simulate the bark. The overall surface of *Killer Hill C.W.* is rich in detail: the aggressively chiseled boulder, full of surface incident, has a relatively matte surface in contrast to that of the more reflective, sinuously patterned trees.

In selecting a subject, Lobe looks for simple shapes that when transformed into monochromatic aluminum shells also read as strong abstract forms. *Mother Maple* (1987–1988), fabricated at a site in Sussex County, New Jersey, and composed from a blocklike rock out of which grows a mature ash and sapling, is a distilled amalgamation of rectangle, cylinder, and line. More than most of Lobe's recent sculptures, it is an assertive, volumetric configuration, intended to be seen in the round. It was made specifically for the Minneapolis Sculpture Garden. Unlike many previous works by Lobe, its seams are carefully fitted together and there are few open or loose-edged areas. In his oeuvre, *Mother Maple* stands as a remarkable fusion of naturalistic and purely geometric elements. Lobe has called it "an echo chamber of art and life." It is both a formal study of volume, mass, line, and texture and an eerie evocation of nature's growth and decay forever fixed in a single moment.

D.H.

1. Quoted in Linda Shearer, Solomon R. Guggenheim Museum, New York, *Young American Artists: 1978 Exxon National Exhibition,* exh. cat., 1978, p. 40.
2. Ibid.
3. Unless otherwise noted, all quotations are from a conversation with the artist, 19 June 1987.

Mother Maple 1987–1988
hammered aluminum
123 x 110 x 123
Commissioned with Lannan Foundation
support for the exhibition
Sculpture Inside Outside
Courtesy the artist and Blum Helman Gallery, New York

Robert Lobe

1945
Born in Detroit, Michigan
1967
B.A., Oberlin College, Oberlin, Ohio
1967–1968
Attended Hunter College, New York

Lives in New York

Selected Solo Exhibitions

1974
Wood Sculpture, Zabriskie Gallery,
New York
1977
Robert Lobe: Recent Sculpture,
Hammerskjold Plaza
Sculpture Garden, New York
1980
Willard Gallery, New York
1981
*Robert Lobe: Hammered Aluminum
Sculpture*, Willard Gallery, New York
1982
Texas Gallery, Houston
1984
Willard Gallery, New York
1986
Willard Gallery, New York
Marian Locks Gallery, Philadelphia
1987
Anderson Gallery, Virginia
Commonwealth University, Richmond
Willard Gallery, New York
(with Harriet Korman)
1988
Blum Helman Gallery, New York

Selected Group Exhibitions

1969
Anti-Illusion: Procedures/Materials,
Whitney Museum of American Art,
New York (catalogue)
Other Ideas, The Detroit Institute of
Arts, Michigan (catalogue)
1970
*1970 Annual Exhibition:
Contemporary American Sculpture,*
Whitney Museum of American Art,
New York (catalogue)
1971
Recent Acquisitions, Whitney Museum
of American Art, New York
Bykert Gallery, New York

1972
Lo Giudice Gallery, New York
Painting and Sculpture Today 1972,
Indianapolis Museum of Art, Indiana
(catalogue)
1973
*1973 Biennial Exhibition:
Contemporary American Art*, Whitney
Museum of American Art, New York
(catalogue)
1974
The Levi Strauss Collection, San
Francisco Museum of Modern Art,
California (catalogue)
Storm King Art Center, Mountainville,
New York
1975
76 Jefferson Street, The Museum of
Modern Art, Art Lending Service,
New York
*Painting, Drawing and Sculpture of the
'60s and '70s from the Dorothy and
Herbert Vogel Collection*, Institute of
Contemporary Art, University of
Pennsylvania, Philadelphia (catalogue)
Storm King Art Center, Mountainville,
New York
1976
A Month of Sundays, P.S. 1, The
Institute for Art and Urban Resources,
Inc., Long Island City, New York
1977
*Wood: An Outdoor Exhibition of
Contemporary Wood Sculpture,*
Nassau County Museum of Fine Art,
Roslyn, New York (catalogue)
Documenta 6, Kassel, West Germany
(catalogue)
1978
Indoor/Outdoor Sculpture Show,
P.S. 1, The Institute for Art and Urban
Resources, Inc., Long Island City,
New York
*Young American Artists: 1978 Exxon
National Exhibition*, Solomon R.
Guggenheim Museum, New York
(catalogue)
1979
Eight Sculptors, Albright-Knox Art
Gallery, Buffalo, New York (catalogue)
Wave Hill: The Artist's View, Wave
Hill, Bronx, New York (catalogue)
Willard Gallery, New York
1981
Selected by Donald Sultan, Texas
Gallery, Houston

The Americans: The Landscape,
Contemporary Arts Museum, Houston
(catalogue)
Trois Dimensions—Sept Americains,
Gillespie-Laage-Salomon, Paris
1982
Willard Gallery, New York
Landscape in Sculpture, Freedman
Gallery, Albright College, Reading,
Pennsylvania (brochure)
1983
*Content in Abstraction: The Uses of
Nature*, The High Museum of Art,
Atlanta (catalogue)
*American Sculptors from the
Permanent Collection*, Solomon R.
Guggenheim Museum, New York
1984
Willard Gallery, New York
*The Houston Festival
American Sculpture*, Margo Leavin
Gallery, Los Angeles
1985
*Louisa Chase—Painting, Robert
Lobe—Sculpture*, Margo Leavin
Gallery, Los Angeles
1986
*About Place: Contemporary American
Landscape*, P.S. 1, The Institute for Art
and Urban Resources, Inc., Long Island
City, New York (catalogue)
In Celebration: 10th Anniversary,
University of Rochester, New York
50th Anniversary Exhibition, Willard
Gallery, New York
1987
1987 Biennial Exhibition, Whitney
Museum of American Art, New York
(catalogue)
*The Allusive Object: Mel Kendrick,
Robert Lobe, Judith Shea*, Barbara
Krakow Gallery, Boston
The Tree Show, North Hall Gallery,
Massachusetts College of Art, Boston
(catalogue)
Sculptor's Drawings, Blum Helman
Gallery, New York
*Emerging Artists 1978–1986:
Selections from the Exxon Series,*
Solomon R. Guggenheim Museum,
New York (catalogue)
*Recent Sculpture: Joel Fisher, Mel
Kendrick, Robert Lobe*, Blum Helman
Gallery, New York
John Duff, Robert Lobe, Al Taylor,
Lorence Monk Gallery, New York

1988
Blum Helman Gallery, New York
The Lay of the Land, Rathbone Gallery,
Russell Sage College, Junior College of
Albany, New York (brochure)

Selected Bibliography

Ratcliff, Carter. Exhibition review,
ARTnews, Vol. 70, December 1971.

Siegel, Jeanne. Exhibition review, *Art in
America*, Vol. 62, September–October
1974.

Smith, Roberta. Exhibition review,
Artforum, Vol. 13, December 1974.

Ashton, Dore. "New York," *Coloquio
Arts*, Lisbon, Vol. 17, October 1975.

Ashbery, John. "The Sculptures of
Summer," *New York Magazine*, 23 July
1979.

Kingsley, April. "The Shapes Arise!,"
Village Voice, 30 July 1979.

O'Beil, Hedy. Exhibition review, *Arts
Magazine*, Vol. 54, June 1980.

Tuchman, Phyllis. Exhibition review, *Art in
America*, Vol. 68, September 1980.

Tennant, Donna. "Impressions," *Houston
Chronicle*, 2 April 1981.

Crossley, Mimi. Exhibition review,
Houston Post, 12 April 1981.

Tennant, Donna. "C.A.M. Exhibit Samples
the Contemporary Landscape,"
Houston Chronicle, 16 April 1981.

Kalil, Susie. "The American Landscape—
Contemporary Interpretations,"
Artweek, Vol. 12, 25 April 1981.

Collings, Matthew. "Nothing Deep,"
Artscribe, No. 30, August 1981.

Wohlfert, Lee. "New York's Young
Sculptors," *Town and Country*,
September 1981.

Larson, Kay. "Robert Lobe," *New York
Magazine*, 21 December 1981.

Gilmartin, David. "Sculptures Recreate
Natural Setting," *Reading Times*,
12 March 1982.

Bannon, Anthony. "Gorge Nature Poses
for Subway Artist," *The Buffalo News*,
14 August 1983.

Baker, Kenneth. "Hammering the
Landscape," *The Christian Science
Monitor*, 20 August 1983.

_____. Exhibition review, *Art in America*,
Vol. 72, May 1984.

Armstrong, Richard. Exhibition review,
Artforum, Vol. 22, May 1984.

Bannon, Anthony. "For Really Real
Realism Try Lobe's 'Devil's Hole,' " *The
Buffalo News*, 7 April 1985.

_____. Exhibition review, *Los Angeles
Times*, 26 April 1985.

Bonenti, Charles. "Sculptor to be in
Residence at Chesterwood Annually,"
Berkshire Eagle, 28 June 1985.

Fay, Stephen. "Figure Eight," *Berkshire
Eagle*, 18 July 1985.

Howlett, Christian. "An Artist in the
House," *Berkshire Week*, 18 July 1985.

Johnson, Ken. "Chesterwood An Outdoor
Gallery of Art," *Times Union*, Albany,
New York, 25 August 1985.

Brenson, Michael. "The Landscape
Maintains Its Hold on American
Artists," *The New York Times*, 9 March
1986.

_____. Exhibition review, *The New York
Times*, 28 March 1986.

Donahoe, Victoria. Exhibition review, *The
Philadelphia Inquirer*, 6 June 1986.

Brenson, Michael. "Art: Whitney
Biennial's New Look," *The New York
Times*, 10 April 1987.

Lou, Vickie. "Letter From L.I.:
'Confrontation is what Modern Art is
all about!,' " *Art/World*, Vol. 11,
15 April 1987.

Miller, Brian. "Running a Cultural
Marathon," *The New York Times*,
24 April 1987.

Larson, Kay. "Good Neighbors," *New
York Magazine*, 27 April 1987.

Hughes, Robert. "Navigating a Cultural
Trough," *Time*, Vol. 129, 11 May 1987.

Walter Martin

Walter Martin's tableaux represent ironic, if not mordant, views of contemporary art and life. He creates enigmatic combinations of found objects and carefully crafted replicas of familiar articles, some of which appear to be on the brink of disintegration. His dreamlike sculptures are at once symbols of a distant past and artifacts of our time as they might look in the future. Martin expresses a strong interest in history and wonders about "the distortions and prejudices we bring to our view of the information that comes down to us."[1] By the same token, he muses about how the souvenirs of today will be comprehended by future generations.

Martin majored in English literature at Old Dominion University in Virginia with the objective of becoming a writer. As an undergraduate he studied briefly at Oxford University in England, concentrating on the work of William Blake. But, dissatisfied with the intangibility of language, he turned to painting—for him a more concrete expressive medium—during his senior year in college. By the time he finished graduate school, he realized that sculpture was his true métier. "The actual physical process of making sculpture gives me the freedom and tranquility to think about what I'm doing and to let my mind wander and cogitate. It's important for me to have some kind of tangible hands-on experience."

By no means did Martin completely abandon his interest in literature, which has continued to be a source for his richly descriptive imagery. In fact, the titles of his sculptures are often taken from novels or lines of poetry, though they are not usually assigned until the pieces are completed. At times, a literary passage will suggest an image for a sculpture, but there is every likelihood that the original idea will be transformed during the evolution of the sculpture. The completed work is then often titled after a completely different source.

Many of Martin's sculptures seem to be narrative fragments, suggesting incidents in cryptic tales, and presented as eerily still *mise-en-scènes*. The old-fashioned easel, canvas, paintbox, and still-life arrangement that constitute *Day is Desire and Night is Sleep* (1985), presents us with a tantalizing, if unexplained, situation. In this haunting studio vignette, has the artist deserted his work or has the creative process even begun? Or, on another level, is this a contemporary evocation and subversion of the *paragone*, the Renaissance discourse about which of the arts—including poetry, painting, and sculpture—is superior? According to Martin, this piece was inspired by a character in Virginia Woolf's *To the Lighthouse*, who attempts time and again to paint an outdoor scene, but is unable to put the first mark on the canvas. By way of explanation, Martin asks, "How do you decide what the first mark will be? Time has passed, the world has passed. Nothing has changed."[2]

Because each of his sculptures requires special technical solutions, Martin uses a variety of improvised tools and processes. An object, such as the grand

Old Fleece Preaching to the Sharks
1985–1986
plaster, steel, rubber, metal
36 x 72 x 84
Collection Walker Art Center
Clinton and Della Walker Acquisition Fund,
1986

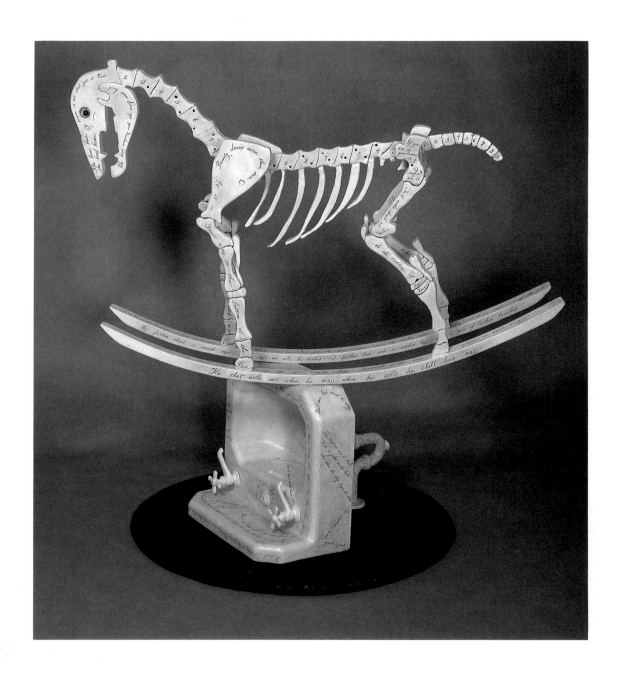

Few words are best   1987
wood, ink, sink, plaster, rubber, oil paint
50¼ x 52 x 35
Collection Penny Pilkington
Courtesy P.P.O.W, New York

(opposite, top)
Day is Desire and Night is Sleep   1985
plaster, wood, mixed media
63¾ x 110
Collection the artist
Courtesy P.P.O.W, New York

(opposite, bottom)
Pastilles of Aconite   1986
wood, plaster, mixed media
64 x 168 x 22
Collection the artist
Courtesy P.P.O.W, New York

Of bodies born up by water   1987
wood, plaster, glass, oil paint, sheet metal
111½ x 20 x 16½
Collection Eileen and Michael Cohen

(opposite)
*Snail, snail come out of your hole/Or else
I'll beat you black as a coal*   1987
styrofoam, wood, rubber, fiberglass,
mixed media
62 x 168 x 65
Collection the artist
Courtesy P.P.O.W, New York

piano of *Snail, snail come out of your hole/Or else I'll beat you black as a coal* (1987), is made of wood, plaster, and styrofoam, and a grandfather clock, *Of bodies born up by water* (1987), is painstakingly crafted from wood. To complete this sculpture of a clock, the artist has attacked it with a woodsman's axe; it stands like a tree in the early stages of being cut down. These fabrications represent an ironic twist on Duchamp's readymades: Duchamp's objects are real, Martin's are like stage props. At their core, Martin's sculptures are as much about illusion as they are about the nature of reality. Things are seldom simply what they appear to be, his art suggests. "I think deception and truth are intrinsically bound and that any object has a timeline," he states, "and somewhere on that timeline, its complex attributes may coalesce into something that appears to be true—that would be the case with art."

Martin's sculptures are often disturbing in their abused and ruined state.

I find the most interesting things are fringed with some sort of penumbra of disintegration and that things usually need to be pushed to the point of falling apart. . . . I take something that's fairly banal from the everyday world that is almost invisible because of its ubiquity, and age it prematurely, drastically, to the point of disintegration. Then it becomes interesting. . . . Things that are decaying are often at their most beautiful and sensual point. The fascination of attraction and repulsion is all locked up in the way things deteriorate.

Worn and weathered, Martin's sculptures have a poignant beauty and a satiric edge. Often his work has an air of imminent disaster, as in the row of bottles falling off a broken shelf in *Pastilles of Aconite* (1986); the grandfather clock about to topple over; and the sink full of perilously stacked dishes of *Holofernes* (1984), which may come tumbling down at any moment. Infused with tension, his sculptures are twentieth-century memento mori, reminders of the transience of all things. They can be read as existentialist statements that romanticize the futility of contemporary existence.

One of Martin's most acerbic works is *Old Fleece Preaching to the Sharks.* Its title refers to a passage in Herman Melville's *Moby Dick* in which Old Fleece, the ship's elderly cook, preaches moderation to a school of hungry sharks greedily attacking and devouring a sperm whale attached to the side of the Pequod. This, of course, is a pointless admonition; Melville's tone is accordingly ironic and his comparison of the sharks' behavior to that of men is a scathing critique of human nature. Similarly, Martin's *Old Fleece* symbolizes greed and frustration. A headless dog sitting in front of a microphone confronts a pile of plaster bones. It is a dog's delight, but Martin's dog has neither the means to speak to nor feast upon his captive bounty; the creature, as Martin has created him, is doomed to an eternity of temptation and non-fulfillment.

Initially the idea of using a dog grew out of John Milton's description of Cerberus, the three-headed beast guarding the Gates of Hell. Though Martin transformed the original allusion by removing the dog's head, the animal nevertheless retains its infernal associations within the context of Melville's "dark vision of an absurdist universe."[3]

Much of Martin's work is highly theatrical. In *Old Fleece,* the dog addressing an audience of bones suggests a private performance, a quality amplified by the presence of an actual microphone. As with live theater, Martin's work often requires a "suspension of disbelief" on the part of the viewer. Once this is accepted, his artful illusionism creates an evocative presentation rich with meaning.

D.H.

1. Unless otherwise noted, all quotations are from a conversation with the artist, 17 June 1987.
2. Conversation with the artist, 30 September 1987.
3. Letter from the artist to Martin Friedman, 30 October 1986.

Walter Martin

1953
Born in Norfolk, Virginia
1977
Private foundation grant for study
abroad, Oxford University
1979
B.A., Old Dominion University,
Norfolk, Virginia
1982
M.F.A., Virginia Commonwealth
University, Richmond

Lives in Brooklyn, New York

Solo Exhibitions

1984
P.P.O.W, New York
1986
P.P.O.W, New York
1988
P.P.O.W, New York

Selected Group Exhibitions

1979
New Painting, Invitational Exhibition,
University Gallery, Old Dominion
University, Norfolk, Virginia
1980
Undiscovered Artists, Jewish
Community Center, Richmond, Virginia
1981
Window Alterations, Richmond,
Virginia
V.C.U. Student Show, Anderson
Gallery, Virginia Commonwealth
University, Richmond
1982
M.F.A. Exhibition, Anderson Gallery,
Virginia Commonwealth University,
Richmond
1984
P.P.O.W, New York
*Behind the Stacks: 4th Annual Artists
Books*, Kathryn Markel Gallery,
New York
1985
57th Between A & D, Holly Solomon
Gallery, New York
East Village at the Centre, Saidye
Bronfman Centre, Montreal
*Sculpture • Objects & Related
Drawings*, Art Palace, New York
Out of Context, Piccadilly Gallery,
London (catalogue)

New Work, P.P.O.W, New York
*A Brave New World • A New
Generation: 40 Artists from New York*,
Udstillingsbygning ved Charlottenborg,
Copenhagen, Denmark (catalogue)
1987
P.P.O.W, New York

Selected Bibliography

Raynor, Vivien. Exhibition review, *The
New York Times*, 30 November 1984.
Shannon, Mark. "Walter Martin," *Arts
Magazine*, Vol. 59, February 1985.
Sichel, Andy. "The Final Appearance of the
Sun," *Downtown*, 18 June 1986.
Panicelli, Ida. "Alice in Wonderland: Letter
from New York II," *NIKE*, July–
September 1986.
Cameron, Dan. Exhibition review, *Flash
Art*, No. 130, October–November
1986.

174

John Newman

Throughout the 1970s, John Newman made two-sided wooden structures which hang perpendicular to a wall. Constructed in relief, each side has a different configuration inscribed within the overall structure. The artist considers these to be primarily formal, even didactic, exercises in cognition.

Newman readily acknowledges a strong debt to Minimal Art and rejects the idea that his work is a reaction against it. Nevertheless, frustrated by its regimented format and programmatic bias, he seeks to make forms that are more expressive. One way to escape Minimalism's pervasive influence was to look for formal precedents outside its conventions, in fact outside the conventions of defined artistic movements either new or old. This led him to such varied phenomena as science, mathematics, and nature for inspiration. He also found himself studying the mechanistic, articulated forms of medieval armor.

An important influence, says Newman, was D'arcy Wentworth Thompson's volume *On Growth and Forms,* originally published in 1918, which discusses the morphological—that is, the structural and mathematical— relationships of organic forms to one another. Thompson illustrated these relationships diagrammatically by means of a warped grid: by plotting the mathematical coordinates of organic forms, he was able to inscribe those shapes within these newly created deformed grids. Aware of Thompson's diagrams, and using the principles of non-Euclidean geometry as a starting point, Newman

began making metal sculptures by bending and otherwise distorting the flat plane so sacred to Minimal Art. For him, he recalls, it was a way of "addressing the emotional quality of abstraction."[1] The resulting complex sculptures were at once organic and mechanical, intuitive and systematic, allusive and non-representational.

The branch of mathematics that has had the greatest impact on Newman's work is topology. He is especially interested in topological equivalence, specifically how one shape can be transformed into another through processes such as bending and pulling. When he began making metal wall pieces in the early 1980s, he constructed their complex curved surfaces by cutting, overlapping, and bending flat sheets of metal. The resulting sculptures, such as *Tolled Belle* (1982) and *Nomen est Numen (Naming is Knowing)* (1984), look as if they have been stretched, pulled, and twisted into shape. Their interlocking, pliant forms seem to defy the rigidity of the metal from which they were made.

Viewed straight on, Newman's wall pieces have a curious iconic power; they read as simple, strong shapes outlined against the wall. But their sculptural impact is inescapable and, as one moves around them, they radically change shape, each vantage presenting a dramatically different configuration. In the 1982 *Tolled Belle,* and *Nomen est Numen,* eccentric shapes radiate out from a central focal point. As in much of his work, these sculptures have a kind of "asymmetrical symmetry"— similar, though slightly modified configurations are repeated throughout, with concave forms echoing convex forms.

Tolled Belle 1982
brass, steel
66 x 35 x 11½
Private collection

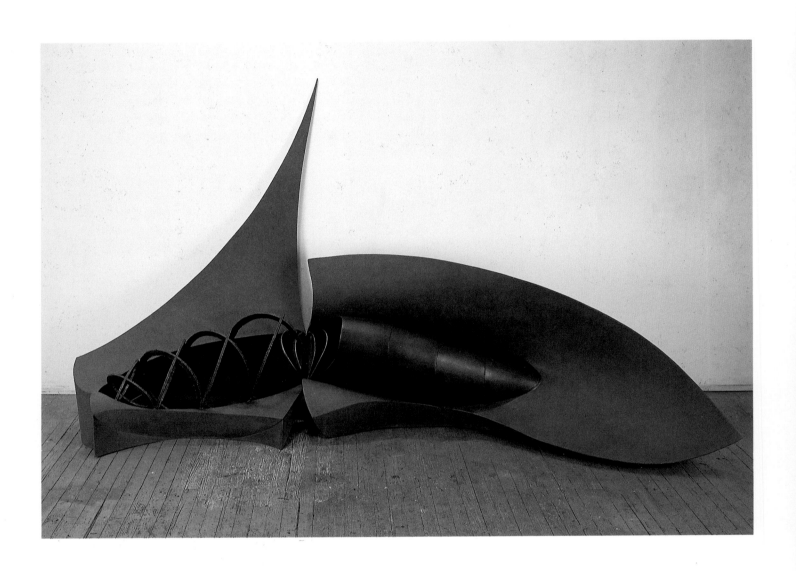

Slow Commotion 1984
steel
68 x 124 x 48
Collection City of Stamford,
Connecticut, Public Art Program

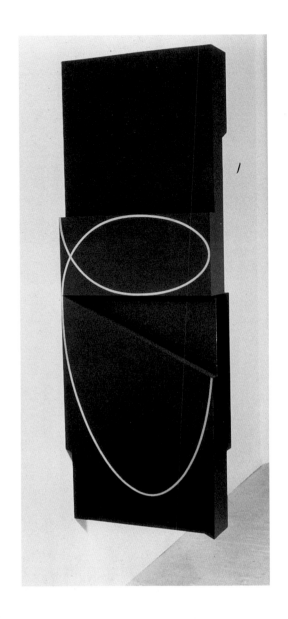
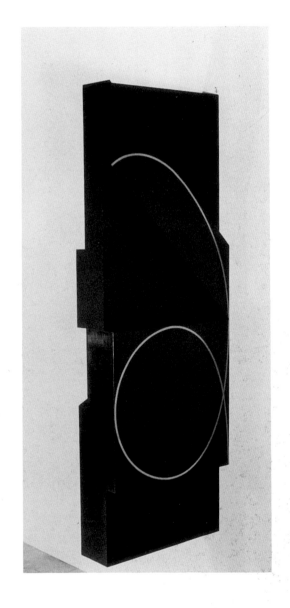

(two views)
Misnomer 1975
graphite on painted wood
63 x 8 x 21
Collection the artist

Drawing for *Nomen est Numen*
(Naming is Knowing) 1984
colored chalk, graphite on paper
106 x 46
Collection Tony Ganz

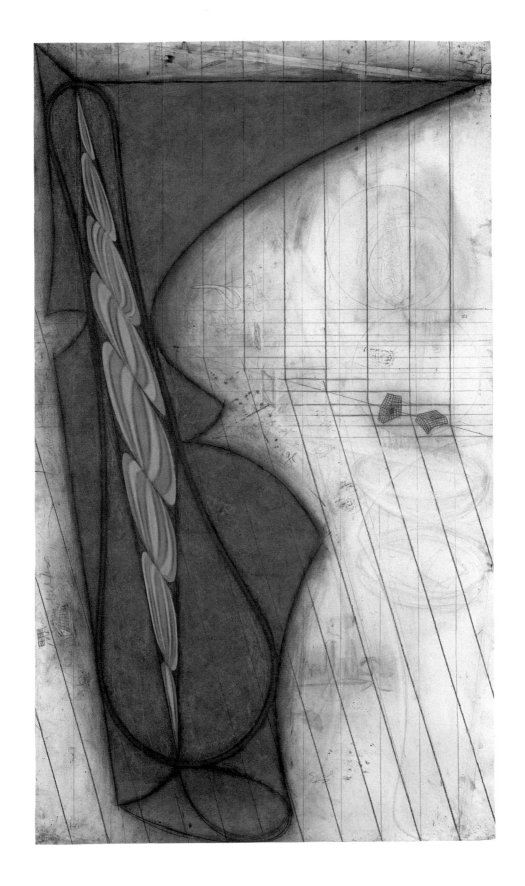

Untitled   1986
colored chalk, oil crayon, graphite on paper
88¼ x 52¼
Collection The Minneapolis Institute of Arts
The Christina N. and Swan J. Turnblad Fund,
1986

Nomen est Numen
(Naming is Knowing)　1984
steel
108 x 37 x 33¼
Collection Phil Schrager

(opposite)
Action at a Distance
(Ghost Version)　1987
aluminum and bronze with lacquer and patina
108 x 62 x 32
Collection The Brooklyn Museum
Purchase Gift of The Contemporary
Arts Council

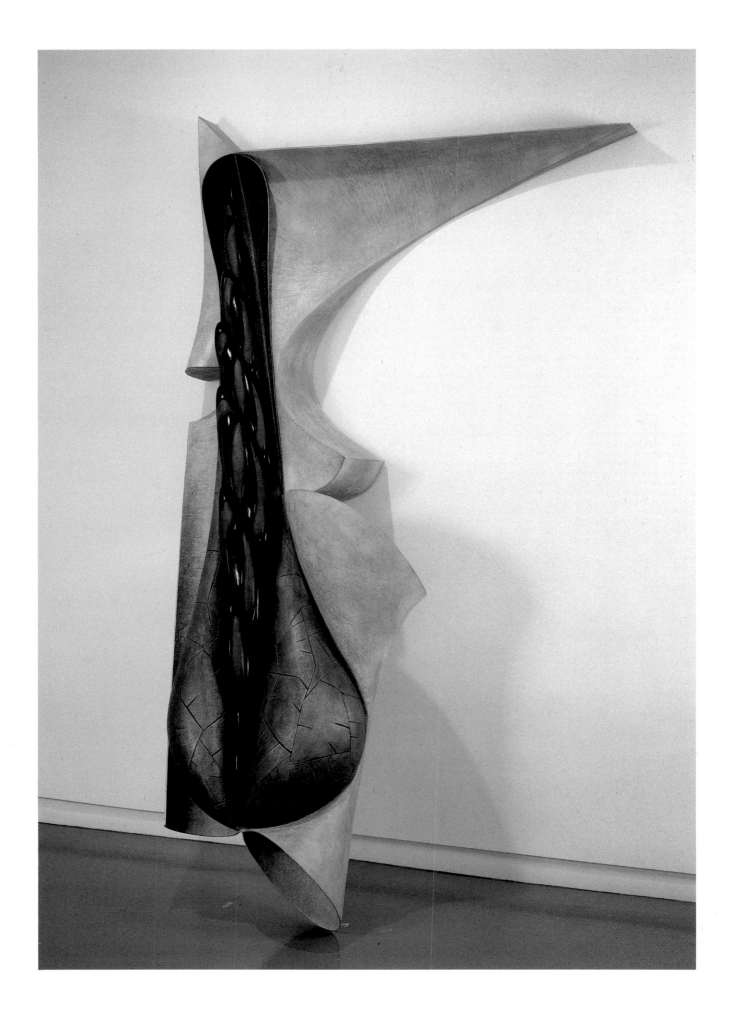

Untitled (Nautilus)   1985
colored chalk, graphite on paper
60 x 60
Collection First Bank System, Inc.,
Minneapolis

Tolled Belle 1987
cast and fabricated aluminum with
chemical dye
48 x 93½ x 48
Collection Mr. Raymond J. Learsy

Untitled (Hanging Judge)   1984
colored chalk, oil stick, graphite on paper
72½ x 66½
Private collection
Courtesy Gagosian Gallery, New York

For example, the hollowed out elliptical shapes of the upper half of *Nomen est Numen* reappear as stacked volumes in its lower half; a double strip arcing upward is counterbalanced below by a tightly twisted screw form.

Although Newman insists that his sculptures are essentially abstractions, still, they are evocative of forms and objects in the real world. The smooth curved surfaces of *Tolled Belle* are reminiscent of medieval armor, and its central image has a masklike quality. The curling sepaloid shapes of *Nomen est Numen* enclose an ovoid projectile resembling an oversized stamen; the overall effect is not unlike a menacing sexual flower. This sculpture is also fraught with mechanical allusions. In a grandly executed drawing related to this piece, the artist has scrawled the word "telescope" in the center of a broadly drawn oval shape. While the corresponding central thrusting element in the sculpture is not a literal representation of such an instrument, the manner in which it projects forward certainly seems inspired by one.

Newman's constructions, with their layered surfaces, also suggest exo-skeletons, fossils, and shells. A chambered nautilus is an especially appropriate metaphor for the artist's sculptures, not only because its curved surfaces are reminiscent of Newman's complex forms, but also in the way both the nautilus and Newman's sculptures are created through accretion over time. The artist's affinity for such organic forms is especially evident in the 1985 drawing, *Untitled (Nautilus)*, that subsequently led to his first large-scale outdoor piece, a commission for the General Mills Corporation in Minneapolis.

The titles Newman assigns to his sculptures are often puns. They emphasize the multiple interpretations of his works and at the same time pay gentle homage to his father, a professor of linguistics. Among Newman's most descriptive puns is the title for the 1984 sculpture, *Slow Commotion*. It was commissioned along with *Air Screw* (1984) for installation in a train station in Stamford, Connecticut. Its title suggests the idea of locomotion (low commotion), and also conveys the slow, lumbering quality of the sculpture. The artist has described this work as "a wall piece that fell down and went splat." At its unveiling, he spoke eloquently of its relationship to its site:

> Sculpture is a fossil of arrested motion and here is where sculpture and [the] railroad link up: too modern to be primitive, too primitive to be futuristic. Wrought by hand as if by Vulcan's forge and not yet the high technology of Sputnik and Challenger.
> Somewhere at rest, about to take off. The slow commotion before departure.[2]

Newman has referred to his sculptures as a cross between sex and science.[3] Certainly a strong sexuality seems to permeate *Action at a Distance (Ghost Version)* (1987). Within its vulvalike structure, a profusion of biomorphic forms cascades. Moreover, one has the sense that these evocative forms may have generated themselves. Newman uses such aggressive, charged images to provoke a strong emotional response in the viewer. Though this sculpture is composed of three independent parts, and though these are finally synthesized into a whole, each of these sections has a distinct formal character. Newman juxtaposes such disparate areas for formal as well as expressive reasons. The contouring shape is made of lacquered aluminum; its metallic surface has an industrial feel. By contrast, the bulbous form of patined aluminum contains heavily worked surfaces; incised lines that read as a kind of drawing are actually remnants of the fabrication process. Finally, the shiny, dark, reflective surface of the cast bronze enhances the seeming liquidity of the forms of this sculpture.

One of Newman's recent works, a floor piece, again titled *Tolled Belle* (1987), consists of two almost identical trumpet shapes connected in the center by a double cylindrical helix. The bell shapes have been elongated and twisted so that one is oriented vertically, the other horizontally. According to the artist, the title is a pun on its bell shape as well as an allusion to the French word for a beautiful woman—an apt reference since, when seen from above, the clearly defined contours of the central void, enhanced by the dark iridescent purple interior, are not unlike an abstracted curvaceous female.

Newman was inspired to make recumbent floor pieces in part, he says, after seeing Giacometti's *Woman with Her Throat Cut* (1932), a provocative, Surrealist sculpture that was intended to lie directly on the floor. While Newman's 1987 *Tolled Belle* bears little direct resemblance to Giacometti's sculpture, nevertheless there are certain affinities in the way both works rise up from the floor in an arcing configuration and in the rhythm of their convex and concave forms. Perhaps most important is the aspect of metamorphosis that is at the heart of both works, though the artists' approaches are entirely opposite. Giacometti transforms the figure to make it abstract. Newman, in contrast, begins with purely abstract forms and through such actions as curving and twisting the flat planes of his materials, invests his work with allusive content.

D.H.

1. Unless otherwise noted, all quotations are from a conversation with the artist 18 June 1987.

2. Artist's notes for a talk delivered at the unveiling of *Slow Commotion* and *Air Screw* in Stamford, Connecticut, 1 December 1987.

3. See Katy Kline, in Hayden Gallery, List Visual Arts Center, Massachusetts Institute of Technology, Cambridge, Mass., *Natural Forms and Forces: Abstract Images in American Sculpture*, exh. cat., 1986, p. 19.

John Newman

1952
  Born in Flushing, New York
1972
  Independent Study Program, Whitney Museum of American Art, New York
1973
  B.A., Oberlin College, Oberlin, Ohio
1975
  M.F.A., Yale University, School of Art, New Haven, Connecticut

  Lives in New York

Selected Solo Exhibitions

1977
  Suzanne Lemberg Usdan Gallery, Bennington College, Bennington, Vermont
  Installations, City University of New York, Graduate Center Mall, New York
  Center for Advanced Visual Studies, Massachusetts Institute of Technology, Cambridge
1979
  Thomas Segal Gallery, Boston
1981
  Reed College, Portland, Oregon
1985
  Daniel Weinberg Gallery, Los Angeles
1986
  Jeffrey Hoffeld & Company, New York
1987
  Jay Gorney Modern Art, New York
1988
  Gagosian Gallery, New York
  Daniel Weinberg Gallery, Los Angeles
  John Newman: Curving the Plane, The New York Academy of Sciences (catalogue)

Selected Group Exhibitions

1975
  Arttransition, Center for Advanced Visual Studies, Massachusetts Institute of Technology, Cambridge
  Sculpture and Drawings, 112 Greene Street, New York
1977
  Between Painting and Sculpture, Worcester Art Museum, Massachusetts
1978
  More Talent, Thomas Segal Gallery, Boston

1979
  Corners: Painterly and Sculptural Work, Hayden Gallery, Massachusetts Institute of Technology, Cambridge (catalogue)
  Six Sculptors, Institute of Contemporary Art, Boston
1980
  Painting in Relief, Whitney Museum of American Art, Downtown Branch, New York
  Black and White, Thomas Segal Gallery, Boston
1981
  New Visions, The Aldrich Museum of Contemporary Art, Ridgefield, Connecticut (catalogue)
1983
  New Sculpture: Icon and Environment, Independent Curators Incorporated, New York (catalogue)
  Drawing it Out, Baskerville + Watson Gallery, New York
  The New Sculpture, Hamilton Gallery, New York
  New Biomorphism and Automatism, Hamilton Gallery, New York
  Willard Gallery, New York
1984
  Drawings, Barbara Toll Fine Arts, New York
  Daniel Weinberg Gallery, Los Angeles
  Lawrence Oliver Gallery, Philadelphia
1985
  1985 Biennial Exhibition, Whitney Museum of American Art, New York
  Working on the Railroad, Whitney Museum of American Art, Fairfield County, Stamford, Connecticut
  Curated by Klaus Kertess, International with Monument, New York
  AIDS Benefit, Daniel Weinberg Gallery, Los Angeles
  Sculptors' Drawings, Diane Brown Gallery, New York
  Between Drawing and Sculpture, Sculpture Center, New York (catalogue)
1986
  Drawings: Carroll Dunham, John Newman, Terry Winters, Jeffrey Hoffeld & Company, New York
  Natural Forms and Forces: Abstract Images in American Sculpture, Hayden Gallery, List Visual Arts Center, Massachusetts Institute of Technology, Cambridge and Bank of Boston Gallery (catalogue)

*Monumental Drawings: Works by
22 Contemporary Americans*, The
Brooklyn Museum, New York
(catalogue)
New Acquisitions: Works on Paper,
Walker Art Center, Minneapolis
Drawings, Barbara Krakow Gallery,
Boston
Sculpture on the Wall, The Aldrich
Museum of Contemporary Art,
Ridgefield, Connecticut
Time after Time: A Sculpture Show,
Diane Brown Gallery, New York
Intuitive Line, Hirschl & Adler Modern,
New York
*Monsters: The Phenomena of
Dispassion*, Barbara Toll Fine Arts,
New York
New Prints, Martina Hamilton Gallery,
New York
Drawings by Sculptors, Nohra Haime
Gallery, New York
Drawings, Knight Gallery, Spirit Square
Center for the Arts, Charlotte,
North Carolina
Works on Paper, Althea Viafora
Gallery, New York
*1976–1986: Ten Years of Collecting
Contemporary American Art—
Selections from the Edward R. Downe,
Jr. Collection*, Wellesley College
Museum, Massachusetts; Knight
Gallery, Spirit Square Center for the
Arts, Charlotte, North Carolina
(catalogue)
1987
*The Structural Image: Sculpture and
Works on Paper by Sculptors*,
Dolan/Maxwell Gallery, Philadelphia
Master Prints, Patricia Heesy Gallery,
New York

Selected Bibliography

Oronato, Ronald J. Exhibition review,
Artforum, Vol. 18, October 1979.
Taylor, Robert. "Corners: Hayden
Gallery," *Boston Globe*, 1 October
1979.
Leja, Michael. "Six Sculptors at the ICA,"
Art in America, Vol. 68, January 1980.
Oronato, Ronald J. Exhibition review,
Artforum, Vol. 18, January 1980.
Pincus-Witten, Robert. "Entries: Big
History, Little History," *Arts Magazine*,
Vol. 54, April 1980.
_____. "Entries: Sheer Grunge," *Arts
Magazine*, Vol. 55, May 1981.
Henry, Gerrit. Exhibition review,
ARTnews, Vol. 82, October 1983.
Levin, Kim. "Top Forms," *Village Voice*,
18 October 1983.
Preston, Malcolm. Exhibition review,
Newsday, 24 April 1984.
"At the Whitney: Zap, Flash and Strange
Sweetness," *International Herald
Tribune*, 13 April 1985.
"Beauty at Railway Stations Explored at
the Whitney," *The New York Times*,
26 May 1985.
McGill, Douglas. Exhibition review, *The
New York Times*, 14 July 1985.
Saunders, Wade. "Talking Objects:
Interviews with Ten Younger
Sculptors," *Art in America*, Vol. 73,
November 1985.
Brenson, Michael. "Art: 8 Artists in
'Between Drawing and Sculpture,'"
The New York Times, 20 December
1985.
Mahoney, Robert. Exhibition review, *Arts
Magazine*, Vol. 60, June 1986.
"Prints & Photographs Published," *Print
Collector's Newsletter*, Vol. 17,
September–October 1986.
Cohen, Ronny. "A New Look at Big
Drawing," *Drawing*, Vol. 8,
September–October 1986.
Silverman, Andrea. "New Editions,"
ARTnews, Vol. 85, October 1986.
Brenson, Michael. "Art: Newman's
Sculpture And Its Links to the 60's,"
The New York Times, 5 December
1986.
Mahoney, Robert. Exhibition review, *Arts
Magazine*, Vol. 61, February 1987.
Smith, Roberta. Exhibition review, *The
New York Times*, 5 June 1987.

Martin Puryear

In 1986, Martin Puryear was approached by Walker Art Center and asked to create a sculpture that would frame the main entrance to the new Minneapolis Sculpture Garden, adjacent to the museum. Deciding in favor of a relatively classical entryway, Puryear designed a pair of gray granite columns. The two pillars are rectangular at one end and taper to a circle at the other. In order to subtly counteract the prevailing symmetry and regularity of the Garden plan, he inverted one of the columns—thus, one stands on its rectangular end and the other on its circular end—effectively transforming them into opposite rather than identical elements. At the Cold Spring Granite Company quarries in central Minnesota, he located a roughly rectangular mass of granite that, when split, yielded two blocks of approximately the same dimensions he intended for his columns. He decided to incorporate as much of this "found" stone as possible. Since the blocks already had several flat, richly textured faces, Puryear cut only what was necessary to give them a square profile. The rounded, lathe-turned surfaces are lightly furrowed, clearly showing the cutting marks. The result is a combination of classical simplicity with a rugged, unpolished finish.

Although these columns represent Puryear's first effort at working in stone on a large scale, they are typical of his work in several respects. The combination of square and conical elements has been a motif in Puryear's work since the mid-1970s. A compressed version of this same basic form is found in *For Beckwourth,* a work from 1980, whose square wooden base is surmounted by an earthen dome. Unlike the monumental solidity of the columns, the squat dome of *For Beckwourth* is evocative of impermanent, rudimentary architecture.

The recurrence of a motif in a number of guises is typical of Puryear's working method: he will repeatedly return to and modify a form or idea he has used before in an effort to mine it for new implications. In speaking of the course of his career, he says, "It's linear in the sense that a spiral is linear. I come back to similar territory at different times. I tend not to discard ideas and move on to totally new territory."[1]

This concern with mutation and evolution reflects interests in history, ethnography, and biology which Puryear has pursued since his childhood in Washington, D.C. His fascination with foreign cultures led him to join the Peace Corps after his graduation from Catholic University in 1963. The two years he spent teaching secondary school in Sierra Leone had a dramatic influence on his artistic career, shifting his interest from painting and drawing to sculpture. He became particularly intrigued by the local traditions in carpentry and building. His daily route to school passed the workshop of a group of village carpenters; Puryear delighted in watching them work and seeing what they produced each day. "Not a power tool in the place," he remembers admiringly, "everything was done by hand."

In large measure as a result of this experience, Puryear prefers to work in wood and construct his sculptures by joining elements together rather than carving them from whole blocks. By

For Beckwourth 1980
earth, wood
40 x 34 x 34
Collection the artist
Courtesy Donald Young Gallery, Chicago

189

Mus   1984
painted wood, wire mesh
26 x 44 x 26
Collection Marne and Jim DeSilva

(opposite)
Timber's Turns   1987
Honduran mahogany, red cedar,
Douglas fir
86½ x 46¾ x 34½
Collection Hirshhorn Museum and
Sculpture Garden, Smithsonian
Institution
Museum Purchase, 1987

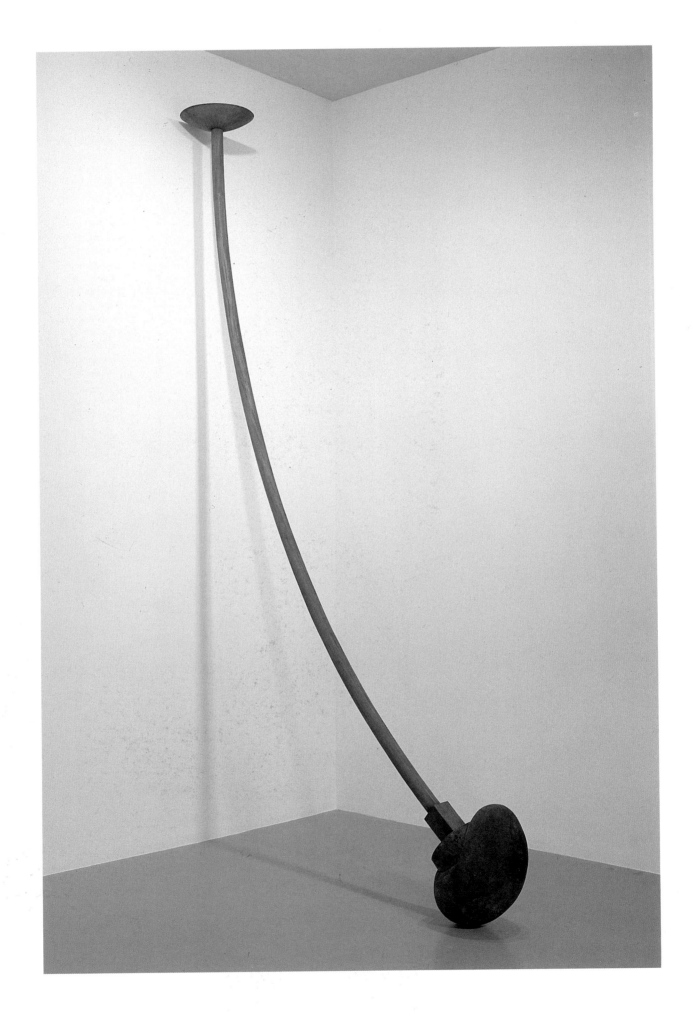

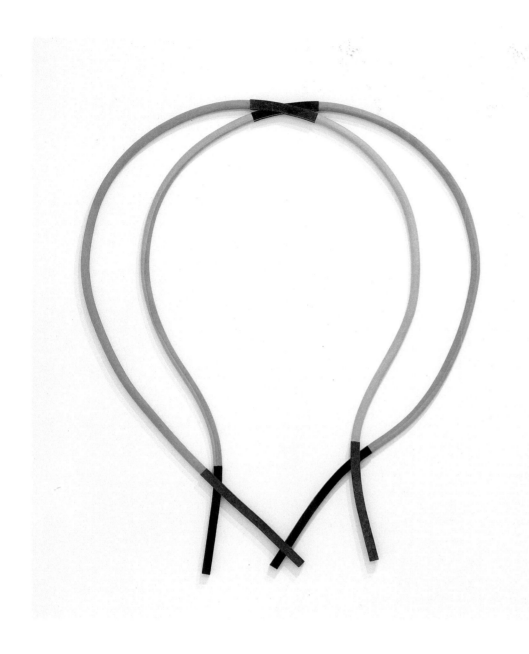

Two Into One   1985
painted wood
74 x 63 x 1⅜
Collection Dr. Beverly R. Rollnick
Courtesy Donald Young Gallery, Chicago

Untitled   1987
bronze
18 x 14 x 6
Collection the artist
Courtesy Donald Young Gallery, Chicago

(opposite)
To Transcend   1987
Honduran mahogany, poplar
169 x 13 x 90
Collection Walker Art Center
Walker Special Purchase Fund, 1988

Generation   1988
red cedar, gourd, paint
101 x 43 x 20
Collection Jane and Leonard Korman

Noblesse O.   1987
red cedar, aluminum paint
98³⁄₈ x 58 x 46
Collection Dallas Museum of Art
General Acquisitions Fund and gift of
The 500, Inc.

Martin Puryear at Cold Spring Granite
Company fabricating *Ampersand* and
installing the sculpture at the main
entrance of the Minneapolis Sculpture
Garden

crafting his sculptures in this fashion he feels that they reveal both the labor and the logic that has gone into them. "I tend not to abrade things, not to use grinders and sanders, but cutting tools: blades, edges. Because then every stroke reads as a decision." Puryear enjoys the sense of history that comes with his techniques; many of his basic tools and methods have been in use for thousands of years. His craftsmanship thus invests his work with a sense of both the intimacy of the maker's touch and, paradoxically, the anonymity of the craftsman. Nonetheless, Puryear emphatically subordinates his role as craftsman to his role as artist. His sculptures read as objects first: only slowly do we come to consider the means by which they have been made.

Puryear's sculptures are so subtly constructed that it is easy to mistake them for objects found in nature. This apparent balance between the natural and the man-made has led to their being termed primitivistic. The artist, however, qualifies this: "I'm as interested in the modern as I am in the primitive; I think I'm interested in where the two meet."

Following his stint in the Peace Corps, Puryear studied at the Swedish Royal Academy of Art for two years; but it was only while in graduate school at Yale University from 1969 to 1971 that he became acquainted with current developments in art. He credits Minimalism, the dominant style in sculpture at the time, with reinforcing his existing predilection for simplicity: "Minimalism legitimized in my mind something I have always focused on—the power of the simple, single thing as opposed to a full-blown complex array of things."[2] Puryear, however, rejected the sensual austerity and intellectual bias of Minimalism. For him, formal simplicity does not equate with psychological simplicity. "My work is very carefully wrought in the sense that there's nothing extra that's just dragging or hanging on—nothing that doesn't have to be there.

You might call it a reductive way of working. Yet at the same time it is intended to reverberate and have a range of possible associations."

One means by which Puryear frequently achieves this associative resonance is to work with familiar forms, whether they are common man-made shapes, forms found in nature, or motifs that he has used before in his own art. By altering their scale, materials, and proportions, he estranges them from their original connotations and endows them with "different realities." The resulting objects are at once vaguely recognizable yet enigmatic.

Because many of his works are hollow floor pieces, they frequently suggest elemental architectural structures transformed into sculptural objects. *For Beckwourth* is based on the dome of Tibetan stupas. Named after a black American frontiersman, its packed earth mound is also reminiscent of the sod houses built by early settlers of the Great Plains.

Though he favors compact, rounded forms, Puryear is less interested in mass and density than in volume, surface, and line. Scattered along the floor and windows of his Chicago home is a vast array of bottles, jars, and other vessels that he has collected over the years. Among his favorites are several lathe-turned wooden containers that echo the shape of the glass bottles they contain and protect. Like these objects, Puryear's hollow sculptures define volume; yet in works like *Timber's Turns* and *Noblesse O.*, both from 1987, he denies the viewer visual access to their interior. "I enjoy the irony of that," says Puryear, "I think a lot of the works are ambiguous because they're so closed. You don't get a sense at all of how thick the walls are." In *Noblesse O.* Puryear has underscored the hollowness of the piece by rubbing aluminum paint into its surface, making it look like sheet metal. By endowing his apparently simple forms with these subtle confusions, Puryear

effectively slows down the viewing process—"It makes you puzzle things out," he says—and promotes an intimate interaction between viewer and sculpture.

In contrast to his volumetric floor pieces, Puryear has also created a number of wall sculptures that are essentially linear. Many of these are wooden loops that resemble oversized neck torques. As with the floor pieces, these wall objects are deceptive in their simplicity. *Two Into One* (1985) is a particularly complex example of this genre. Its two interwoven loops of wood change color where they meet in the center of the piece, creating a sense of confusion as to which is which. In addition, though they read as simple lines from a distance, upon close examination the viewer discovers that the loops repeatedly shift between flat and rounded profiles.

To Transcend (1987) is unusual in Puryear's work in its reliance on both wall and floor for support. Like *For Beckwourth*, it plays organic form against ideal, geometric form; at one end of an elegantly curved shaft is a podlike base which rests on the ground, at the other end, held far above the viewer's head, is a more ethereal circular disk, its thin edge barely touching the wall. The piece appears to balance precariously on its globular base, but it is in fact perfectly stable. Like so many of Puryear's sculptures, *To Transcend* harmonizes opposing themes—organic and geometric, natural and ideal, stability and instability—in a paradoxically simple form.

P.W.B.

1. Unless otherwise noted, all quotations are from a conversation with the artist, 5 December 1987.
2. Quoted in Hugh M. Davies and Helaine Posner, "Conversations with Martin Puryear," University of Massachusetts, Amherst, *Martin Puryear*, exh. cat., 1984, p. 32.

(two views)
Ampersand 1987–1988
granite
east column: 163 x 36 x 36
west column: 167 x 36 x 38
Commissioned for the exhibition
Sculpture Inside Outside
Collection Walker Art Center
Gift of Margaret and Angus Wurtele,
1988

Martin Puryear

1941
Born in Washington, D.C.
1963
B.A., Catholic University of America, Washington, D.C.
1966–1968
Swedish Royal Academy of Art, Stockholm
1971
M.F.A., Yale University, New Haven, Connecticut

Lives in Chicago

Solo Exhibitions

1968
Grona Palletten Gallery, Stockholm
1972
Fisk University Museum of Art, Nashville, Tennessee
Henri Gallery, Washington, D.C.
1973
Henri Gallery, Washington, D.C.
1977
The Corcoran Gallery of Art, Washington, D.C.
1978
Protetch-McIntosh Gallery, Washington, D.C.
1979
Protetch-McIntosh Gallery, Washington, D.C.
1980
Young-Hoffman Gallery, Chicago
Museum of Contemporary Art, Chicago (brochure)
Joslyn Art Museum, Omaha, Nebraska (brochure)
1981
Delahunty Gallery, Dallas
and/or Gallery, Seattle
1982
McIntosh/Drysdale Gallery, Washington, D.C.
Young-Hoffman Gallery, Chicago
1983
Donald Young Gallery, Chicago
1984
University Gallery, University of Massachusetts at Amherst (catalogue)
1985
Margo Leavin Gallery, Los Angeles
Donald Young Gallery, Chicago
University Art Museum, Berkeley, California (brochure)

1987
Chicago Public Library Cultural Center (catalogue)
Carnegie-Mellon University Art Gallery, Pittsburgh (brochure)
Donald Young Gallery, Chicago
David McKee Gallery, New York
1988
McIntosh/Drysdale Gallery, Washington, D.C.

Selected Group Exhibitions

1962
Annual Exhibition, Baltimore Museum of Art, Maryland
1965
USIS Gallery, Freetown, Sierra Leone
1967
Stockholm Biennial Exhibition, Liljevachs Konsthall
1971
Prints and Paintings by Black Artists, University of Wisconsin, Madison
1972
New Talent at Maryland, University of Maryland Art Gallery, College Park
1977
The Material Dominant, Pennsylvania State University Museum of Art, University Park (catalogue)
Artpark, Lewiston, New York (catalogue)
1978
Young American Artists: 1978 Exxon National Exhibition, Solomon R. Guggenheim Museum, New York (catalogue)
The Presence of Nature, Whitney Museum of American Art, New York (catalogue)
1979
1979 Biennial Exhibition, Whitney Museum of American Art, New York (catalogue)
Customs and Culture, Creative Time, Inc., New York
Wave Hill, Bronx, New York (catalogue)
1980
Afro-American Abstraction, P.S. 1, The Institute for Art and Urban Resources, Inc., Long Island City, New York
Black Circle, Montgomery Ward Gallery, University of Illinois at Chicago Circle
Chicago, Chicago, Contemporary Arts Center, Cincinnati, Ohio

1981

1981 Biennial Exhibition, Whitney Museum of American Art, New York (catalogue)

Instruction Drawings, Cranbrook Academy of Art Museum, Bloomfield Hills, Michigan (catalogue)

Artists' Parks and Gardens, Museum of Contemporary Art, Chicago (catalogue)

The New Spiritualism: Transcendent Images in Painting and Sculpture, Oscarsson Hood Gallery, New York (catalogue)

1982

Invitational Exhibition, David Winton Bell Gallery, List Art Center, Brown University, Providence, Rhode Island (catalogue)

FAF:PFPAFP: Form and Function: Proposals for Public Art for Philadelphia, Pennsylvania Academy of the Fine Arts, Philadelphia (catalogue)

74th American Exhibition, The Art Institute of Chicago (catalogue)

American Abstraction Now, The Institute of Contemporary Art, The Virginia Museum of Art, Richmond (catalogue)

Afro-American Abstraction, The Art Museum Association, New York (catalogue)

1983

Five Sculptors/NOAA, Seattle Art Museum

1984

An International Survey of Recent Painting and Sculpture, The Museum of Modern Art, New York (catalogue)

Proposals and Projects: World's Fairs, Waterfronts, Parks and Plazas, Rhona Hoffman Gallery, Chicago

Primitivism in 20th Century Art: Affinity of the Tribal and the Modern, The Museum of Modern Art, New York (catalogue)

1985

Chicago Sculpture International/ Mile 4, Chicago International Art Exposition (catalogue)

Anniottanta, Galleria Communale d'Arte Moderna, Bologna

Transformations in Sculpture: Four Decades of American and European Art, Solomon R. Guggenheim Museum, New York (catalogue)

1986

Natural Forms and Forces: Abstract Images in American Sculpture, Hayden Gallery, List Visual Arts Center, Massachusetts Institute of Technology and Bank of Boston (catalogue)

After Nature, Germans van Eck, New York (brochure)

Individuals: A Selected History of Contemporary Art, 1945–1986, The Museum of Contemporary Art, Los Angeles (catalogue)

Three Artists/Three Visions, Charlotte Crosby Kemper Gallery, Kansas City Art Institute, Missouri

1987

Structure to Resemblance: Work by Eight American Sculptors, Albright-Knox Art Gallery, Buffalo, New York (catalogue)

Emerging Artists 1978–1986: Selections from the Exxon Series, Solomon R. Guggenheim Museum, New York (catalogue)

Selected Bibliography

Bourdon, David. Exhibition review, *Art in America*, Vol. 62, January/February 1974.

Richard, Paul. "A Shrine of Cedar and Hide," *The Washington Post*, 30 July 1977.

Zimmer, William. "Art for the Me Decade," *SoHo Weekly News*, 1 March 1979.

Crary, Jonathan. "Martin Puryear's Sculpture," *Artforum*, Vol. 18, October 1979.

Artner, Alan. "Martin Puryear, Museum of Contemporary Art," *Chicago Tribune*, 22 February 1980.

Hughes, Robert. "Going Back to Africa—as Visitors," *Time*, 31 March 1980.

Schulze, Franz. "Puryear Works: Elegant Simplicity," *Chicago Sun-Times*, 18 May 1980.

Tully, Judd. "The Chicago art scene," *Flash Art*, No. 103, Summer 1981.

Artner, Alan. "Martin Puryear," *Chicago Tribune*, 25 June 1982.

Schulze, Franz. "It's All in a Matter of Course with New MCA Gift Wrapping," *Chicago Sun-Times*, 27 June 1982.

Brenson, Michael. "Sculpture: Puryear Postminimalism," *The New York Times*, 10 August 1984.

Silverthorne, Jeanne. Exhibition review, *Artforum*, Vol. 23, December 1984.

Tomkins, Calvin. "Perceptionist at All Levels," *The New Yorker*, 3 December 1984.

Kirshner, Judith Russi. Exhibition review, *Artforum*, Vol. 23, Summer 1985.

Taylor, Sue. "Poetic resonance marks Puryear's new sculpture," *Chicago Sun-Times*, 23 October 1985.

Arnason, H.H. *History of Modern Art*, New York: Harry N. Abrams, 1986, pp. 685–686.

Moser, Charlotte. Exhibition review, *ARTnews*, Vol. 85, January 1986.

Plagens, Peter. "I Just Dropped in to See What Condition My Condition Was In . . . ," *Artscribe*, No. 56, February/March 1986.

Madoff, Steven Henry. "Sculpture Unbound," *ARTnews*, Vol. 85, November 1986.

Morgan, Ann Lee. "Martin Puryear: Sculpture as Elemental Expression," *New Art Examiner*, Vol. 14, May 1987.

Westerbeck, Colin. Exhibition review, *Artforum*, Vol. 25, May 1987.

Brenson, Michael. "Maverick Sculptor Makes Good," *The New York Times Magazine*, 1 November 1987.

_____. "Shaping the Dialogue of Mind and Matter," *The New York Times*, 22 November 1987.

Schwabsky, Barry. "The Obscure Objects of Martin Puryear," *Arts Magazine*, Vol. 62, November 1987.

Morgan, R.C. "American Sculpture and the Search for a Referent," *Arts Magazine*, Vol. 62, November 1987.

Judith Shea

Judith Shea's spare, elegant figures are essentially about the nature, language, and history of sculpture. Though her hollowed-out figural fragments of stiffened felt, bronze, or cast iron reflect her early training as a clothing designer, and though the theme of clothing still has rich associations for her, her philosophical and technical approaches to form are those of a sculptor.

Upon receiving a degree in fashion design from Parsons School of Design in 1969, she worked in that field for a year, only to conclude that designing clothes was too restrictive: "I wanted out," she says. In addition to returning to school part-time for her B.F.A., two experiences in particular directed Shea toward making sculpture. One was working in a store in the United Nations building that sold clothing from around the world. There, she recalls, she began thinking about clothing in sculptural terms: "My idea of the conception of clothes as being so different, depending on where you came from, became a whole theoretical premise of what I wanted to do."[1]

The other decisive occurrence was in 1974, when she decided to conduct a workshop on the structure of clothes at Artpark in Lewiston, New York. There she met several sculptors, including Jene Highstein, Richard Nonas, and Suzanne Harris, who were working in a Minimalist style, and through her association with them she realized that there could be another forum for her work. In the pared-down geometry of Minimalist sculpture she found affinities to her own work.

The evolution of Shea's sculpture reflects a transition from the use of clothing as abstract form to its use as a surrogate for the human presence. Her early sculptures of the mid-1970s were items of clothing composed of basic geometric shapes such as squares, rectangles, and triangles. Hung flat on the wall, these works were clearly related to a Minimalist vocabulary of limited shapes and repeating elements; as Shea says, they were "clothes as primary structures." She followed these with a series of freestanding sheet metal and heavy paper garments that explored the idea of clothing as three-dimensional form.

By 1979, Shea returned to a two-dimensional format, creating sewn fabric silhouettes. These clothing forms such as dresses, sleeves, bodices, and trousers, were hung from rods or pinned directly to the wall and, though often anatomically incorrect, functioned as human surrogates. Eventually, to make her forms more gestural, Shea stiffened the cloth with plaster, paste, paint, wax, or Rhoplex. The results were three-dimensional reliefs. Inspired by the research she was doing for a lecture on medieval armor at The Metropolitan Museum of Art, she began experimenting with cast metal in her own work. With the aid of technicians at the Johnson Atelier in nearby Princeton, she developed a method of direct casting from shapes made of cloth saturated with hot wax. This technique, which she still uses today, enabled her to work more quickly and directly and "to build the figure from the inside out."

Enduring Charms 1986
cast iron, copper
dress: 36 x 14 x 10½
pyramid: 4 x 6 x 6
Collection Walker Art Center
Clinton and Della Walker Acquisition Fund,
1986

Peplum   1983
cast iron
18½ x 10 x 3
Collection Mr. and Mrs. William J.
Magavern II

Proxy   1981
acrylic, canvas
16¾ x 11 x 7
Collection Martin Sklar

(opposite)
The Christening   1987
bronze, cast marble
dress: 60 x 16 x 13
broken column, left: 13¾ x 34 x 13¾
broken column, right: 46 long, 8¼ diam.
Collection Robert F. Fogelman

He and She 1984
bronze
12 x 53 x 43
Private collection

(opposite)
Che Cosa Dice? 1986
bronze, oak
62 x 41 x 48½
Collection Mr. and Mrs. Armand J. Castellani

Untitled (study for
Custom Angle) 1985
colored pencil, graphite on paper
26 x 19
Collection Dorace M. Fichtenbaum

Untitled (first study for
Endless Model) 1986
graphite on paper
26 x 19
Collection the artist

Study for *Without Words*   1987
pastel, charcoal, graphite on paper
28 x 26
Collection Walker Art Center
Gift of Jeanne and Richard Levitt, 1988

Judith Shea installing *Without Words*

Without Words   1988
bronze, cast marble, limestone
78 x 80 x 118
Commissioned for the exhibition
Sculpture Inside Outside
Collection Walker Art Center
Gift of Jeanne and Richard Levitt, 1988

Different Destiny 1988
cast stone, cast bronze
59 x 16 x 42
Collection Dr. Harold and Elaine L. Levin

Shea's first fully three-dimensional cast works were done in 1982 and are simplified, reclining torsos laid on the floor. She preferred to work with fragments of the figure in order to make her work more compact:

It was [a way] of getting down to [the] essence of [a] human presence or human energy without the extraneous parts. The center of the torso, or some portion [of it] seemed to contain the presence. You didn't need arms, legs, or a head to represent the human presence.

Around this time her work became more fully figurative. The general architectural drapery associated with early classical Greek sculpture influenced the character of her work, as is evident in such sculptures as Black Dress (1983), and Standing There (1984). These solitary, hollow female forms, more often than not scaled to the artist's own figure, are not only formal examinations of interior and exterior space and gesture, but they are also metaphorical vessels for emotions. The "figureless" voids are like empty containers into which the viewer is free to project personal psychological responses.

As Shea's figures grew increasingly anatomical in detail and gave up some of their rigid formality, they began to suggest movement, often through a subtle striding position. In late 1983, she began to combine male and female figures in her pieces, a process that resulted in complex formal as well as psychological resonances. In He and She, a 1984 bronze, Shea presented a reclining female form enclosed within a man's overcoat sprawled out on the floor. The dialogue between male and female, protector and protected, active and passive is heightened by the tensions that are generated between the open form of the coat and the closed form of the female figure.

In an effort to avoid an exclusively narrative reading of her work, and to minimize the interpretation of her garments as male and female figures, in 1985 Shea decided to juxtapose figurative and geometric elements within specific works, thus establishing dialogues between dissimilar entities. To her solitary standing and seated figures she added such forms as cubes and pyramids. Sometimes these cryptic shapes were held on the laps of the figures, other times they were placed on the floor. Shea uses such ageless images she says, "as symbols of history, of art, of a specific period or a specific place." Enduring Charms (1986), consists of a hollow, columnar, full-length skirt made of iron; in front of it on the floor, like a mysterious energy center, rests a copper pyramid. Reminiscent as Shea's figure is of antique Greek and Egyptian statuary, it is also strongly contemporary. Like other simplified dress forms she uses, it is based on an evening dress that belonged to her mother. And, as Shea adds, the tight little skirt is back in fashion. Paired with the pyramid, symbol of ancient art and architecture, it invites speculation about the relationship between contemporary art and its historical precedents.

The individual elements of Enduring Charms activate one another through their opposite characteristics. The figure's minimalistic skirt, vaguely organic in form, suggests an immediate human presence; the pyramid, in contrast, is cool, abstract, and impenetrable. The sculpture is thus a metaphoric objectification of the artist's desire to reconcile her proclivity for description with her regard for the Minimalist aesthetic.

In a recent ambitiously scaled outdoor sculpture, Without Words (1988), consisting of two bronze figures and a fragment of an ancient Egyptian head replicated in cast marble, Shea continues her explorations of the dialogue between contemporary life and antiquity. As she points out, the head fragment, based on an Eighteenth Dynasty sculpture of Queen Tiye, establishes a specific historical reference.[2] Incorporating the ancient head was clearly the next step in the evolution of her work—a realization of the desire "to get involved technically in something that was more explicitly figurative; to truly understand traditional figurative sculpture through the process of re-creating it."

As the fulcrum of the tripartite composition, the head fragment is the psychological focus of both the Hera-like female figure and the unoccupied coat. The invisible presence in the coat would seem to be actively contemplating the sensuous stone fragment, while the classicized standing female, rendered in subtle contrapposto, appears aloof. Shea's sculpture is purposefully ambiguous. As she has said, "I'm much more interested in what you can imagine is about to happen rather than in 'this is what is happening here.'" For her, the implied gesture is more powerful than the specific one. In Without Words, the emotional resonance is heightened both by the enigmatic character of the figures and the tension between them.

Without Words reflects Shea's new ambitions as a sculptor. Her early sartorial fragments were small-scale, private explorations of structure. Today, she is excited by the possibilities of working with new materials and techniques to create more complex compositions. Her work has become more inclusive as she seeks to incorporate both the history of art and a complex range of human emotions into her sculpture.

D.H.

1. Unless otherwise noted, all quotations are from a conversation with the artist, 15 June 1987.
2. Queen Tiye was the wife of Amenhotep III and the mother of Akhnaton. The original head at The Metropolitan Museum of Art is made of yellow jasper and dated ca. 1417–1379 B.C.

Judith Shea

1948
Born in Philadelphia, Pennsylvania
1969
Grad., Fashion Design, Parsons School of Design, New York
1975
B.F.A., Parsons/New School, New York

Lives in New York

Selected Solo Exhibitions

1976
Studio Project, The Clocktower, The Institute for Art and Urban Resources, Inc., New York
1980
Judith Shea: Clothing Constructions, Willard Gallery, New York
1981
Judith Shea: Sculpture as Clothing, 80 Washington Square East Galleries, New York University, New York
Willard Gallery, New York
1983
Willard Gallery, New York
Dart Gallery, Chicago
1984
Viewpoints: Judith Shea, Nick Vaughn, Walker Art Center, Minneapolis (brochure)
1985
Robert Moskowitz: Recent Paintings and Pastels/Judith Shea: Recent Sculpture, Hayden Gallery, List Visual Arts Center, Massachusetts Institute of Technology, Cambridge; Knight Gallery, Spirit Square Center for the Arts, Charlotte, North Carolina (catalogue)
1986
Judith Shea: New Sculptures, Morris Gallery, Pennsylvania Academy of the Fine Arts, Philadelphia (brochure)
Willard Gallery, New York
1988
Curt Marcus Gallery, New York
Judith Shea, La Jolla Museum of Contemporary Art, California (catalogue)

Selected Group Exhibitions

1974
Artpark, Lewiston, New York (catalogue)
1975
Artpark, Lewiston, New York
1976
Rooms P.S. 1, P.S. 1, The Institute for Art and Urban Resources, Inc., Long Island City, New York (catalogue)
The Handwrought Object, 1776–1976, Herbert F. Johnson Museum of Art, Cornell University, Ithaca, New York (catalogue)
1977
Collection in Progress: 200 or So Selections from the Collection of Milton Brutten and Helen Herrick, Moore College of Art Gallery, Philadelphia (catalogue)
1978
Willard Gallery, New York
1979
Clothing Constructions, Los Angeles Institute of Contemporary Art
Material Pleasures, Institute of Contemporary Art, University of Pennsylvania, Philadelphia; Museum of Contemporary Art, Chicago, 1980 (catalogue)
1980
Fabric into Art, Amelie A. Wallace Gallery, State University of New York, College at Old Westbury (catalogue)
Seven Artists, Neuberger Museum, State University of New York, College at Purchase (catalogue)
1981
1981 Biennial Exhibition, Whitney Museum of American Art, New York (catalogue)
Summer Pleasures, Barbara Gladstone Gallery, New York
The Soft Land/Il Soffice Paese, Palazzo Farnese, Ortona, Italy (catalogue)
Figuratively Sculpting, P.S. 1, The Institute for Art and Urban Resources, Inc., Long Island City, New York
Parafunction, Barbara Gladstone Gallery, New York
1982
Art Materialized: Selections from the Fabric Workshop, The New Gallery for Contemporary Art, Cleveland, Ohio (catalogue)
Willard Gallery, New York
By the Sea, Barbara Toll Fine Arts, New York

Painting and Sculpture Today, 1982, Indianapolis Museum of Art, Indiana (catalogue)
1983
1984 —A Preview, Ronald Feldman Fine Arts, New York (catalogue)
Directions 1983, Hirshhorn Museum and Sculpture Garden, Washington, D.C. (catalogue)
Day in/Day out: Ordinary Life as a Source for Art, Freedman Gallery, Albright College, Reading, Pennsylvania (catalogue)
The New Sculpture, Hamilton Gallery, New York
The Sixth Day: A Survey of Recent Developments in Figurative Sculpture, The Renaissance Society at The University of Chicago (catalogue)
Artist/Critic, White Columns, New York
Sculpture Now, The Institute for Contemporary Art, Virginia Museum of Fine Arts, Richmond (brochure)
1984
Four Sculptors: Ritual and Artifact, Zabriskie Gallery, New York (brochure)
Art and Use: Scott Burton, R.M. Fischer, Judith Shea, Milwaukee Art Museum, Wisconsin (brochure)
Artist in the Theater, Hillwood Art Gallery, C.W. Post Center, Long Island University, Brookville, New York; Guild Hall Museum, East Hampton, New York (catalogue)
American Sculpture, Margo Leavin Gallery, Los Angeles
1985
Affiliations: Recent Sculpture and its Antecedents, Whitney Museum of American Art, Fairfield County, Stamford, Connecticut (catalogue)
Body & Soul: Aspects of Recent Figurative Sculpture, The Contemporary Arts Center, Cincinnati, Ohio (catalogue)
1986
Painting and Sculpture Today 1986, Indianapolis Museum of Art, Indiana (catalogue)
50th Anniversary Exhibition, Willard Gallery, New York
Works on Paper, Althea Viafora Gallery, New York
Willard Gallery, New York
Contemporary Cutouts, Whitney Museum of American Art at Philip Morris, New York (catalogue)

Drawings, Barbara Krakow Gallery, Boston

1987

Standing Ground: Sculpture by American Women, The Contemporary Arts Center, Cincinnati, Ohio (catalogue)

The Allusive Object: Mel Kendrick, Robert Lobe, Judith Shea, Barbara Krakow Gallery, Boston

Structure to Resemblance: Work by Eight American Sculptors, Albright-Knox Art Gallery, Buffalo, New York (catalogue)

Bronze, Plaster and Polyester, The Goldie Paley Gallery, Moore College of Art, Philadelphia

Sculptors on Paper: New Work, Madison Art Center, Wisconsin (catalogue)

Sculpture: Looking into Three Dimensions, Anchorage Museum of History and Art, Alaska

1988

Works on Paper, Curt Marcus Gallery, New York

Selected Bibliography

Greenwood, Susan. "Artist Constructs Clothes that Allow Fabric to Flow," *Niagara Gazette*, 24 August 1975.

McConathy, Dale. "Clothes (that Become You)," *Art-Rite*, No. 11–12, Winter–Spring 1976.

Schwartz, Barbara. Exhibition review, *Craft Horizons*, Vol. 36, August 1976.

Shea, Judith. "Style: The Art of Clothing," *Craft Horizons*, Vol. 38, October 1978.

Askey, Ruth. "Clothing Constructions," *Artweek*, Vol. 10, 16 June 1979.

Anderson, Alexandra. "Painting by the Yard," *SoHo Weekly News*, 28 June 1979.

Frank, Peter. "Museums on the Metroliner," *Village Voice*, 16 July 1979.

Flood, Richard. Exhibition review, *Artforum*, Vol. 18, October 1979.

Rickey, Carrie. "Art of Whole Cloth," *Art in America*, Vol. 67, November 1979.

Connor, Maureen. "Form Follows Fashion," *Artforum*, Vol. 18, December 1979.

Burton, Scott, et al. "Situation Esthetics: Impermanent Art and the Seventies Audience," *Artforum*, Vol. 18, January 1980.

Rickey, Carrie. "Of Crystal Palaces and Glass Houses," *Village Voice*, 14 April 1980.

Raynor, Vivien. "Art: Two Women Take Crafts to Higher Plane," *The New York Times*, 27 June 1980.

Nadelman, Cynthia. "Fabric In Art," *ARTnews*, Vol. 79, September 1980.

Cohen, Ronny. "Energism: An Attitude," *Artforum*, Vol. 19, September 1980.

Silverthorne, Jeanne. Exhibition review, *Artforum*, Vol. 19, October 1980.

Larson, Kay. "For the first time women are leading not following," *ARTnews*, Vol. 79, October 1980.

Cohen, Ronny. Exhibition review, *Art in America*, Vol. 68, October 1980.

Donahue, Michael. "Wealth of Images Dots Modern Show," *Memphis Press-Scimitar*, 4 December 1980.

Ashbery, John. "An Exhilarating Mess," *Newsweek*, Vol. 98, 23 February 1981.

Schjeldahl, Peter. "The Hallelujah Trail," *Village Voice*, 18 March 1981.

Smith, Roberta. "Biennial Blues," *Art in America*, Vol. 69, April 1981.

Morgan, Stuart. "Animal House: The Whitney Biennial," *Artscribe*, No. 29, June 1981.

Larson, Kay. "Sculpting Figuratively," *New York Magazine*, Vol. 14, 16 November 1981.

Morris, Robert. "American Quartet," *Art in America*, Vol. 69, December 1981.

Siegel, Jeanne. "Figuratively Sculpting P.S. 1 (Long Island)," *Art Express*, March 1982.

Shea, Judith. "Beyond Fashion: Mariano Fortuny," *Art in America*, Vol. 70, November 1982.

——. "Valentino," book review, *Artforum*, Vol. 21, December 1982.

Stein, Judith. "The Artist's New Clothes," *Portfolio*, Vol. 5, January–February 1983.

Peacock, Mary. "V," *Village Voice*, 1 February 1983.

Cohen, Ronny and Peggy Cyphers. "The First Energist Book," *New Observations*, March 1983.

Bernard, April. "Notes," *Vanity Fair*, May 1983.

Gessner, Liz. "Apparel Art," *Gentlemen's Quarterly*, May 1983.

Levin, Kim. "Top Forms," *Village Voice*, 24 May 1983.

Moser, Charlotte. "Renaissance Show Surveys 10 Years of Using Human Form in Sculpture," *The New York Times*, 29 May 1983.

Liebmann, Lisa. Exhibition review, *Artforum*, Vol. 22, September 1983.

Henry, Gerrit. Exhibition review, *ARTnews*, Vol. 82, October 1983.

Lichtenstein, Therese. Exhibition review, *Arts Magazine*, Vol. 58, November 1983.

Aver, James. Exhibition review, *Milwaukee Journal*, 27 November 1983.

Princenthal, Nancy. Exhibition review, *ARTnews*, Vol. 84, February 1985.

Cohen, Ronny. Exhibition review, *Artforum*, Vol. 23, February 1985.

Westfall, Stephen. Exhibition review, *Art in America*, Vol. 73, March 1985.

Gill, Susan. Exhibition review, *ARTnews*, Vol. 84, April 1985.

Saunders, Wade. "Talking Objects: Interviews with Ten Younger Sculptors," *Art in America*, Vol. 73, November 1985.

Van Wagner, Judy Collischan. "Judith Shea: A Personal Balance," *Arts Magazine*, Vol. 61, January 1987.

Gill, Susan. Exhibition review, *ARTnews*, Vol. 86, January 1987.

Peter Shelton

By the time he reached the fifth grade, Peter Shelton knew the names of all the bones and muscles of the human body. Later, at Pomona College in the early 1970s, he was a pre-med student. Not surprisingly, then, the human figure has played a major role in his art. Disparate as the forms of his sculpture may seem at first glance, ranging from architectural steel and canvas structures to delicately lacquered fiberglass wall pieces, his imagery centers on what may be termed the phenomenology of the body. His aim is to create an art that breaks down the distinction between the mind and the body by provoking a psychological response to a physical situation.

Shelton's earliest major statement as an artist was SWEATHOUSE *and little principals*, a 1979 installation that established the essential concerns of his sculpture. This work consisted of a small, steel hutlike chamber located amid a veritable forest of totemic objects. The latter, consisting of steel forms suspended on thin rods, alluded to various body parts through the size and placement of the forms relative to the viewer's body. The heart, for example, was represented by a small box raised to chest level by a steel rod. Shelton refers to the sensibility informing these objects as his own brand of "perverse Minimalism."[1]

The two main elements of SWEATHOUSE *and little principals,* the chamber and the totems, offered fundamentally different experiences. Shelton intended that, in wandering through the field of totems, viewers would become "psychically dismembered," their attention diverted to specific parts of their bodies as they encountered each element. For Shelton, "consciousness resides in the whole body, it isn't something that resides only in the head; and depending on what parts of you I touched, I would elicit different parts of consciousness. In a way it's very Oriental, as if there are different ideas located in different parts of the body."

If the totems presented viewers with an experience of viewing the body as a collection of parts, entering the hut provided a more integrated experience of the body. With its small dimensions, the hut was like a shell, making the viewer/participant acutely aware of his sensory perceptions. While standing before it, one inevitably imagined what it would be like inside the hut; once inside, the viewer had to reconcile the difference between the imagined and the actual experience.

These distinctions between actual and projected experience, between inside and outside, and between the body as object and as sensation have persisted in Shelton's work. In the early 1980s, he created a series of canvas and steel structures that combined aspects of sculpture, architecture, and theater in an effort to break down the traditional distinctions between audience, performer, and artwork. Upon entering the works, the viewer/participant became subject to the psychological sensations stimulated by his physical interaction with the spaces created by the architecture. The relationship between the architecture and the viewer's body was underscored by the use of translucent shellacked cloth walls which

Stiffshirt 1983
steel
30 x 58 x 11
Collection Barry and Gail Berkus

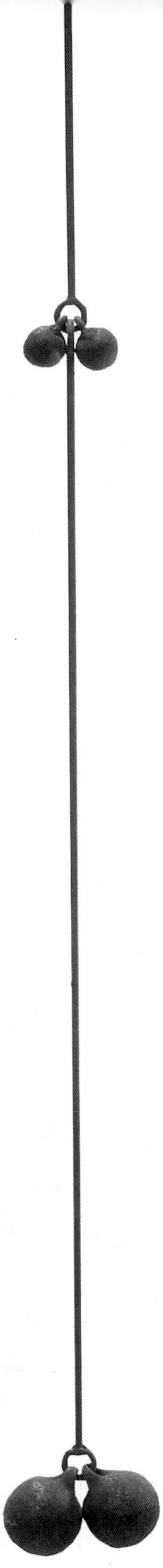

Eyesballs   1983
cast iron
36 x 5 x 2½
Private collection

(opposite, top)
MAJORJOINTS *hangers and squat*
(detail)   1983–1984
steel, cast iron, cement
Installation at L.A. Louver and Malinda
Wyatt Galleries
Venice, California

(opposite, bottom)
SWEATHOUSE *and little principals*
(detail)   1977–1982
steel
Installation at Contemporary Arts Forum
Santa Barbara, California

219

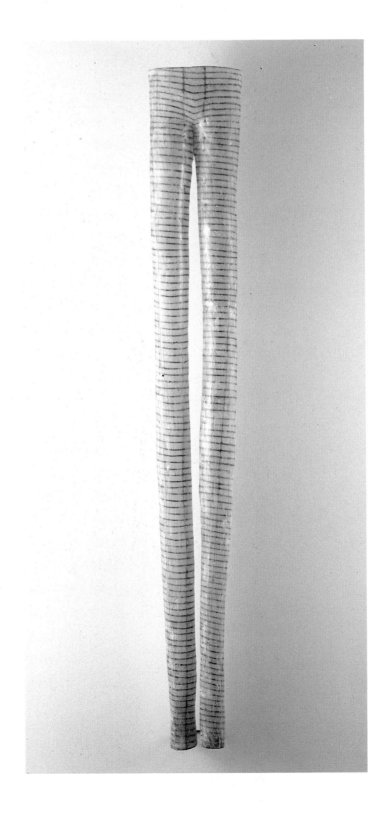

Skinnywhitelegs   1983–1985
mixed media
60 x 9 x 6
Collection Donald and Judy Kay

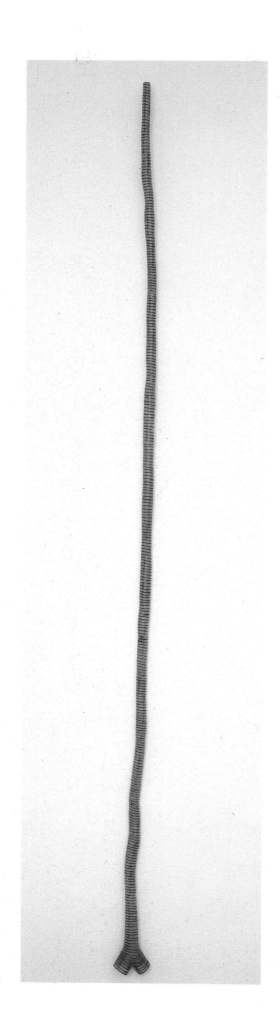

Windpipe   1983–1986
mixed media
108½ x 5 x 2½
Collection Marjorie and Michael Fasman

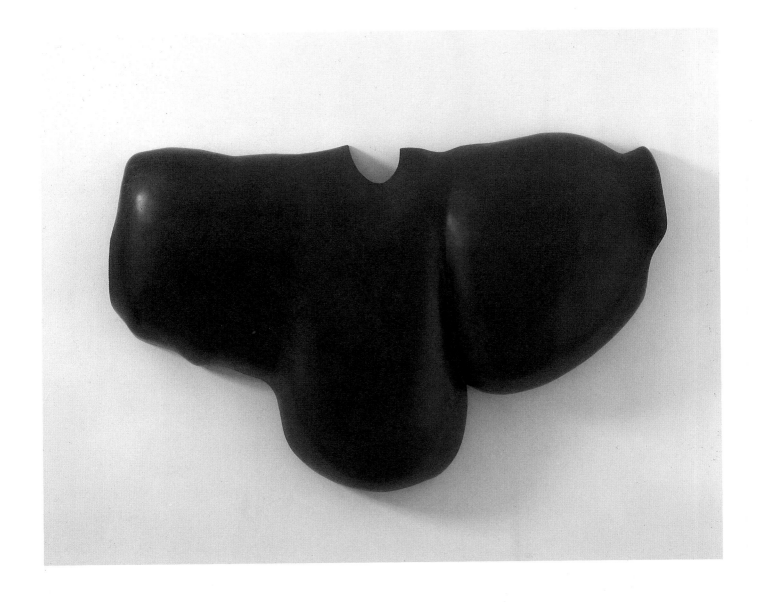

Fireshirt   1985–1986
mixed media
39 x 60 x 11
Collection Stanley and Pauline Foster

(opposite)
Armout   1986
mixed media
63 x 45 x 4½
Collection Barry and Gail Berkus

Misterleaner 1988
graphite, charcoal on Mylar
82¼ x 36
Collection Walker Art Center
Walker Special Purchase Fund, 1988

(opposite)
Bigflatsack 1984–1986
cast iron
41 x 45 x 5½
Collection Walker Art Center
Butler Family Fund, 1987

Study for BLACKVAULT*falloffstone*
1987
graphite, charcoal on vellum
23¹⁵⁄₁₆ x 35¹⁵⁄₁₆
Collection Walker Art Center
Acquired with Lannan Foundation
support in conjunction with the exhibition
Sculpture Inside Outside, 1988

took on a distinctly membranous quality. In Shelton's words, it was "as if you had taken your skin off and hung it up on poles around you."

Since 1983, the overt representation of the figure and its parts has become an increasingly important part of Shelton's art. For a complex 1983–1984 installation, MAJORJOINTS *hangers and squat,* he created a number of elements in cast iron and concrete. As with the *little principals* of his first installation, these were intended to create a dialogue with the viewer's body. Shelton views some of these elements, such as *Stiffshirt,* a hollow cast iron torso with outspread arms, as "tight-fitting architecture" into which a viewer could project himself. Others, like *Eyesballs,* with its two sets of iron balls suspended by a rod from the ceiling, provide whimsical objectifications of isolated body parts.

An ambitiously scaled installation from 1985–1986, *floatinghouse*DEADMAN was related to SWEATHOUSE *and little principals* in its juxtaposition of a central architectural element with a series of figure-related objects. The major element was a wood and paper structure, reminiscent of traditional Japanese architecture, which was suspended off the ground by cast-iron deadweights, or deadmen. The plan of this building was in the form of a spread-eagled human figure that looked as if it had, in Shelton's words, "swallowed the nave and apse of a small church." Viewers entered the figure from one extremity, an arm or a leg, and left by another. As they walked through the glowing, gently swaying structure, they were metaphor-ically passing through a human body, a fact they would probably only notice when they saw a small model of the building that served as one of the dead-weights. The cast-iron counterweights provided a contrast to the instability of the *floatinghouse* by their insistent solidity. An iron chair, for example, was so dense and heavy that anyone who sat on it felt insubstantial by comparison.

Shelton first used fiberglass to make molds for a number of the cast-iron elements in his installations, but for the past several years he has been using it as a material in its own right to create lightweight sculptures that hang on the wall. In works such as *Fireshirt* (1985–1986), Shelton molded the fiberglass over an intricately assembled wire armature and coated it with layers of resin and lacquer, often of different colors. He then sanded the lacquer down to allow the underlying colors to shine through. He began making these objects as an alternative to his installations, where questions of scale, expense, and labor often restricted what he could do. "These works are nice for me because they're sensual, they're immediate, and they're responsive to manipulation," he says, "They're like making drawings."

For Shelton, these hollow wall pieces act as metaphoric skins or shells and they are often distorted to humorously accentuate body functions or gestures. "I think of them as things that you are in front of, that mirror you a bit, but they're all stretched out of shape." In *Windpipe* (1983–1986), for example, an elongated trachial canal grossly exaggerates the act of inhaling. Shelton exploits the lightweight nature of fiberglass to give his forms a buoyant look that betrays their source, which is frequently in dreams. The parodic humor of these corporeal exaggerations is reminiscent of California Funk Art of the 1960s, a heritage Shelton readily acknowledges.

For *Sculpture Inside Outside,* Shelton has created a two-part outdoor piece, BLACKVAULT*falloffstone* (1988), which continues his investigation of figure-oriented architecture. One element is a black cement vault elevated off the ground by a steel truss system. It is a personally-scaled room whose lateral dimensions barely exceed one's reach: from the center of the vault, one cannot quite touch the walls to either side. From outside, the vault is impressive in its

immense weight and dense, rock-encrusted surface, but once inside, its dark smooth walls and resonant acoustics create a surprisingly airy, meditative space. The second element is a metal shell in the shape of a figure that cantilevers out from a rock base. A viewer who lies down in the form is locked into an open-armed position and denied any visual referents to determine his position relative to the ground. With both forms, then, the viewer/participant is isolated in the private world of his own body and imagination.

P.W.B.

1. All quotations are from a conversation with the artist, 19 June 1987.

Peter Shelton fabricating BLACKVAULT
in Seattle and installing
BLACKVAULT*falloffstone* in the
Minneapolis Sculpture Garden

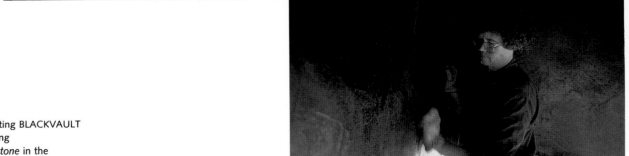

BLACKVAULT*falloffstone*   1988
cast concrete, steel, aluminum, stone
BLACKVAULT: 142 x 105 x 197
falloffstone: 53 x 67 x 116
Commissioned with Lannan Foundation
support for the exhibition
Sculpture Inside Outside
Courtesy the artist and L.A. Louver
Gallery, Inc., Venice, California

Peter Shelton

1951
    Born in Troy, Ohio
1973
    B.A., Pomona College, Claremont,
    California
1974
    Trade certifications, Hobart School of
    Welding Technology, Troy, Ohio
1979
    M.F.A., University of California,
    Los Angeles

    Lives in Los Angeles

Selected Solo Exhibitions

1980
    Artpark, Lewiston, New York
    (catalogue)
    BROWNROOMS, Los Angeles
    Contemporary Exhibitions, Inc.
1981
    NECKWALL *footscreen, sleeper*,
    Malinda Wyatt Gallery, Venice,
    California
1982
    white, round, HEAD, Artists Space,
    New York
    trunknuts WHITEHEAD, *floater*,
    Open Space Gallery, Victoria, British
    Columbia, Canada (catalogue)
    SWEATHOUSE *and little principals*,
    Santa Barbara Contemporary Arts
    Forum (catalogue)
1984
    MAJORJOINTS *hangers and squat*,
    L.A. Louver and Malinda Wyatt
    Galleries, Venice, California
    pipegut, waterseat and STANDSTILL,
    Portland Center for the Visual Arts,
    Portland, Oregon (brochure)
1986
    *floatinghouse*DEADMAN, University
    Gallery, University of Massachusetts at
    Amherst
    Peter Shelton: Recent Sculpture,
    L.A. Louver Gallery, Inc., Venice,
    California
1987
    *floatinghouse*DEADMAN, Wight Art
    Gallery, University of California,
    Los Angeles (catalogue)
1988
    Des Moines Art Center, Iowa
    (catalogue)

Selected Group Exhibitions

1977
    Art in Public Places, Cheney Cowles
    Memorial Museum, Spokane,
    Washington (catalogue)
1979
    Wight Art Gallery, University of
    California, Los Angeles (installation of
    SWEATHOUSE *and little principals*)
1980
    *Architectural Sculpture—History and
    Documents*, Los Angeles Institute of
    Contemporary Art (installation of
    BIRDHOUSE *holecan* at Chapman
    College, Orange, California)(catalogue)
    Sculpture 1980, The Maryland
    Institute, College of Art, Baltimore
    (catalogue)
    *Maquettes and Models—Art with
    Architectural Concerns*, Los Angeles
    Municipal Art Gallery
1981
    Divola, Picot, Shelton, Libra Gallery,
    Claremont Graduate School of Fine
    Arts, Claremont, California
    With More than One Sense,
    Los Angeles County Museum of Art
    The Intimate Object, The Downtown
    Gallery, Los Angeles
1982
    Forgotten Dimension, Fresno Arts
    Center, California (catalogue)
    *Une Experience Museographique:
    Echange Entre Artistes 1931–1982
    Pologne-USA*, Musée d'Art Moderne
    de la Ville de Paris (catalogue)
1983
    Public Comments, Center on
    Contemporary Art, Seattle
1984
    Constructed Metal: Modern Sculpture,
    College of Creative Studies, University
    of California, Santa Barbara (brochure)
    Aperto 84, XLI Esposizione
    Internazionale d'Arte, La Biennale di
    Venezia (catalogue)
1985
    Anniottanta, Galleria Communale
    d'Arte Moderna, Bologna (catalogue)
1987
    Avant-Garde in the Eighties,
    Los Angeles County Museum of Art
    (catalogue)
    California Figurative Sculpture, Palm
    Springs Desert Museum, California
    (catalogue)

Invitational Exhibition, Curt Marcus
Gallery, New York
1988
Elements: Five Installations, Whitney
Museum of American Art at Philip
Morris, New York (catalogue)
*Abstract Expressions: Recent
Sculpture*, Lannan Museum,
Lake Worth, Florida (catalogue)
Striking Distance, The Museum of
Contemporary Art, Los Angeles
(brochure)

Selected Bibliography

Fahr, Barry. "Enigmatic Architecture,"
Artweek, Vol. 11, 21 June 1980.
Huntington, Richard. "Artpark Does Its
Best to Get Rid of Middleman," *Buffalo
Courier-Express*, 13 July 1980.
Larson, Kay. "Is There a Crimp in the
Beauty Parlor," *Village Voice*,
10 September 1980.
Muchnic, Suzanne. "Sprawling
Sculptures," *Los Angeles Times*,
2 November 1980.
Brodhead, Wendy. "Protection and
Entrapment," *Artweek*, Vol. 11,
22 November 1980.
Schipper, Merle. "Peter Shelton's Places
and Spaces," *Images and Issues*,
Vol. 1, Spring 1981.
Pincus, Robert L. Exhibition review,
Los Angeles Times, 1 May 1981.
Drohojowska, Hunter. "Peter
Shelton—Art Pic of the Week,"
L.A. Weekly, 1 May 1981.
Knight, Christopher. "Your Place or
Shelton's," *Los Angeles Herald
Examiner*, 10 May 1981.
Blaine, Michael. "Formalist Shelter,"
Artweek, Vol. 12, 16 May 1981.
Perreault, John. "Park's Lot," *The SoHo
Weekly News*, 25 August 1981.
Wortz, Melinda. "A Tropical Sleeper,"
ARTnews, Vol. 80, October 1981.
Lewison, David. "Nebulae of Color,"
Artweek, Vol. 12, 7 November 1981.
Wilson, Raymond L. "Small Metaphors,"
Artweek, Vol. 13, 1 May 1982.
Amos, Robert. Exhibition review,
Vanguard, Vol. 11, October–November
1982.
Timberman, Marcy. "Peter Shelton:
The Power of the Ordinary," *Artweek*,
Vol. 13, 27 November 1982.
Hicks, Mary. Exhibition review, *Images
and Issues*, Vol. 3, March–April 1983.

Wortz, Melinda. Exhibition review,
ARTnews, Vol. 82, May 1983.
Hackett, Regina. "Public Comments,"
Seattle Post-Intelligencer, 7 December
1983.
Schipper, Merle. "Plausible Dream," *Arts
and Architecture*, Vol. 3, 1984.
Pincus, Robert L. Exhibition review,
Los Angeles Times, 24 March 1984.
Glowen, Ron. "Morphology and
Material," *Artweek*, Vol. 15, 26 May
1984.
Gardner, Colin. "Art Scan," *Images and
Issues*, Vol. 5, July–August 1984.
Panza di Biumo, Giuseppe. "La Biennale,"
Domus, No. 652, July–August 1984.
Gendel, Milton. "Report from Venice,
Cultured Pearls at the Biennale," *Art in
America*, Vol. 72, September 1984.
Groot, Paul. "Closed Quotes," *Artforum*,
Vol. 23, September 1984.
Muchnic, Suzanne. "2 Sculptors Earn
Young Talent Prize," *Los Angeles
Times*, 24 June 1985.
Drohojowska, Hunter. "The Prize,"
Los Angeles Herald Examiner, 25 June
1985.
Cabutti, Lucio. "Uno Squardo Sugli Anni
Ottanta—Bologna E Altre Città," *Arte*,
Vol. 15, July–August 1985.
Wright, Patricia. "A house levitates," *The
Hampshire Gazette*, Springfield,
Massachusetts, 25 February 1986.
McKenna, Kristine. Exhibition review,
Los Angeles Times, 5 December 1986.
Conrad, Barnaby. "Peter Shelton,"
Horizon, Vol. 30, January–February
1987.
Mallinson, Constance. Exhibition review,
Art in America, Vol. 75, February 1987.
Knight, Christopher. " 'DEADMAN'
exhibit exudes life," *Los Angeles
Herald Examiner*, 26 February 1987.
Anderson, Michael. Exhibition review,
L.A. Weekly, 27 February 1987.
Bulmer, Marge. Exhibition review, *Reader*,
Los Angeles, 27 February 1987.
Wakefield, Sanford Suzan. "Shelton's
installation: 'light, blond and
buoyant,' " *The Outlook*, 27 February
1987.
Bijvoet, Marga. "Engaging the
Viewer/Participant," *Artweek*, Vol. 18,
28 February 1987.
Muchnic, Suzanne. "Exploring a House
that Floats," *Los Angeles Times*,
2 March 1987.

Gardner, Colin. Exhibition review,
Artforum, Vol. 25, May 1987.
Clothier, Peter. "Peter Shelton: Dwellings
in the Abstract," *ARTnews*, Vol. 86,
September 1987.
Levin, Kim. "Art Walk," *Village Voice*,
5 January 1988.
Brenson, Michael. "A Transient Art Form
With Staying Power," *The New York
Times*, 10 January 1988.
_____. "Fossilization Evolves Into A
Modern Metaphor," *The New York
Times*, 31 January 1988.

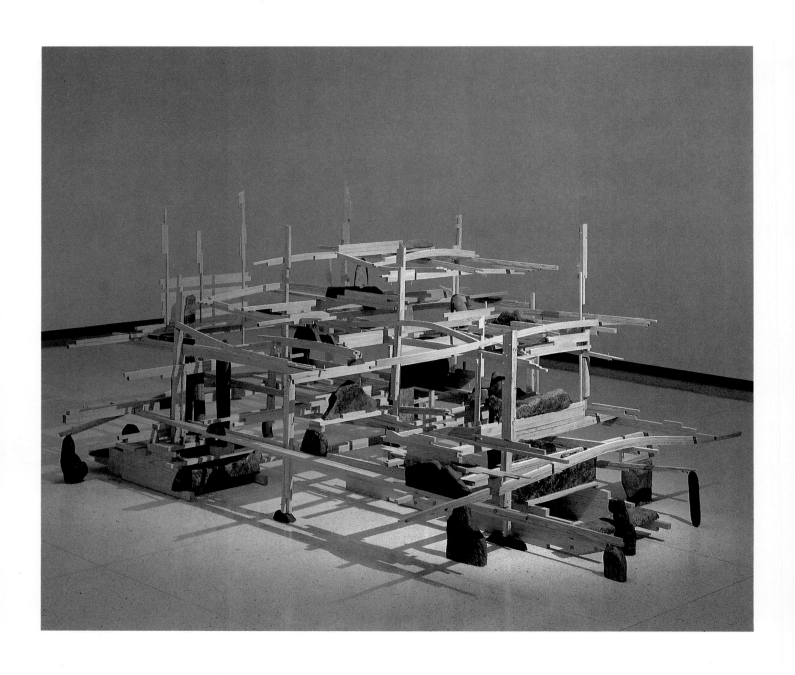

Michael Singer

The intricate constructions of wood and stone created by Michael Singer are like visual symphonies: individual elements, repeated and interwoven, coalesce into a harmonious whole. Evident in his indoor as well as his outdoor sculpture is a deep respect for nature. Natural materials take on new identity as components of metaphorical statements about nature's cyclical phenomena.

In 1971, Singer abandoned New York for a small town in Vermont to begin an exploration of and interaction with the natural environment that continues today. He began by observing his immediate surroundings, "researching" its innate rhythms, and trying to understand his place within the larger order of nature. Initially, his probing of nature resulted in sculptures that were unobtrusive, even recessive. A group of early pieces, the Situation Balance Series, evolved from his close observations of a beaver bog and its ecology. By leaning fallen trees over one another and using tree stumps as fulcrums, he sought to balance these elements to achieve a quality of weightlessness in his constructions. In speaking of this period of work, Singer has said:

> I cut trees so they would split as though a windfall caused such an occurrence. I painted many of the cut ends to conceal the whiteness of the raw wood. It became an absolute rule that there should be no sign of human presence. Part of my obsession about the absence of humans in these works came from the shame I felt about being part of a culture that has systematically destroyed the natural environment. . . . Eventually I accepted my role in the environment as more than observer, manager, researcher. I understood this role as an artist.[1]

Concurrent with his Vermont pieces of the early 1970s, Singer also explored the landscape of Long Island saltwater marshes, utilizing elements he found there in another group of environmental sculptures. He formed these by bundling phragmites—a marsh reed indigenous to this area—within a bamboo armature and placing these throughout the landscape. In the early and mid-1970s, he continued to work on various projects, known as the Ritual Series, in locations from Long Island to the Florida Everglades. In these, he favored such materials as bamboo, phragmites, and jute. Fragile and flexible, these outdoor installations suggested tenuously drawn lines afloat in space, their configurations subtly modified by changing conditions of light and wind. Increasingly, Singer took such variables into account as he formed and placed his pieces. Many of these works were intentionally designed to be short-lived and were located in secluded areas that were difficult to reach. The audience for them was limited to the hardy few who could find them. It was, however, the process of understanding the adaptation of a sculpture to a specific site that was most important to the artist.

The word "ritual" appears repeatedly in Singer's titles and the idea of ritual underlies all of his work. Initially, he chose the term for its poetic, equivocal quality, though its meaning has become more

Cloud Hands Ritual Series 1982–83
wood, stone
70¾ x 112 x 147
Collection Walker Art Center
Walker Special Purchase Fund, 1986

Cloud Hands Ritual Series 1982–83
(details)

First Gate Ritual Series 5/30/84
chalk, ink, collage on paper
50 x 38
Collection Rose Art Museum, Brandeis
University, Waltham, Massachusetts
Rose Purchase Fund

Situation Balance Series
Beaver Bog   1971–1973
hemlock trees, jute rope
Located, Marlboro, Vermont
(no longer extant)

Ritual Balance Series 12/75
phragmites, rocks, bricks, wood
144 x 192 x 192
Collection Australian National Gallery,
Canberra

Cloud Hands Ritual Series 80/81
pine, ash, rocks
57 x 171½ x 201
Collection Louisiana Museum of
Modern Art
Humlebaek, Denmark

First Gate Ritual Series 6/12/84
charcoal, ink wash, chalk, collage
on paper
47⅞ x 37⅝
Collection Solomon R. Guggenheim
Museum, New York
Anonymous Gift, 1986

Ritual Series/Syntax   1985
granite, fieldstone
120 x 144 x 60
Collection the artist

inclusive over the years. It came to symbolize the repetitive actions necessary to make his work, as well as his growing appreciation of nature through sustained viewing and experience. "Today, the role of ritual as it relates to my own work is that it allows one to be in contact with something that is not ordinarily in his life."[2]

In late 1975, with the first of his indoor works, *Ritual Balance Series 12/75,* Singer established a formal vocabulary that would serve as the basic syntax for subsequent pieces. Wooden strips and bunches of reed were used to define the horizontal and vertical axes of his new interior space-oriented sculptures. The forms in *Ritual Balance Series 12/75* strongly evoke natural phenomena: arching strips of wood suggest the flow of water over rocks; reed bundles are reminiscent of the upward thrust of trees; and the overall structure itself, carefully balanced on rocks and bricks, alludes to nature's tenuous but ever present equilibrium.

The spare architectural framework established by Singer in *Ritual Balance Series 12/75* has become increasingly complex in subsequent works. One of these, *Cloud Hands Ritual Series 1982–83* consists of subtly bowed ash strips laid over and under stones. The stones, selected for their form and color, are carefully altered to enhance their vertical and horizontal orientation. Earlier, Singer had used rocks mainly to demarcate a site; here they function both as supports and as objects to be supported. Within the overall rhythm and flow of *Cloud Hands Ritual Series 1982–83* they provide visual punctuation, serving as points of focus throughout the piece. Because of their durable character, they symbolize universal or geological time in Singer's art. Framed and sometimes partially concealed by the strips of wood, the stones become objects of contemplation. In contrast to the stones, the wood, being the more perishable material, and more easily shaped by the artist's intervention,

symbolizes historical time, says Singer. "The wood," he muses, "is the human response to the natural occurrence of the stone."

Much has been written of Singer's absorption with Eastern thought and aesthetics. While undeniable associations exist, such as the calligraphic quality of his sculpture, his formal vocabulary and philosophic approach were well defined by the time he first visited Japan in 1981. What he found there, he says, was a confirmation of many of his own attitudes. Whatever the sequence of events, Singer's work has decided affinities with the attitudes of Asian philosophy and art. The title of *Cloud Hands Ritual Series 1982–83* derives from a movement in *tai chi.* The wooden configurations throughout it suggest torii, the entrance gates to Shinto shrines. Indeed, the gate concept is integral to much of his work. As he observes, gates in Western culture are a means of keeping people out, while in Eastern thought, they define spiritual as well as physical passage. The open network of woven slats and stones that comprises a Singer sculpture invites the viewer to visually enter the piece, as it were, and to undertake a metaphorical journey of discovery.

Since 1980, the forms in Singer's sculptures have become increasingly solid. The once airy, linear components are now denser, more opaque shapes; weight-lessness has given way to a new emphasis on gravity. If his earlier works deal with issues of light and air—"the surface of our existence," then it can be said that his work of the 1980s makes reference to the earth and to its underlying structure. In addition to wood and rocks, Singer now uses slabs of slate and granite. Moreover, he often places his configurations on elevated platforms within three-sided structures that isolate the work from its surroundings and give it a frontal orientation.

Each of Singer's sculptures represents a clarification of an idea suggested in

preceding work. In *Ritual Series 1988/ Retellings*, he has again placed the work on a platform, but removed the enclosing walls and oriented the sculpture in such a way that the viewer must walk around to see it in its entirety. A dense wooden wall divides the work into two distinct areas: on one side is a structure composed of wood and "found" stones, on the other side is a reticulated rack. Interspersed throughout the latticed rack are examples of the elements that comprise the structure on the other side of the wall. The rack thus serves as an index to the forms of the other structure. It is as if Singer were presenting the basic elements of his visual language.

Because *Ritual Series 1988/Retellings* cannot be comprehended from a single vantage point, it must be viewed sequentially. This process of slow discovery can be likened to one's experiences in the landscape: it is only through sustained viewing that one comes to understand the intricacies of Singer's complex work.

D.H.

1. Quoted by Diane Waldman, in Solomon R. Guggenheim Museum, New York, *Michael Singer,* exh. cat., 1984, p. 17.
2. Unless otherwise noted, all quotations are from a conversation with the artist, 14 June 1987.

Ritual Series 1988/Retellings
wood, stone
72 x 150 x 360
Courtesy Sperone Westwater,
New York

Ritual Series 1988/Retellings (detail)

Michael Singer

1945
Born in Brooklyn, New York
1967
B.F.A., Cornell University, Ithaca, New York
1966
Yale University Norfolk Program, Norfolk, Connecticut
1968
Graduate study, Rutgers University, New Brunswick, New Jersey

Lives in Vermont

Selected Solo Exhibitions

1975
Sperone Westwater Fischer, New York
1976
Michael Singer/MATRIX 24, Wadsworth Atheneum, Hartford, Connecticut (brochure)
1977
Works by Michael Singer, Dalrymple Gallery, Smith College Museum of Art, Northampton, Massachusetts (catalogue)
Art Museum of South Texas, Corpus Christi
Michael Singer: Sculptures, Neuberger Museum, State University of New York, College at Purchase (brochure)
Greenburgh Nature Center, Scarsdale, New York
1978
Sperone Westwater Fischer, New York
1979
Portland Center for the Visual Arts, Oregon
School Of Visual Arts, New York
Michael Singer: MATRIX/BERKELEY 25, University Art Museum, University of California at Berkeley (brochure)
1980
Michael Singer: New Work, The Renaissance Society at The University of Chicago (brochure)
1981
Michael Singer: Ritual Series Photographs and Drawings, Galerie Zabriskie, Paris
Sperone Westwater Fischer, New York
1983
J. Walter Thompson Art Gallery, New York

1984
Michael Singer, Solomon R. Guggenheim Museum, New York (catalogue)
1986
Sperone Westwater, New York
1987
Michael Singer: Ritual Series Retellings, The Fine Arts Center Art Gallery, State University of New York at Stony Brook (catalogue)
Michael Singer: Ritual Series, Santa Barbara Contemporary Arts Forum (indoor); Santa Barbara Botanic Garden (outdoor), California (brochure)
1988
Sculptor and Architect: A Collaboration (with Michael McKinnell), Jewett Arts Center, Wellesley College Museum, Massachusetts

Selected Group Exhibitions

1970
Light and Environment, The Hudson River Museum, Yonkers, New York
1971
Ten Young Artists: Theodoron Awards, Solomon R. Guggenheim Museum, New York (catalogue)
1975
Museum Collection: Recent American Art, Solomon R. Guggenheim Museum, New York
1976
Ideas on Paper: 1970–1976, The Renaissance Society at The University of Chicago (brochure)
Nine Sculptors: On the Ground, In the Water, Off the Wall, Nassau County Museum of Fine Art, Roslyn Harbor, New York
1977
Documenta 6, Kassel, West Germany (catalogue)
1978
Drawings and Other Works on Paper, Sperone Westwater Fischer, New York
1979
1979 Biennial Exhibition, Whitney Museum of American Art, New York (catalogue)
Eight Sculptors, Albright-Knox Art Gallery, Buffalo, New York (catalogue)
1980
The Brown Invitational Exhibition, Bell Gallery, List Art Center, Brown University, Providence, Rhode Island

Skulptur in 20. Jahrhundert, Wenkenpark Riehen/Basel, Riehen, Switzerland (catalogue)
Drawings: The Pluralist Decade, 39th Venice Biennale; Institute of Contemporary Art, University of Pennsylvania, Philadelphia (catalogue)
Aycock/Holste/Singer, Fort Worth Art Museum, Texas
1981
Contemporary Americans: Museum Collection and Recent Acquisitions, Solomon R. Guggenheim Museum, New York
New Dimensions in Drawing, 1950–1980, The Aldrich Museum of Contemporary Art, Ridgefield, Connecticut (catalogue)
Mythos & Ritual in der Kunst der 70er Jahre, Kunsthaus Zurich, Switzerland (catalogue)
6 Decades: Collecting, Heckscher Museum, Huntington, New York
Variants: Drawings by Contemporary Sculptors, Sewall Art Gallery, Rice University, Houston (catalogue)
Natur-Skulptur, Kunstverein Stuttgart, West Germany (catalogue)
1982
Awards in the Visual Arts 1, National Museum of American Art, Washington, D.C. (catalogue)
Common Ground: Five Artists in the Florida Landscape, The John and Mable Ringling Museum of Art, Sarasota, Florida (catalogue)
Vermont Visions, Brattleboro Museum and Art Center, Vermont
1983
Merz, Nauman, Singer, Venezia, Sperone Westwater, New York
Recent Acquisitions, Solomon R. Guggenheim Museum, New York
1984
Large Drawings, Ezra and Cecile Zilkha Gallery, Center for the Arts, Wesleyan University, Middletown, Connecticut (catalogue)
Art on Paper, Weatherspoon Art Gallery, Greensboro, North Carolina
Drawings by Sculptors: Two Decades of Non-Objective Art in the Seagram Collection, Montreal Museum of Fine Arts (catalogue)
Primitivism in 20th Century Art: Affinity of the Tribal and the Modern, The Museum of Modern Art, New York (catalogue)

1985
Transformations in Sculpture: Four Decades of American and European Art, Solomon R. Guggenheim Museum, New York (catalogue)
1986
Sculpture/Aspen, The Aspen Art Museum, Colorado (catalogue)
1987
Nineteenth Bienal de São Paulo, Brazil (brochure)

Selected Bibliography

Russell, John. "Michael Singer Blends Nature with Art at a Show Here," *The New York Times*, 27 December 1975.

Kingsley, April. "Sculpture Gets New Energy," *The SoHo Weekly News*, 1 January 1976.

Grove, Nancy. Exhibition review, *Arts Magazine*, Vol. 50, February 1976.

Zucker, Barbara. Exhibition review, *ARTnews*, Vol. 75, February 1976.

Collins, Tara. "Michael Singer," *Arts Magazine*, Vol. 50, February 1976.

Foote, Nancy. Exhibition review, *Artforum*, Vol. 14, March 1976.

Gussow, Alan. "Let's Put the Land in Landscapes," *The New York Times*, 14 March 1976.

Forgey, Benjamin. "Art Is Where You Find It; Even in the Marshlands," *Washington Star*, 14 May 1976.

Kuspit, Donald B. Exhibition review, *Art in America*, Vol. 64, July–August 1976.

Ratcliff, Carter. Exhibition review, *Artforum*, Vol. 15, October 1976.

"Voll bespielt," *Der Spiegel*, 28 February 1977.

"The Younger Generation: A Cross Section," *Art in America*, Vol. 65, September–October 1977.

Baker, Elizabeth C. "Report from Kassel Documenta VI," *Art in America*, Vol. 65, September–October 1977.

Siegel, Jeanne. "Notes on the State of Outdoor Sculpture at Documenta 6," *Arts Magazine*, Vol. 52, November 1977.

Linker, Kate. "Michael Singer: A Position In, and On, Nature," *Arts Magazine*, Vol. 52, November 1977.

Shirey, David L. "A One-Sculpture Show at the Neuberger," *The New York Times*, 20 November 1977.

Forgey, Benjamin. "Art out of nature which is about nothing but nature," *Smithsonian*, Vol. 8, January 1978.

Maeve, Bee. "The Gallery Connection," *Ocular*, Vol. 3, Fall 1978.

Stevens, Mark. "Browser's Delights," *Newsweek*, Vol. 96, 13 November 1978.

Russell, John. "Michael Singer," *The New York Times*, 17 November 1978.

Sheffield, Margaret. "Natural Structures: Michael Singer's Sculpture and Drawings," *Artforum*, Vol. 17, February 1979.

Shapiro, Lindsay Stamm. Exhibition review, *Craft Horizons*, Vol. 39, February 1979.

Hughes, Robert. "Roundup at the Whitney Corral," *Time*, Vol. 115, 26 February 1979.

Zimmer, William. "Art for the Me Decade," *SoHo Weekly News*, 1 March 1979.

Edelman, Sharon. "Sculpture Show Weaves Art and Architecture," *Buffalo Evening News*, 20 March 1979.

Muller, Marion. "Biennial Fashions," *The New Leader*, 26 March 1979.

Whelan, Richard. "Discerning trends at the Whitney," *ARTnews*, Vol. 78, April 1979.

Huntington, Richard. "Albright Sculpture Exhibit a Treat," *Buffalo Courier Express*, 1 April 1979.

McCaslin, Walt. "Just getting there is half the fun," *Journal Herald*, Dayton, Ohio, 14 April 1979.

Saunders, Wade. "Art Inc.: The Whitney's 1979 Biennial," *Art in America*, Vol. 67, May–June 1979.

Albright, Thomas. "Disintegrating Sculpture and Relics," San Francisco Chronicle, 5 September 1979.

Boettger, Suzaan. Exhibition review, *Daily Californian*, Berkeley, Vol. 10, 21 September 1979.

_____. "Environments for Experience," *Oakland Artweek*, 22 September 1979.

Baker, Kenneth. "Hewing to the line: Sculpture for meditation," *The Boston Phoenix*, 12 February 1980.

Marvel, Bill. "Unlikely trio puts on stunning show," *Dallas Times Herald*, 28 November 1980.

Ayers, Robert. Exhibition review, *Artscribe*, No. 33, February 1982.

Phillips, Deborah C. Exhibition review, *ARTnews*, Vol. 81, March 1982.

Caldwell, John. "Contemporary Artists in Summit Exhibit," *The New York Times*, 28 March 1982.

Kuspit, Donald B. "Caves and Temples," *Art in America*, Vol. 70, April 1982.

Loft, Kurt. "Five Artists Find Common Ground in New Exhibit at Ringling Museum," *The Tampa Tribune*, 16 June 1982.

Ratcliff, Carter. "A Season in New York," *Art International*, Vol. 25, September–October 1982.

Feinberg, Jean E. "Michael Singer: Ritual Series," *Arts Magazine*, Vol. 57, June 1983.

Glueck, Grace. Exhibition review, *The New York Times*, 13 April 1984.

"Album: Michael Singer," *Arts Magazine*, Vol. 58, May 1984.

Bois, Yve-Alain. "La Pensée Sauvage," *Art in America*, Vol. 73, April 1985.

Phillips, Deborah. Exhibition review, *ARTnews*, Vol. 84, May 1985.

Brenson, Michael. "How Sculpture Freed Itself From the Past," *The New York Times*, 15 December 1985.

Phillips, Patricia C. Exhibition review, *Artforum*, Vol. 24, April 1986.

Taylor, Susan M. "'7 Moon Ritual Series 1985': A New Print by Michael Singer," *Print Collector's Newsletter*, Vol. 17, January–February 1987.

Lipson, Karin. "Singer: Serenity in Wood and Stone," *Newsday*, 27 March 1987.

Harrison, Helen A. "Viewing a Sculpture," *The New York Times*, 29 March 1987.

Hugo, Joan. "Astute Balancing Acts," *Artweek*, Vol. 18, 5 December 1987.

Robert Therrien

Robert Therrien has created an art of laconic resonance which is curiously at odds with the celebrated flash and glitter of the Los Angeles area in which he works. For the past decade, he has restricted himself to a limited lexicon of forms—including a steepled church, a snowman, a pointed arch, a keystone, a trumpet, a keyhole, a bent triangle—subtly varying their scale, proportions, dimensions, color, and materials in an effort to coax new implications from familiar subjects. Whether rendered in relief or as freestanding works, his sculptural silhouettes hover between representation and abstraction: while recognizable as specific images, they are so reductive and devoid of detail that they border on the nonobjective. Therrien's work is deceptive in its simplicity. Though his forms are minimal in their rendering, they are surprisingly complex in their impact, subtly shifting between two- and three-dimensionality, between object and image, between the familiar and the unfathomable, between muteness and eloquence.

Many of Therrien's forms are rooted in childhood memories: "I try to stay with themes or objects or sources I can trace back to my personal history. The further back I can trace something as being meaningful to me in some way or another . . . the more I am attracted to it."[1] He underscores this concern with the past by giving his surfaces a smooth, worn look, as if they had been polished by repeated handling.

There is something childlike in the simplified rendering of his images. Therrien still has a stencil book he owned as a child that taught young artists how to draw things with a combination of simple geometric forms, precisely the system he uses today. But Therrien's reductive tendency is also a legacy of his education in the early 1970s, when Minimalist aesthetics were dominant. This combination of Minimalist heritage and allusion to childhood is particularly pronounced in the image of the snowman, a motif that Therrien has been working with since the early 1980s. It first appealed to him because of its elemental nature. As he puts it: "The first sculpture that anyone ever made for decorative purposes might have had that structure—a pile of three rocks."[2] Just as importantly, however, Therrien remembers making snowmen as a child and imagines that this activity represents most children's first attempt at making sculpture.

Though his images are personal in origin, the process of reduction and simplification serves to render them universal. They expand beyond the realm of personal icons to become archetypal symbols. The snowman becomes a symbol for human presence. The steepled church, derived from the churches he remembers seeing as a boy in Chicago, becomes emblematic of the concept of church. Stripped of all detail save its irregular silhouette, the motif loses its specificity; it is a blank form to be filled by the viewer's own memories and reflections. Therrien tinkers endlessly with his images in an effort to come up with the "perfect" representation, the one that can absorb the widest variety of associations.

no title 1987
enamel on bronze
14¹¹⁄₁₆ x 11³⁄₈ x 2¾
Collection Walker Art Center
Gift of the artist, 1987

247

Keystone 1982
oil, wax on wood
14¾ x 27⅝ x 35½
The Eli and Edythe L. Broad Collection

(opposite)
no title 1986
mixed media on bronze
35 x 15 x 16
Collection Walker Art Center
Walker Special Purchase Fund, 1987

no title   1986
bronze
100 x 78½ x 12½
Collection Walker Art Center
Walker Special Purchase Fund, 1987

no title   1986
oil on canvas mounted on wood
96 x 64
Collection the artist
Courtesy Leo Castelli Gallery, New York

The tendency toward abstraction in Therrien's art is abetted by his working process, which includes rendering the same images in drawings, reliefs, and freestanding sculptures. Each medium has the capacity to alter the way a form is perceived and interpreted. One of the most compelling examples of this metamorphic potential is the bent triangle or cone. Conceived as a two-dimensional image, it originally represented a highly simplified perspective view of road or railroad track receding to a point on the horizon. Once Therrien transformed it into a relief, however, the illusion of perspectival recession became elusive; the shape had become an object and resembled a dunce's cap bent at the peak. Rendered as a freestanding sculpture, a bent cone, its earliest "life" as a receding road was completely lost; instead it looked surprisingly similar to another Therrien motif, the broad-based pitcher.

Therrien accentuates the metamorphic quality of his forms through his emphasis on silhouette. The three-dimensionality of his objects is often lost at a distance; as the work is approached and its full form becomes apparent, the viewer's initial reactions are subject to change. His relief in the form of a pointed arch swells out from the wall along a central axis that resembles the keel of a boat. This bulge is invisible from a distance and the pointed shape looks like a lancet window of a Gothic church. Only when the viewer gets relatively close to the piece does the association with a boat become apparent.

Such multivalence is essential to Therrien's art and becomes particularly potent when various works are installed together. Because he limits himself to combinations of a few basic geometric shapes, his diverse motifs can take on unexpected similarities. The keystone, for example, when elongated, resembles the bottom part of the coffin; the snowman, when reduced to a few inches in height, resembles the keyhole. The trumpet is an inverted and elongated version of the bent cone. Ideally, a single room will contain only three or four sculptures, leaving each piece relatively isolated and permitting it to resonate without undue interference in the viewer's consciousness. To enter such a room is to enter a peculiar universe in which objects are at once isolated yet interrelated, reticent yet filled with shadowy allusion.

P.W.B.

1. Quoted in Wade Saunders, "Talking Objects: Interviews with Ten Younger Sculptors," *Art in America,* vol. 73, November 1985, p. 136.
2. Ibid.

Robert Therrien

1947
Born in Chicago, Illinois

Lives in Los Angeles

Selected Solo Exhibitions

1975
Ruth S. Schaffner Gallery, Los Angeles
1977
Ruth S. Schaffner Gallery, Los Angeles
1978
Holly Solomon Gallery, New York
1979
Los Angeles Institute of Contemporary Art
1980
Otis Art Institute of the Parsons School of Design, Los Angeles
1982
Ace Gallery, Los Angeles
1984
The Museum of Contemporary Art, Los Angeles (catalogue)
1985
Ace Gallery, Los Angeles
1986
Leo Castelli Gallery, New York
1986–1987
Leo Castelli Gallery, New York (a series of three installations)
1987
Hoshour Gallery, Albuquerque, New Mexico (publication: collaboration with Robert Creeley and Michel Butor)
Konrad Fischer Gallery, Düsseldorf
1988
Leo Castelli Gallery, New York

Selected Group Exhibitions

1974
Young California, Ruth S. Schaffner Gallery, Los Angeles
1975
Nine Artists, Occidental College Gallery, Los Angeles
1977
Visual Incantations, Los Angeles Contemporary Exhibitions
Four Californians, La Jolla Museum of Contemporary Art, California (catalogue)
1980
Sculpture in California 1975–1980, San Diego Museum of Art (catalogue)

1982
  Quiet Commitment, Fisher Gallery, University of Southern California, Los Angeles
1984
  Awards in the Visual Arts 3, Southeastern Center for Contemporary Art, Winston-Salem, North Carolina (catalogue)
  Four Sculptors, Ace Gallery, Los Angeles
  Aperto 84, XLI Esposizione Internazionale d'Arte, La Biennale di Venezia (catalogue)
1985
  1985 Biennial Exhibition, Whitney Museum of American Art, New York (catalogue)
1986
  III Works, Hoshour Gallery, Albuquerque, New Mexico
  Major Acquisitions Since 1980: Selected Paintings and Sculpture, Whitney Museum of American Art, New York
  Abstraction, Hans Strelow Gallery, Düsseldorf
  Individuals: A Selected History of Contemporary Art, 1945–1986, The Museum of Contemporary Art, Los Angeles (catalogue)
1987
  Structure to Resemblance: Work by Eight American Sculptors, Albright-Knox Art Gallery, Buffalo, New York (catalogue)
  Leo Castelli y sus Artistas, Centro Cultural Arte Contemporaneo, Polanco, Mexico (catalogue)
  New Work by Kossuth, Morris, Oldenburg, Serra, Stella, Therrien, Leo Castelli Gallery, New York
  A Collecting Partnership: Highlights of California Art Since 1945, Newport Harbor Art Museum, Newport Beach, California (catalogue)
  small scale sculpture LARGE SCALE SCULPTURE, The Atlanta College of Art, Georgia (catalogue)
  Abstract Expressions: Recent Sculpture, Lannan Museum, Lake Worth, Florida (catalogue)
1988
  Inaugural Exhibition, Magasin 3, Stockholm (catalogue)

Selected Bibliography

Wilson, William. "Young California," *Los Angeles Times,* 22 March 1974.

Seldis, Henry. Exhibition review, *Los Angeles Times,* 19 December 1975.

Muchnic, Suzanne. "Four Abstractionists—Krebs, Spence, Therrien, Georgesco," *Artweek,* Vol. 8, 27 August 1977.

Marmer, Nancy. Exhibition review, *Los Angeles Times,* 21 October 1977.

Keeffe, Jeffrey. Exhibition review, *Artforum,* Vol. 16, January 1978.

Frank, Peter. Exhibition review, *Village Voice,* November 1978.

Olejarz, Harold. "Robert Therrien," *Arts Magazine,* Vol. 53, December 1978.

Muchnic, Suzanne. "Le Va, Therrien, Two Extremes," *Los Angeles Times,* 9 April 1980.

Drohojowska, Hunter. "Pick of the Week," *L.A. Weekly,* 12 March 1982.

Knight, Christopher. "Artist Robert Therrien Tackles Figure-Ground Relationships," *Los Angeles Herald Examiner,* 14 March 1982.

Hicks, Emily. "To Discourage Preconceptions," *Artweek,* Vol. 13, 27 March 1982.

Bebb, Bruce. "Therrien's Objects: Dialogue in Space," *The Contemporary,* Museum of Contemporary Art, Los Angeles, Spring 1984.

Muchnic, Suzanne. "Bigger is Better at Contemporary Museum," *Los Angeles Times,* 15 March 1984.

Delgado, Michael. "Pick of the Week," *L.A. Weekly,* 23 March 1984.

Drohojowska, Hunter. "One Person Shows 'In Context,'" *Los Angeles Herald Examiner,* 23 March 1984.

Knight, Christopher. "MOCA's Second Show Reveals a Museum in Search of a Future," *Los Angeles Herald Examiner,* 25 March 1984.

Wilson, William. "'In Context' The Subtext is Religion," *Los Angeles Times,* 22 April 1984.

Menzies, Neal. "Beautiful Mysterious Objects," *Artweek,* Vol. 15, 5 May 1984.

Panza di Biumo, Giuseppe. "La Biennale," *Domus,* No. 652, July–August 1984.

Mallinson, Constance. Exhibition review, *Art in America,* Vol. 72, October 1984.

Muchnic, Suzanne. Exhibition review, *Los Angeles Times,* 15 February 1985.

Drohojowska, Hunter. "Therrien at Flow Ace," *L.A. Weekly,* 8 March 1985.

Russell, John. "Art: Whitney Presents Its Biennial Exhibition," *The New York Times,* 22 March 1985.

Plagens, Peter. "Nine Biennial Notes," *Art in America,* Vol. 73, July 1985.

Cabutti, Lucio. "Uno Squardo Sugli Anni Ottanta—Bologna E Altre Città," *Arte,* Vol. 15, July–August 1985.

Saunders, Wade. "Talking Objects: Interviews with Ten Younger Sculptors," *Art in America,* Vol. 73, November 1985.

Raynor, Vivien. "Art: Robert Therrien Is Showing 28 Works," *The New York Times,* 6 June 1986.

Shields, Kathleen. "Albuquerque Letter," *Artspace,* Summer 1987.

Morgan, Robert C. "American Sculpture and the Search for a Referent," *Arts Magazine,* Vol. 62, November 1987.

Meg Webster

"I think of my work in an elemental way—circles, triangles, squares, earth, water, air, plants, wood."[1] From nature's basic elements, Meg Webster fashions pure, reductivist shapes, a 1980s synthesis of the Minimalist and Earthworks aesthetics of the previous two decades.

Webster began using natural materials in 1980. Working with sand, earth, and gravel, she created primal shapes that were derived from the inherent character of these substances. Discussing her working method she says, "It's not forcing the form, it's the form growing out of the material." Her earliest sculptures included a sand hummock resembling a hot cross bun with a cross incised into its surface, four symmetrical packed earth mounds, and a sharply defined square with a circular depression in its center made of gravel. Though the starkness of their shapes certainly recalled Minimalist sculpture, their sensuous texture and the precariousness of her materials represented quite a departure from the industrial objects, such as the hard-edged structures of metal, glass, and plastic favored by Donald Judd, Sol LeWitt, and other exemplars of purist geometry.

By 1982, Webster was making what she termed "living" sculptures. *Two Hills for Passage*, exhibited as part of her M.F.A. thesis exhibition at Yale University in 1983, consisted of two packed earth mounds from which grass grew, thanks to fluorescent lights suspended over the pieces. The piece required continued maintenance, and tending it was an important part of the artist's process. As the grass grew, the sculpture was in constant, though subtle, flux. Webster's work presented a paradox: grass grown indoors somehow seemed unnatural, but at the same time this anomalous sculpture heightened the viewer's awareness of natural processes.

By 1984, the scale of her sculpture had grown, allowing the viewer to move around inside the large works. For a 1984 installation at the Mattress Factory in Pittsburgh, Webster made three enclosures: a truncated cone of packed earth, a tall wooden rectangular box, and a pyramidal shape made of hay. These structures, which she has referred to as "pre-architecture," were both organic and architectonic. Each, with its unique form and texture, offered the viewer a distinctive physical as well as aesthetic experience. Unlike much Conceptual and Minimal Art, the appeal of Webster's work is primarily sensual, and in this regard she says, "I'd like the viewer's physical, sensory perception to be heightened."

The six-foot-high packed earth cone, large enough to accommodate a single visitor, was entered through a narrow vertical slot. The viewer was enclosed within a cool, curving, womblike wall that absorbed and muffled all sound. The musty earth also elicited an olfactory response. To enter the ten-foot-high wooden box, the viewer had to walk up a steep ramp. Inside, a pair of facing benches allowed just enough room for two visitors to sit knee to knee. Access to the third structure, the pyramid of hay, was by means of a ladder. Once again, aroma was a factor: the viewer was immediately confronted with the sweet smell as well as

Moss Bed 1988
peat moss, moss
12 x 94 x 72
Courtesy the artist and Barbara
Gladstone Gallery, New York

Hot Cross   1980
sand
12 x 36 x 36
Detail of installation at Leavenworth Street
San Francisco

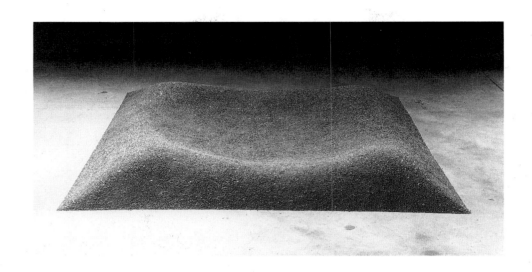

Four Square   1980
gravel
4 x 48 x 48
Detail of installation at Leavenworth Street
San Francisco

Four Mounds   1980
earth
36 x 36 overall
Detail of installation at Leavenworth Street
San Francisco

(top)
Untitled   1984
packed earth
72 x 72
Detail of installation at the Mattress Factory
Pittsburgh

(center)
Untitled   1984
wood
120 x 60 x 60
Detail of installation at the Mattress Factory
Pittsburgh

(bottom)
Untitled   1984
hay
132 x 132 x 132
Detail of installation at the Mattress Factory
Pittsburgh

Hollow 1984–1985
packed earth, perennials
25 ft diam., 90 ft long
Installation at the Nassau County
Museum of Fine Art, Roslyn Harbor,
New York

Two Hills for Passage   1983
packed earth, grass, fluorescent lights
48 x 84 diam. each
Detail of M.F.A. Thesis Exhibition, Yale
University, New Haven, Connecticut

Glen 1988
earth, steel, plants, fieldstone
142 x 504 x 510
Commissioned with Lannan Foundation
support for the exhibition
Sculpture Inside Outside
Courtesy the artist and Barbara
Gladstone Gallery, New York

Meg Webster constructing *Glen*

Glen 1988
earth, steel, plants, fieldstone
142 x 504 x 510
Commissioned with Lannan Foundation
support for the exhibition
Sculpture Inside Outside
Courtesy the artist and Barbara
Gladstone Gallery, New York

the rough texture of the hay. In contrast to the restrictive spaces of the wood and earth pieces, Webster's abstract hayloft provided room to recline for those who wanted to enjoy fully being in the piece. As an ensemble encountered in sequence, experiencing this trio of works was like participating in a performance. Their configuration directed the viewer to assume three basic postures: standing, sitting, and reclining. Within these organic environments, one became especially conscious of these actions.

For a 1987 installation at the Peekskill Gallery in New York, Webster created other interior pieces such as a cylinder of tightly packed earth, a rectangular moss bed, a spiral of sticks, and a triangular vertical steel structure which she filled to the rim with water. Each object animated its surroundings. More important perhaps, each seemed on the brink of dissolution. Would the packed earthen walls disintegrate, would the water overflow its container and flood the room? Such possibilities generated palpable tension.

Evident as her debt to Minimalist sculpture is, the sources of her imagery are equally in the Earth Art movement of the 1970s. The relationship of Webster's work to the Earth projects of Robert Smithson, Nancy Holt, Robert Morris, and Michael Heizer, whom Webster worked for in 1983, is most evident in her outdoor sculpture. Her first major outdoor commission was *Hollow*, a packed earth structure which she completed in 1985 on a site at the Nassau County Museum of Fine Art in Roslyn Harbor, New York. From the outside, *Hollow* resembled a large cylinder, gently tapering at the top and partially submerged in the ground. Architectural in scale—its interior walls measured ten feet high—it vaguely suggested the dwelling of some primitive society. From the exterior, its severe geometry and relatively uninflected surface gave no hint of what lay inside. The visitor approached the piece by walking down a ninety-foot long, gently

sloping dirt path. Given the length of the walkway and its gradual descent below ground, approaching and penetrating the work assumed ritual significance. Entering the sculpture through its slotlike portal, one encountered a lush interior—a great mass of brightly colored flowering plants.

Two rock seats were provided from which visitors could contemplate this rich profusion of plants. In the Nassau piece, as in her other outdoor works, Webster wants to intensify the viewer's perception of nature. "I'm not making nature, surely," she has said, "but I'm pulling [the viewer] to it." A viewer able to return several times over a period of months to this meditative environment could not help but focus on nature's processes. As the seasons changed, so did Webster's sculpture.

Glen (1988), another large-scale enclosed sculpture, commissioned for the Minneapolis Sculpture Garden, is Webster's most site-specific outdoor work to date. It consists of a circular depression carved into the slope that forms the eastern border of the Garden, and it was constructed in response to the surrounding landscape. Two triangular steel walls that serve as retaining walls form a strongly sculptural entryway to the interior of the piece and establish a ceremonial nexus between its interior and exterior. The terraced interior of *Glen* is planted with carefully arranged flowering plants. The overall effect is like a pointillist canvas: the varicolored flowers are like dots of paint that merge to create an allover surface. Webster's "canvas," however, is rich with texture and scent.

Webster's environmental structures are distinguished by their strong spatial quality and the way in which they enhance a sense of place by surrounding the viewer. For such earth structures, she prefers a circular form because it is primary and enclosing, like embracing arms. Webster has also characterized her planted works as womanly and sexual, not only because of their womblike quality and the

nurturing attention required to maintain them, but also because the works must be penetrated in order to be fully experienced. In spring, especially, the pieces are alive with possibility; procreation occurs over and over by insects pollenating the flowers, investing her work with the spirit of birth and regeneration.

Although Webster, by her own account, never actively participated in the rhetoric of Minimalism, she nevertheless believes her work "continues the dialogue" with its aesthetic principles. In expressing her relationship to Minimalism, she says, "I'm coming at it because of the geometry . . . and the need to present an idea or concept." By her use of organic materials such as earth, hay, and plants, in combination with the cool vocabulary of Minimalist sculpture, Webster creates sensuous animate forms.

D.H.

1. Unless otherwise noted, all quotations are from a conversation with the artist, 1 July 1987.

Meg Webster

1944
Born in San Francisco
1963–1964
Attended Mary Baldwin College,
Staunton, Virginia
1976
B.F.A., Old Dominion University,
Norfolk, Virginia
1983
M.F.A., Yale University, School of Art,
New Haven, Connecticut

Lives in New York

Selected Solo Exhibitions

1980
Leavenworth Street, San Francisco
1983
Two Walls: Meg Webster, Donald
Judd's exhibition space, Spring Street,
New York
1984
Installation: Meg Webster, Mattress
Factory, Pittsburgh
1986
Excerpts from Circuit, Art Galaxy,
New York
Meg Webster Part I, Forecast Gallery,
Peekskill, New York
1987
*Meg Webster Part II: Additions,
Subtractions, Reformations*, Forecast
Gallery, Peekskill, New York
1988
Barbara Gladstone Gallery, New York

Selected Group Exhibitions

1980
*From the Land: An Exhibition of
Earth-Related Works by Three
Northeastern Artists*, Brattleboro
Museum & Art Center, Vermont
(brochure)
1984
*Tom Bills   Hank De Ricco   Meg
Webster: Outdoor Installations,*
Nassau County Museum of Fine Art,
Roslyn Harbor, New York (catalogue)
1986
*Robert Gober, Nancy Shaver, Alan
Turner, Meg Webster*, Cable Gallery,
New York
Sculpture in Place, Borough of
Manhattan Community College, City
University of New York
1987
*Kindred Spirits: Nancy Brett, Shalvah
Segal, Meg Webster*, Hillwood Art
Gallery, C.W. Post Campus, Long
Island University, Brookville, New York
(catalogue)
The New Poverty, John Gibson Gallery,
New York (catalogue)
Paula Cooper Gallery, New York
1988
Media Post Media, Scott Hanson
Gallery, New York (catalogue)
Utopia Post Utopia, The Institute of
Contemporary Art, Boston (catalogue)
*Deer Manger, A Dress Pattern,
Farthest Sea Water, And A Signature*,
303 Gallery, New York

Selected Bibliography

Karson, Robin. "The Good Earth,"
Landscape Architecture, Vol. 74,
March–April 1984.
Lowry, Patricia. "Organic Installation
Compelling," *The Pittsburgh Press*,
27 September 1984.
Miller, Donald. "Artist's Environmental
Work Brings Viewers Back to Earth,"
Pittsburgh Post-Gazette, 13 October
1984.
Homisak, Bill. "Mud, Wood & Hay,"
Dialogue, Vol. 7, November–December
1984.
Baker, Kenneth. Exhibition review, *Art in
America*, Vol. 73, May 1985.
Braff, Phyllis. "Sculpture Inspired by the
Site," *The New York Times*, 12 May
1985.
Indiana, Gary. "The Hollow," *Village
Voice*, 15 October 1985.
_____. "United States," *Village Voice*,
20 May 1986.
Artner, Alan G. "What's New In Art?,"
Chicago Tribune, 29 June 1986.
Sugiura, Kunie. "From Abroad, News from
New York: Meg Webster, 'Circuit,'"
Bijutse Tee, Tokyo, September 1986.
Princenthal, Nancy. Exhibition review, *Art
in America*, Vol. 74, November 1986.
Zimmer, William. "A Minimalist's Look at
Nature Opens New Peekskill Gallery,"
The New York Times, 18 January 1987.

Steven Woodward

For the past several years, Steven Woodward has been intrigued with the idea of modifying architectural forms associated with solidity and permanence to create dynamic sculptures evocative of motion, change, and instability. "I want to take a straight line and curve it," he says, "to take something and turn it into something else, to show its potential or show that things aren't what we think they are."[1]

Woodward's interest in bringing together antithetical qualities may well reflect his early experience with blown glass while a student at St. Cloud State University. There he spun molten glass into sinuous forms that set and hardened as they cooled. He abandoned glass blowing in 1976 in favor of the greater freedom he found in making sculpture from a diversity of materials.

After moving to Minneapolis in 1980, Woodward worked intensely on a series of relief sculptures made from cameras. Typically, he would dismantle a camera and methodically file the parts until they were only a fraction of an inch deep. When the parts were reassembled, the camera appeared intact but was in fact almost completely flat. He then framed the camera in a flat plaster field painted a glossy white to resemble photographic paper. Wryly referring to these works as "dense-packs," Woodward says he was striving to compress an object into as compact a form as possible while still leaving it recognizable. They are also an expression of the sculptor's habitual distrust of photography; by flattening the camera, Woodward subjected it to the same distortion that a photograph imposes on three-dimensional objects.

In 1982 Woodward followed these camera sculptures with a large relief tableau of a kitchen. Here he cut a number of objects—a refrigerator, a microwave oven, wooden cabinets, a Formica counter and floor tile—in such a fashion that although the work is only an inch deep, it appears to recede into deep space according to classic Renaissance rules of perspective.

Woodward modified this idea in a 1983 work titled *Ship of Fools*. From one end, this twelve-foot-tall and twenty-seven-foot-long sculpture looked like an inverted roof gable, its peak resting on the floor. At the other end, the "roof" narrowed to a sharp point, resembling the prow of a boat. *Ship of Fools* extended into three dimensions the illusory perspective of the kitchen tableau in that, as Woodward puts it, it involved "taking an object and bringing it out to just a point."

The idea for *Ship of Fools* occurred to him one day when he was repairing the roof of a house, an occupation he had taken up to support himself after leaving college. The blue sky and sharp line of the ridge of the roof reminded him of a ship knifing through water. He constructed the piece as if he were building a gable—with the base of its triangle on the ground—and accentuated its rooflike quality by covering the surface with black tar paper. Only after he had finished constructing it did he roll the sculpture over: "It was literally turning architecture on its head," he recalls. What had been a stable, practical A-frame structure was

Another Conundrum 1988
wood, modified bitumen, steel, paint
130 x 102 x 374¾
Commissioned with Lannan Foundation support for the exhibition
Sculpture Inside Outside
Courtesy the artist

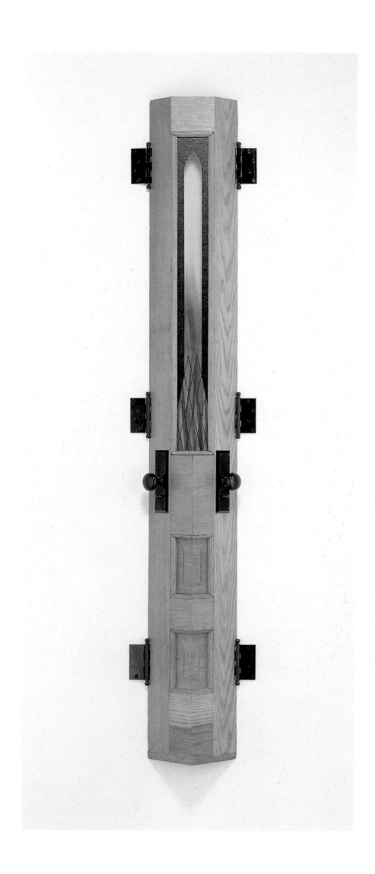

Christian Rockets   1984
wood, glass, paint, metal
84 x 17 x 5½
Collection John and Lee Mannillo

(opposite)
Untitled   1986
slate tiles, veneer on plywood
slate wall: 120 x 120 x ½
chair: 35¼ x 20 x 18½
Collection the artist

Obelique 1988
wood, metal, glass
110 x 23 x 25½
Collection Walker Art Center
Jerome Foundation Purchase Fund for
Emerging Artists, 1988

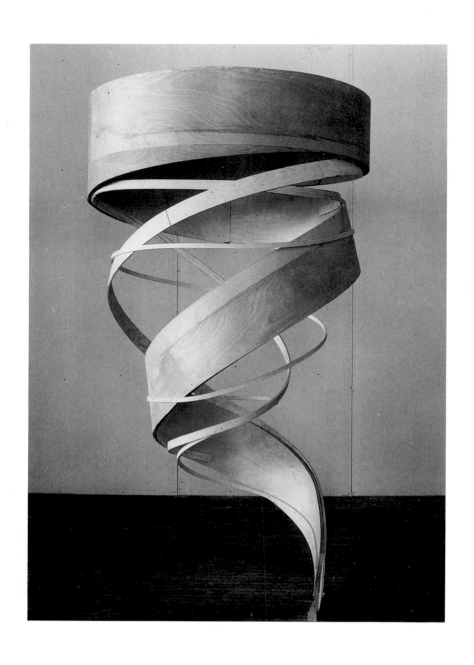

Two models for proposed
Walker Art Center lobby installation
wood
Courtesy the artist

Steven Woodward in his studio
constructing *Another Conundrum* and
installing the work on Walker Art Center
roof terrace

(opposite and overleaf)
Another Conundrum   1988
wood, modified bitumen, steel, paint
130 x 102 x 374¾
Commissioned with Lannan Foundation
support for the exhibition
Sculpture Inside Outside
Courtesy the artist

transformed into an unstable, purely aesthetic object. "By inverting it, suddenly I was making sculpture." To the artist, the union of the roof—"stationary, permanent, secure"—and the boat—"always moving, always at sea, always under threat of storm"—synthesized the seemingly opposing themes of stability and motion.

For the Walker Art Center's *Sculpture Inside Outside* exhibition, Woodward has created an outdoor version of *Ship of Fools*. The earlier sculpture had been held upright simply by propping it against a wall, but for the Walker commission, named *Another Conundrum*, Woodward added a gable to the side of the piece to serve as a supporting element. Perhaps the most important distinction between the two works results from the effect of sunlight on the interior of the hull. The raw pine gives off a golden light that floods out of the gable windows and provides a sharp contrast to the dense blackness of the roofing material.

Woodward spent 1984–1985 in residence at P.S. 1 in New York, a non-profit organization that awards studio and exhibition space to young artists. Reacting to the crush and congestion of the city, he began a series of sculptures characterized by a sense of compressed energy. These were made from doors that he sliced vertically and reassembled to form thin columns. In addition to compacting the doors into a small amount of space, sculptures such as *Christian Rockets* (1984), with its tall, narrow proportions and bilateral symmetry, underscore the essential relationship between doors and the human form.

Continuing his work with roofing materials, Woodward created an untitled work in 1986 made from slate tiles salvaged from the roof of P.S. 1. The piece is comprised of a small slate chair set before a wall of slate. The heaviness of the slate and the reduced proportions of the seat give the sculpture a remarkable sense of weight and density. Mindful of the fact

that P.S. 1 was originally a school, Woodward was also taking advantage of slate's associations with blackboards to make a sly allusion to the boredom of school days.

Returning to Minnesota in 1986, Woodward began experimenting with making curved, wavelike forms from boards and sheets of plywood, an idea that eventually led to his proposal for a twenty-five-foot-tall wooden tornado, reminiscent of Tatlin's *Monument to the Third International* turned on its head, for the lobby of Walker Art Center. Using a form common to the windblown Midwest, the sculpture would drop from the lobby skylight and descend in a series of sinuous curves to a point on the floor, its spiraling lines contrasting with the spare geometry of the architecture.[2]

In this and other recent works, Woodward says he is looking "to replicate nature in a semi-mechanical fashion." In *Obelique* (1988) he achieves this effect while fusing the door and whirlwind motifs. He has sliced a wooden door and wrapped it around a vertical bridge beam, creating a powerful sense of compression. The work is an effective demonstration of Woodward's continuing desire to transform familiar materials into unexpected forms.

P.W.B.

1. All quotations are from a conversation with the artist, 8 October 1987.
2. At the time of this printing, this project had not yet been realized.

Steven Woodward

1953
    Born in Little Falls, Minnesota
1976
    B.A., St. Cloud State University, St. Cloud, Minnesota

    Lives in Minneapolis

Solo Exhibitions

1985
    Bim Bam Botterham, The Stokker Stikker Gallery, New York (with Lily van der Stokker)

Selected Group Exhibitions

1984
    Annual Juried Exhibition, The Queens Museum, Flushing, New York (catalogue)
    National and International Studio Program Artists, The Clocktower, The Institute for Art and Urban Resources, Inc., New York (catalogue)
    Sculpture Chicago '84, South Loop Planning Board, Chicago (catalogue)
    Four Sculptors, School of Associated Arts, St. Paul
    Five Jerome Artists, Minneapolis College of Art and Design (catalogue)
1985
    Public Art, The Tilted Arc Controversy, Storefront for Art and Architecture, New York
    National and International Studio Program Artists, The Clocktower, The Institute for Art and Urban Resources, Inc., New York (catalogue)

Selected Bibliography

Lyon, Christopher. "Profiles of 'Sculpture Chicago '84' artists," *Chicago Sun-Times*, 26 August 1984.

Brotman, Barbara. "Sculptors let people decide what's art," *Chicago Tribune*, 27 September 1984.

Shipp, E.R. "Chicago Watches as 10 Sculptures Grow," *The New York Times*, 2 October 1984.

Busk, Celeste. "Sculptures on trek over to River City," *Chicago Sun-Times*, 3 February 1985.

Preston, Malcom. "A juried exhibition at the Queens Museum," *Newsday*, 25 June 1985.

Acknowledgments

The preparation of the exhibition *Sculpture Inside Outside* and this accompanying volume involved the participation of many individuals and institutions. Of paramount importance was the cooperation of the seventeen artists whose work is represented in the exhibition and publication. Their patience and assistance during numerous studio visits and discussions with those of us involved in the selection process provided valuable insights into the highly diverse creative processes that have engendered their imagery. Without their wholehearted support this project could not have been realized. Special thanks are due the many individuals and institutions who graciously allowed us to borrow their works of art. To part even briefly with sizable sculptures is no small inconvenience, but nevertheless there were few refusals of our requests for loans. It is a pleasure to credit the generosity of all these lenders, listed on the opposite page.

I especially want to acknowledge the cooperation of the galleries representing the artists whose works appear in *Sculpture Inside Outside.* Their staffs were extremely helpful in providing important information about these artists and in helping to locate works by them in various collections.

Determining the structure of this exhibition and publication involved considerable review and discussion among Walker Art Center staff members. Contributing substantially to this effort were Donna Harkavy and Peter Boswell who, as Curatorial Associates for *Sculpture Inside Outside,* were involved in virtually all of its aspects during its two years of development. As part of the effort to gain information about important stylistic currents in recent American sculpture, they visited studios, galleries, and museum exhibitions throughout the country. During the course of preparing this exhibition, they were in frequent communication with the artists represented and contributed the essays on individual artists to this volume. Mark Kramer, Coordinator of Exhibition Installations, provided invaluable services overseeing and coordinating the installation of the commissioned works in the Minneapolis Sculpture Garden; the installation of the interior section of *Sculpture Inside Outside* in Walker Art Center's galleries was skillfully accomplished by our technical crew under the direction of Stephen Ecklund, Exhibition Crew Manager. On page 288, other staff contributions to the exhibition are recognized.

MF

276

Lenders to the Exhibition

Phoebe Adams
Mr. and Mrs. Harry W. Anderson
Barry and Gail Berkus
Art Berliner and Anita Ettinger
Lois and Bruce Berry
Steven and Cecile Biltekoff
Blum Helman Gallery, New York
The Eli and Edythe L. Broad Collection
The Brooklyn Museum, New York
Laura L. Carpenter
Mr. and Mrs. Armand J. Castellani
Leo Castelli Gallery, New York
Cava Gallery, Philadelphia
Eileen and Michael Cohen
Dallas Museum of Art
Elaine Werner Dannheisser
Susan and Leland David Collection
Mr. and Mrs. Julius E. Davis
Marne and Jim DeSilva
Michael Egan
Marjorie and Michael Fasman
Dorace M. Fichtenbaum
First Bank System, Inc., Minneapolis
Robert F. Fogelman
Stanley and Pauline Foster
Peter Freeman
Gagosian Gallery, New York
Tony Ganz
Germans van Eck Gallery, New York
Barbara Gladstone Gallery, New York
Robert Gober
Greenberg Gallery, St. Louis
Solomon R. Guggenheim Museum, New York
Brower Hatcher
Jene Highstein
Hirshhorn Museum and Sculpture Garden,
    Smithsonian Institution, Washington, D.C.
Anne and William J. Hokin
Donald and Judy Kay
Robert M. Kaye
Jin Soo Kim
Jane and Leonard Korman
L.A. Louver Gallery, Inc., Venice, California
Mr. Raymond J. Learsy
Dr. Harold and Elaine L. Levin
Donald Lipski

Sylvia Lipski
Robert Lobe
Mr. and Mrs. William J. Magavern II
John and Lee Mannillo
Curt Marcus Gallery, New York
Walter Martin
Drs. Stephen and Linda McMurray
Michael Klein, Inc., New York
The Minneapolis Institute of Arts
Museum of Contemporary Art, Chicago
Mr. and Mrs. Raymond D. Nasher
The Oliver-Hoffmann Collection
John Newman
P.P.O.W, New York
The Pennsylvania Academy of the
    Fine Arts, Philadelphia
Penny Pilkington
The Progressive Corporation
Martin Puryear
Dr. Beverly R. Rollnick
Rose Art Museum, Brandeis University,
    Waltham, Massachusetts
Dr. and Mrs. Louis E. Rossman
Phil Schrager
Judith Shea
Jeffrey T. and Kay D. Shea
Peter Shelton
Mr. and Mrs. Joseph Samuels Sinclair
Michael Singer
Martin Sklar
Joan Sonnabend
Sperone Westwater, New York
City of Stamford, Connecticut,
    Public Art Program
Storm King Art Center,
    Mountainville, New York
Robert Therrien
Walker Art Center
Meg Webster
Penny and Mike Winton
Steven Woodward
Donald Young Gallery, Chicago
Four private collections

Selected Bibliography

Exhibition Catalogues

Alloway, Lawrence. *American Pop Art*. New York: Whitney Museum of American Art, 1974.

Anti-illusion: Procedures/Materials. New York: Whitney Museum of American Art, 1969.

Arte Povera, Antiform: Sculptures 1966–1969. Bordeaux: Centre d'Arts Plastiques Contemporains, 1982.

Artpark: The Program in Visual Arts. Lewiston, New York: Artpark, 1976–1984.

Auping, Michael. *Common Ground: Five Artists in the Florida Landscape*. Sarasota, Florida: John and Mable Ringling Museum of Art, 1982.

Beardsley, John. *Probing the Earth: Contemporary Land Projects*. Washington, D.C.: Hirshhorn Museum and Sculpture Garden, 1977.

Beyond the Plane: American Constructions, 1930–1965. Trenton, New Jersey: New Jersey State Museum, 1983.

Bussmann, Klaus and Kasper König. *Skulptur Projekte in Münster 1987*. Cologne: DuMont Buchverlag, 1987.

Carl Andre, Robert Barry, Daniel Buren, Jan Dibbets. . . . New York: Seth Siegelaub, 1969.

Carnegie International. Pittsburgh: The Carnegie Museum of Art, 1985.

Celant, Germano. *Conceptual Art, Arte Povera, Land-Art*. Turin: Galleria Civica d'Arte Moderna, 1970.

————. *The Knot Arte Povera at P.S. 1*. New York: P.S. 1, 1985.

Contemporary American Sculpture: Selection 1. New York: Whitney Museum of American Art, 1966.

Contemporary American Sculpture: Selection 2. New York: Whitney Museum of American Art, 1969.

Content: A Contemporary Focus 1974–1984. Washington, D.C.: Hirshhorn Museum and Sculpture Garden, 1984.

Dabrowski, Magdalena. *Contrasts of Form: Geometric Abstract Art 1910–1980*. New York: The Museum of Modern Art, 1985.

Develing, Enno. *Minimal Art*. Gravenhage: Haags Gemeentemuseum, 1968.

Documenta III, IV, V, VI, VII, VIII. Kassel, Germany: 1964, 1968, 1972, 1977, 1982, 1987.

Door Beeldhouwers Gemaakt/Made by Sculptors. Amsterdam: Stedelijk Museum, 1978.

Earth Art. Ithaca, New York: Andrew Dickson White Museum, Cornell University, 1970.

Earthworks: Land Reclamation as Sculpture. Seattle: Seattle Art Museum, 1979.

Eight Sculptors: The Ambiguous Image. Minneapolis: Walker Art Center, 1966.

Elsen, Albert E. *The Partial Figure in Modern Sculpture: From Rodin to 1969*. Baltimore: The Baltimore Museum of Art, 1969.

Europe in the Seventies: Aspects of Recent Art. Chicago: The Art Institute of Chicago, 1977.

Figures/Environments. Minneapolis: Walker Art Center, 1970.

Five Artists at NOAA: A Casebook on Art in Public Places. Seattle: Real Comet Press, 1985.

Fourteen Sculptors: The Industrial Edge. Minneapolis: Walker Art Center, 1969.

Fox, Howard N. *Metaphor: New Projects by Contemporary Sculptors*. Washington D.C.: Hirshhorn Museum and Sculpture Garden, 1982.

Geldzahler, Henry. *New York Painting and Sculpture 1940–1970*. New York: The Metropolitan Museum of Art, 1969.

Glozer, Laszlo. *Westkunst: Zeitgenössische Kunst seit 1939.* Cologne: Museen der Stadt Köln, 1981.

Guggenheim International Exhibition 1967: Sculpture from Twenty Nations. New York: Solomon R. Guggenheim Museum, 1967.

Haskell, Barbara. *Blam! The Explosion of Pop, Minimalism and Performance 1958–1964.* New York: Whitney Museum of American Art, 1984.

Hulten, Pontus. *Futurismo e Futurismi.* Venice: Palazzo Grassi, 1986.

_____. *The Machine as Seen at the End of the Mechanical Age.* New York: The Museum of Modern Art, 1968.

Jonge Engelse Beeldhouwers. Amsterdam: Stedelijk Museum, 1967.

Lippard, Lucy R. *Soft Sculpture.* New York: American Federation of Arts, 1968.

Live in your Head: When Attitudes Become Form: Works-Concepts-Processes-Situations-Information. Bern: Kunsthalle, 1969.

McShine, Kynaston. *Information.* New York: The Museum of Modern Art, 1970.

_____. *An International Survey of Recent Painting and Sculpture.* New York: The Museum of Modern Art, 1984.

Marshall, Richard. *Developments in Recent Sculpture.* New York: Whitney Museum of American Art, 1981.

Monumenta: A Biennial Exhibition of Outdoor Sculpture. Newport, Rhode Island: Newport County Arts Council, 1974.

Nash, Steven A., ed. *A Century of Modern Sculpture: The Patsy and Raymond Nasher Collection.* New York: Rizzoli in conjunction with Dallas Museum of Art, 1987.

The Nathan Manilow Sculpture Park. University Park, Illinois: Governors State University Foundation, 1987.

Natural Forms and Forces: Abstract Images in American Sculpture. Cambridge, Massachusetts: MIT Committee on the Visual Arts, 1986.

9 Artists/9 Spaces. Minneapolis: Minnesota State Arts Council and Walker Art Center, 1970.

The Object Transformed. New York: The Museum of Modern Art, 1966.

Phillips, Lisa. *The Third Dimension: Sculpture of the New York School.* New York: Whitney Museum of American Art, 1984.

Pier + Ocean: Construction in the Art of the Seventies. London: Hayward Gallery, 1980.

Plous, Phyllis. *7 + 5 Sculptors in the 1950s.* Santa Barbara: University Art Museum, University of California, Santa Barbara, 1976.

Primary Structures: Younger American and British Sculptors. New York: The Jewish Museum, 1966.

Qu'est-ce Que la Sculpture Moderne?. Paris: Musée National d'Art Moderne, Centre Georges Pompidou, 1981.

A Quiet Revolution: British Sculpture since 1965. Chicago: Museum of Contemporary Art, 1987.

Quintessence: The Alternative Spaces Residency Program. Nos. 1–6. Dayton, Ohio: City Beautiful Council, Wright State University Department of Art and Art History, 1978–1984.

Recent American Sculpture. New York: The Jewish Museum, 1964.

Rogers-Lafferty, Sarah. *Body & Soul: Aspects of Recent Figurative Sculpture.* Cincinnati: Contemporary Arts Center, 1985.

Rowell, Margit. *The Planar Dimension: Europe, 1912–1932.* New York: Solomon R. Guggenheim Museum, 1979.

Rubin, William, ed. *Primitivism in 20th Century Art: Affinity of the Tribal and the Modern.* New York: The Museum of Modern Art, 1984.

Scale and Environment: 10 Sculptors. Minneapolis: Walker Art Center, 1977.

Sculpture: A Generation of Innovation. Chicago: The Art Institute of Chicago, 1967.

Sculpture Made in Place: Dill, Ginnever, Madsen. Minneapolis: Walker Art Center, 1976.

Sculpture Off the Pedestal. Grand Rapids, Michigan: Women's Committee of the Grand Rapids Art Museum, 1973.

The Sculpture Show: Fifty Sculptors at the Serpentine and the South Bank. London: Hayward Gallery and Serpentine Gallery, 1983.

Sculpture: The Tradition in Steel. Roslyn Harbor, New York: Nassau County Museum of Fine Art, 1983.

Seitz, William C. *The Art of Assemblage.* New York: The Museum of Modern Art, 1961.

Selz, Peter. *Directions in Kinetic Sculpture.*
Berkeley, California: University Art
Museum, University of California at
Berkeley, 1966.

Seven Sculptors. Philadelphia: Institute of
Contemporary Art—University of
Pennsylvania, 1965.

Sitings. La Jolla, California: La Jolla
Museum of Contemporary Art, 1986.

Six in Bronze. Williamstown,
Massachusetts: Williams College
Museum of Art, 1983.

'60 '80 Attitudes, Concepts, Images.
Amsterdam: Stedelijk Museum, 1982.

SkulpturSein. Düsseldorf: Städtische
Kunsthalle, 1986.

*Sonsbeek 86: Internationale Beelden
Tentoonstelling International
Sculpture Exhibition.* Utrecht,
The Netherlands: Veen Reflex, 1986.

Space Invaders. Regina, Saskatchewan:
MacKenzie Art Gallery, University of
Regina, 1985.

*Structure to Resemblance: Work by Eight
American Sculptors.* Buffalo,
New York: Albright-Knox Art Gallery,
1987.

Tableaux: Nine Contemporary Sculptors.
Cincinnati: Contemporary Arts Center,
1982.

Tuchman, Maurice. *American Sculpture of
the Sixties.* Los Angeles: Los Angeles
County Museum of Art, 1967.

20 American Artists: Sculpture 1982.
San Francisco: San Francisco Museum
of Modern Art, 1982.

*Two Hundred Years of American
Sculpture.* New York: Whitney
Museum of American Art, 1976.

*Urban Encounters: Art, Architecture,
Audience.* Philadelphia: Institute of
Contemporary Art—University of
Pennsylvania, 1980.

A View of a Decade. Chicago: Museum of
Contemporary Art, 1977.

Waldman, Diane. *Transformations in
Sculpture: Four Decades of American
and European Art.* New York: Solomon
R. Guggenheim Museum, 1985.

Wallis, Brian. *Damaged Goods: Desire and
the Economy of the Object.* New York:
The New Museum of Contemporary
Art, 1986.

Works for New Spaces. Minneapolis:
Walker Art Center, 1971.

Books

Ashton, Dore. *American Art since 1945.*
New York: Oxford University Press,
1982.

_____. *Modern American Sculpture.*
New York: Harry N. Abrams, 1968.

Battcock, Gregory, ed. *Idea Art.* New York:
Dutton, 1973.

_____, ed. *Minimal Art: A Critical
Anthology.* New York: Dutton, 1968.

Beardsley, John. *Art in Public Places.*
Washington D.C.: Partners for Livable
Places, 1981.

_____. *Earthworks and Beyond:
Contemporary Art in the Landscape.*
New York: Abbeville Press, 1984.

_____. *A Landscape for Modern
Sculpture: Storm King Art Center.*
New York: Abbeville Press, 1985.

Burnham, Jack. *Beyond Modern
Sculpture: The Effects of Science and
Technology on the Sculpture of This
Century.* New York: George Braziller,
1968.

_____. *Great Western Salt Works: Essays
on the Meaning of Post-Formalist Art.*
New York: George Braziller, 1974.

Calas, Nicolas and Elena. *Icons and Images
of the Sixties.* New York: Dutton, 1971.

Celant, Germano. *Ambiente/Arte dal
Futurismo alla Body Art.* Venice:
Alfieri, 1977.

_____. *Art Povera.* New York: Praeger,
1969.

Craven, Wayne. *Sculpture in America.*
New York: Thomas Y. Crowell, 1968.

Cummings, Paul. *Artists in Their Own
Words.* New York: St. Martin's Press,
1979.

Davies, Peter and Tony Knipe, eds. *A Sense
of Place: Sculpture in Landscape.* Tyne
and Wear, England: Ceolfrith Press,
1984.

Elsen, Albert E. *Origins of Modern
Sculpture: Pioneers and Premises.*
New York: George Braziller, 1974.

Friedman, Martin, ed. *Twentieth Century
Sculpture Walker Art Center:
Selections from the Collection.*
Minneapolis: Walker Art Center, 1969.

Giedion-Welcker, Carola. *Contemporary
Sculpture: An Evolution in Volume and
Space.* New York: George Wittenborn
Inc., 1960.

Goldwater, Robert. *What is Modern
Sculpture?.* New York: The Museum of
Modern Art, 1969.

Greenberg, Clement. *Art and Culture: Critical Essays.* Boston: Beacon Press, 1961.

Hammacher, Abraham Marie. *The Evolution of Modern Sculpture: Tradition and Innovation.* New York: Harry N. Abrams, 1969.

Harris, Stacy Paleologos, ed. *Insights/On Sites: Perspectives on Art in Public Places.* Washington, D.C.: Partners for Livable Places, 1984.

Herbert, Robert, ed. *Modern Artists on Art.* Englewood Cliffs, New Jersey: Prentice-Hall, 1964.

Hunter, Sam. *American Art of the 20th Century.* New York: Harry N. Abrams, 1973.

Hunter, Sam and John Jacobus. *Modern Art From Post-Impressionism to the Present: Painting, Sculpture, Architecture.* New York: Harry N. Abrams, 1976.

Johnson, Ellen H., ed. *American Artists on Art from 1940 to 1980.* New York: Harper & Row, 1982.

_____. *Modern Art and the Object.* New York: Harper & Row, 1976.

Krauss, Rosalind E. *The Originality of the Avant-Garde and Other Modernist Myths.* Cambridge, Massachusetts: MIT Press, 1985.

_____. *Passages in Modern Sculpture.* Cambridge, Massachusetts: MIT Press, 1977.

Kultermann, Udo. *The New Sculpture: Environments and Assemblages.* New York: Praeger, 1968.

Licht, Fred. *A History of Western Sculpture: 19th & 20th Centuries.* Greenwich, Connecticut: New York Graphic Society, 1967.

Lippard, Lucy R. *Overlay: Contemporary Directions in the Visual Arts.* New York: Pantheon Books, 1983.

_____. *Six Years: The Dematerialization of the Art Object from 1966 to 1972.* New York: Praeger, 1973.

Lodder, Christina. *Russian Constructivism.* New Haven and London: Yale University Press, 1983.

Lucie-Smith, Edward. *Art Now: From Abstract Expressionism to Superrealism.* New York: William Morrow and Company, 1977.

_____. *Late Modern: The Visual Arts since 1945.* New York: Praeger, 1969.

Maillard, Robert, ed. *Dictionary of Modern Sculpture.* New York: Tudor Publishing Company, 1962.

Meilach, Dona Z. *Soft Sculpture and Other Soft Art Forms.* New York: Crown, 1974.

Meyer, Ursula. *Conceptual Art.* New York: Dutton, 1972.

Müller, Gregoire. *The New Avant-Garde: Issues for the Art of the Seventies.* New York: Praeger, 1972.

Rickey, George. *Constructivism: Origins and Evolution.* New York: George Braziller, 1967.

Rose, Barbara. *American Art Since 1900.* New York: Praeger, 1975.

_____. *Readings in American Art, 1900–1975.* New York: Holt, Rinehart & Winston, 1975.

Rosenberg, Harold. *The Anxious Object: Art Today and its Audience.* New York: Horizon Press, 1964.

_____. *Art on the Edge: Creators and Situations.* New York: MacMillan, 1975.

_____. *Artworks and Packages.* New York: Horizon Press, 1969.

Rubin, William. *Dada and Surrealist Art.* New York: Harry N. Abrams, 1968.

Russell, John and Suzi Gablik. *Pop Art Redefined.* New York: Praeger, 1969.

Sculptures in the Rijksmuseum Kröller-Müller. Otterlo, The Netherlands: Rijksmuseum Kröller-Müller, 1981.

Seitz, William C., ed. "Contemporary Sculpture," *Arts Yearbook 8.* New York: The Art Digest, Inc., 1965.

Selz, Jean. *Modern Sculpture: Origins and Evolution.* New York: George Braziller, 1963.

Seuphor, Michel. *The Sculpture of This Century: Dictionary of Modern Sculpture.* New York: George Braziller, 1960.

Sonfist, Alan, ed. *Art in the Land: A Critical Anthology of Environmental Art.* New York: Dutton, 1983.

Trier, Eduard. *Form and Space: Sculpture of the Twentieth Century.* New York: Praeger, 1968.

Tucker, William. *Early Modern Sculpture.* New York: Oxford University Press, 1974.

_____. *The Language of Sculpture.* London: Thames & Hudson, 1974.

Index

Page numbers in bold type indicate illustrations. Works of art are listed in alphabetical order following the artist's name.

Reproduction Credits

ART on FILE/Colleen Chartier   66 (top), 228 (top left; top right)
Christian Baur, courtesy Max Protetch Gallery, New York   67
Gregory Benson   78
Courtesy Andrea Blum   71
Blum Helman Gallery, New York   158
Grace Borgenicht Gallery, New York 90 (right)
Ed Brandon, courtesty Van Voorst Van Beest Gallery, The Hague   144
Joan Broderick, courtesy Lawrence Oliver Gallery, Philadelphia   82, 83
Rudolph Burckhardt, courtesy Leo Castelli Gallery, New York   25, 39
Geoffrey Clements, courtesy Paula Cooper Gallery, New York   101
The Cleveland Museum of Art 52 (bottom)
Anthony Cosentino   113
Dallas Museum of Art   195
D. James Dee, courtesy Paula Cooper Gallery, New York   96, 100, 102
D. James Dee, courtesy Metro Pictures, New York   30
M. Lee Fatherree   76
M. Lee Fatherree, courtesy John Berggruen, San Francisco   91
Allan Finkelman, courtesy Sidney Janis Gallery, New York   20 (bottom)
Robert Gober, courtesy Paula Cooper Gallery, New York   98
Solomon R. Guggenheim Museum, New York   79
Glenn Halvorson for Walker Art Center cover, frontispiece, 6, 18, 32, 48, 60, 81, 85, 88, 90 (left), 99, 106, 109, 111, 114, 115, 116 (top right), 117, 123, 127, 129, 130, 134, 136, 138, 139, 142, 153, 156, 161, 162, 166, 174, 180, 183, 188, 193 (top), 196, 198, 199, 202, 204, 206, 208, 209, 211, 225, 226, 229, 232, 234, 246, 248, 250, 254, 261, 263, 266, 268, 269, 270, 271, 272, 273, 274

Courtesy Brower Hatcher   110
Biff Henrich   159, 207
Bruce C. Jones, courtesy Leo Castelli Gallery, New York   69
Michael Klein, Inc., New York 122 (top), 126
Kouros Gallery, New York   51
Peter Latner for Walker Art Center 84 (center; bottom), 116 (bottom left; bottom right), 128, 152 (center left; bottom left; top right; bottom right), 210, 228 (bottom left; bottom right), 262
Robert Lobe   160
Richard Long   56
Curt Marcus Gallery, New York   92, 93
Marlborough Gallery, New York 21, 26
Daniel J. Martinez, courtesy Michael Klein, Inc., New York   120, 124
McIntosh/Drysdale Gallery, Washington, D.C.   194
The Metropolitan Museum of Art, courtesy Muriel Kallis Newman   55
Robert Miller Gallery, New York   53
The Minneapolis Institute of Arts   28
Courtesy Mary Miss   62
Andrew Moore, courtesy Paula Cooper Gallery, New York   103
Museum für Moderne Kunst, Frankfurt   42
The Museum of Modern Art, New York   34, 35, 36, 37, 52 (top)
William Nettles, courtesy L.A. Louver, Gallery, Inc., Venice, California   224
Courtesy John Newman   177
Bill Orcutt, courtesty Curt Marcus Gallery, New York   205, 212
Douglas M. Parker Studio 190, 249, 251
Pelka/Noble   176, 178, 179, 182, 184
Philadelphia Museum of Art 50 (center)

Quicksilver   108
Adam Reich, courtesy P.P.O.W, New York   168, 171
Adam Reich, courtesy Holly Solomon Gallery, New York   66 (bottom)
Estate of Theodore Roszak   50 (top)
Barbara Runnette, courtesy Michael Klein, Inc. New York   122 (bottom)
Nancy L. Safford   116 (top left; center left)
Peter Shelton   219
Michael Singer   236
Courtesy Michael Singer   237
SITE Projects, Inc.   70
David Stansbury   235, 238, 239, 240, 242, 243
Ivan Dalla Tana, courtesy Gagosian Gallery, New York   181
Michael Tropea   137, 149
Tom Vinetz, courtesy L.A. Louver Gallery, Inc., Venice, California 216, 218, 220, 221, 222, 223
Walker Art Center   8, 9, 10, 11, 13, 14, 16, 20 (top), 22, 24, 40, 50 (bottom)
Ruth V. Ward   112
John Webb, courtesy Mark Lancaster   38
Courtesy Meg Webster and Barbara Gladstone Gallery, New York 256, 257, 258, 259, 260
Brian Weil, courtesy P.P.O.W, New York   169, 170
Paul Yonchek   80, 84 (top)
Donald Young Gallery, Chicago 191, 192, 193 (bottom)
Dorothy Zeidman, courtesy Germans van Eck, New York 145, 146, 147, 148, 150, 152 (top left)
Joe Ziolkowski, courtesy Museum of Contemporary Art, Chicago   125